T0345169

Smart Distributed Embedded Systems for Healthcare Applications

This book discusses the applications and optimization of emerging smart technologies in the field of healthcare. It further explains different modeling scenarios of the latest technologies in the healthcare system and compares the results to better understand the nature and progress of diseases in the human body, which would ultimately lead to early diagnosis and better treatment and cure of diseases with the help of distributed technology.

- Covers the implementation models using technologies such as artificial intelligence, machine learning, and deep learning with distributed systems for better diagnosis and treatment of diseases.
- Gives in-depth review of technological advancements like advanced sensing technologies such as plasmonic sensors, usage of RFIDs, and electronic diagnostic tools in the field of healthcare engineering.
- Discusses possibilities of augmented reality and virtual reality interventions for providing unique solutions in medical science, clinical research, psychology, and neurological disorders.
- Highlights the future challenges and risks involved in the application of smart technologies such as cloud computing, fog computing, IOT, and distributed computing in healthcare.
- Confers to utilize the AI and ML and associated aids in healthcare sectors in the post-Covid 19 period to revitalize the medical setup.

Contributions included in the book will motivate technological developers and researchers to develop new algorithms and protocols in the healthcare field. It will serve as a vast platform for gaining knowledge regarding healthcare delivery, healthcare management, healthcare in governance, and health monitoring approaches using distributed environments. It will serve as an ideal reference text for graduate students and researchers in diverse engineering fields including electrical, electronics and communication, computer, and biomedical fields.

Explainable AI (XAI) for Engineering Applications

Series Editors:

Aditya Khamparia and Deepak Gupta

Explainable AI (XAI) has developed as a subfield of artificial intelligence, focusing on exposing complex AI models to humans in a systematic and interpretable manner. This area explores and discusses the steps and models involved in making intelligent decisions. This series will also cover the working behavior and explain the ability of powerful algorithms such as neural networks, ensemble methods including random forests, and other similar algorithms to sacrifice transparency and explainability for power, performance, and accuracy in different engineering applications related to the real world. Aimed at graduate students, academic researchers, and professionals, the proposed series will focus on key topics including XAI techniques for engineering applications, explainable AI for deep neural network predictions, explainable AI for machine learning predictions, XAI-driven recommendation systems for automobile and manufacturing industries, and explainable AI for autonomous vehicles.

Deep Learning in Gaming and Animations: Principles and Applications
Vikas Chaudhary, Moolchand Sharma, Prerna Sharma, and Deevyankar Agarwal

Artificial Intelligence for Solar Photovoltaic Systems: Approaches, Methodologies and Technologies
Bhavnesh Kumar, Bhanu Pratap, and Vivek Shrivastava

Smart Distributed Embedded Systems for Healthcare Applications
Preeti Nagrath, Jafar A. Alzubi, Bhawna Singla, Joel J. P. C. Rodrigues, and A. K. Verma

For more information about this series, please visit: https://www.routledge.com/Explainable-AI-XAI-for-Engineering-Applications/book-series/CRCEAIFEA

Smart Distributed Embedded Systems for Healthcare Applications

Edited by

Preeti Nagrath, Jafar A. Alzubi, Bhawna Singla,
Joel J. P. C. Rodrigues, and A. K. Verma

CRC Press

Taylor & Francis Group
Boca Raton London New York

CRC Press is an imprint of the
Taylor & Francis Group, an **Informa** business

First edition published 2023
by CRC Press
6000 Broken Sound Parkway NW, Suite 300, Boca Raton, FL 33487-2742

and by CRC Press
4 Park Square, Milton Park, Abingdon, Oxon, OX14 4RN

CRC Press is an imprint of Taylor & Francis Group, LLC

ISBN: 9781032183473 (hbk)
ISBN: 9781032183497 (pbk)
ISBN: 9781003254119 (ebk)

DOI: 10.1201/9781003254119

Typeset in Times
by codeMantra

Contents

Preface

Embedded systems is the smart integration of hardware and software, which has many applications. Initially, embedded systems were introduced in the field of healthcare to cater to medical issues. Now, the amalgamation of smart distributed embedded systems with digital technologies such as artificial intelligence, cloud computing, IOT, NLP, augmented reality, virtual reality, and fog computing are used, and they prove to be a boon in the field of health and medicine. The new features offered by smart distributed technologies have accelerated the growth in the health industry. This book would be helpful to academicians, researchers, students, and technology developers for the development of better and optimized methods in healthcare.

This book provides in-depth comprehensive information on the latest research in the area of health and medicine on smart distributed embedded technologies. Chapter 1, "Healthcare Engineering Using AI and Distributed Technologies", discusses the transformation of healthcare with distributed computing. The chapter highlights the impact, challenges, benefits, and limitations of AI in the healthcare industry. The chapter also features AI-based robots in the healthcare ecosystem. Chapter 2, "Cloud Computing in Healthcare: A Systematic Study", elaborates on medicinal solutions provided by cloud computing using cloud-based molecular simulation tools and cloud-based medical imaging solutions. Application of fog computing in healthcare is also discussed.

Chapter 3, "Medical Information Extraction of Clinical Notes and Pictorial Visualization of Electronic Medical Records Summary Interface", highlights the NLP technique that enables users to quickly fetch and comprehend the patient's medical history and current data using Open NLP-trained Time-Entity model.

Chapter 4, "Investigations on RFID-Enabled Healthcare Usage and Adoption Issues", highlights that RFID has the potential for monitoring, tracking, and storing read data in real time. The chapter discusses various advantages provided by RFID technology. When RFID is linked, it can provide valuable process-integrated decision support based on current medical knowledge. It can also use patient data for research and healthcare reporting in a variety of ways. The chapter anticipates an RFID-enabled smart hospital in the future, which will combine RFID and wireless technology to provide a variety of healthcare services.

Chapter 5, "Photonic Crystal Fiber Plasmonic Sensor for Applications in Medicine", elaborates on how newly developed plasmonic materials/meta-materials can be a part of the overall development of sensing technology and can be used in medical equipment. Chapter 6, "Augmented Reality as a Boon to Disability", provides comprehensive coverage on the application of augmented reality for physically challenged, visually impaired, mentally challenged people, and other special children.

Chapter 7, "Augmented and Virtual Reality: Transforming the Future of Psychological and Medical Sciences", elaborates on immersive technologies, such as virtual reality and augmented reality, that play a significant role in developing a stimulating environment to help doctors perform surgeries, children with autism disorder develop their communication skills, and psychologists provide simulated situations to patients suffering from different neurological disorders. Chapter 8, "Artificial Intelligence in Healthcare: Perspectives from Post-Pandemic Times", emphasizes to best utilize the AI algorithms, ML techniques, and associated aids in health-care sectors in the post-pandemic times to revitalize the medical setup. Chapter 9, "Bioweapons v/s Computer-Based Counter Measure Techniques and Mathematical Modelling for the Prediction of COVID-19", provides an in-depth study of genetically engineered pathogens and their countermeasure techniques based on computer and artificial intelligence. The chapter examines several genetically engineered illnesses as well as the impact of biological agents. In the instance of a pandemic, artificial intelligence, big data, computer vision, computer-aided systems, and IoT-based systems are offering solutions. Computer-assisted surgery is extremely beneficial to doctors.

Chapter 10, "Evolution of Healthcare Sector and Evolving Cyber Attacks—A Summary", summarizes the evolution of the healthcare industry from healthcare 1.0 to healthcare 4.0. The chapter also highlights the need of Healthcare 4.0 from cyber-attacks, as it is necessary to secure patients' information in healthcare organiza-tions. Chapter 11, "Improving Cardiovascular Health by Deep Learning", highlights the next-generation machine learning and applications of artificial intelligence for cardiovascular health.

Editors

Dr. Preeti Nagrath is working as an Associate Professor in Bharati Vidyapeeth's College of Engineering. She has more than 19 years of academic experience and has obtained her B.Tech., M.Tech., and Ph.D. in Computer Science and Engineering. Her areas of research are network security, delay tolerant networks, machine learning, and deep learning. She is a member of ISTE. She has more than 60 research papers in SCI-indexed journals, highly reputed journals, and international conferences. She is working on government-funded DST project on women security. She has chaired many sessions in international conferences. She has been appointed as a reviewer in many conferences and journals. She has organized many faculty development programs, workshops, hackathons, and guest lectures. She has mentored teams in Smart India Hackathons. She is Associate Editor of *Journal of Multi-Disciplinary Engineering Technologies*, published by Bharati Vidyapeeth's College of Engineering, New Delhi.

Jafar A. Alzubi is an Associate Professor at Al-Balqa Applied University, School of Engineering, Jordan. He received his Ph.D. in advanced telecommunications from Swansea University, Swansea, UK (2012); Master of Science degree (Hons.) in electrical and computer engineering from New York Institute of Technology, New York, USA (2005); and Bachelor of Science degree (Hons.) in electrical engineering, majoring in electronics and communications, from the University of Engineering and Technology, Lahore, Pakistan (2001). Jafar works and researches in multi- and inter-disciplinary environments involving machine learning, classification and detection of web scams, internet of things, wireless sensor networks, cryptography, and using algebraic–geometric theory in channel coding for wireless networks. He managed and directed few projects funded by the European Union. A cumulative research experience of over 10 years resulted in publishing more than 60 papers in high-impact journals. Currently, he is a senior IEEE member and is serving as an editor for *IEEE Access*, and Wireless Sensor Networks area editor for *Turkish Journal of Electrical Engineering and Computer Sciences*. In addition, he is an editorial board member and a reviewer in many other prestigious journals in computer engineering and the science field. He is also managing several special issues in high-impact journals.

Dr. Bhawna Singla has received her doctorate degree from Thapar University, Patiala, India. She is currently working as Professor of Computer Science and Engineering Department, PIET College of Engineering and Technology, Samalkha, Panipat, India. She organized and participated in several national-level seminars and conferences. She has more than 15 years of rich academic experience. She has published more than 25 research papers in international journals/conferences and edited books. She is on the editorial board and in the review panel of many international journals. She organized a national-level seminar on "Mobile Computing and Mobile Applications Development (MOBAPP-2014)," which is dedicated to state-of-the-art research on mobile computing and its application including services. She participated in the organizing activities of an international conference on emerging technologies—ICET-2014, Futuristic Technologies (ICFT 2019).

Joel J. P. C. Rodrigues [FELLOW, IEEE & AAIA] is with the College of Computer Science and Technology, China University of Petroleum, Qingdao, China; and senior researcher at the Instituto de Telecomunicações, Portugal. Prof. Rodrigues is an Highly Cited Researcher (Clarivate), N. 1 of the top scientists in computer science in Brazil (Research.com), the leader of the Next Generation Networks and Applications (NetGNA) research group (CNPq), Member Representative of the IEEE Communications Society on the IEEE Biometrics Council, and the President of the scientific council at ParkUrbis—Covilhã Science and Technology Park. He was Director for Conference Development—IEEE ComSoc Board of Governors, an IEEE Distinguished Lecturer, Technical Activities Committee Chair of the IEEE ComSoc Latin America Region Board, a Past-Chair of the IEEE ComSoc Technical Committee (TC) on eHealth and the TC on Communications Software, a Steering Committee member of the IEEE Life Sciences Technical Community and Publications co-Chair. He is the editor-in-chief of the International Journal of E-Health and Medical Communications and editorial board member of several high-reputed journals (mainly, from IEEE). He has been general chair and TPC Chair of many international conferences, including IEEE ICC, IEEE GLOBECOM, IEEE HEALTHCOM, and IEEE LatinCom. He has authored or coauthored about 1100 papers in refereed international journals and conferences, 3 books, 2 patents, and 1 ITU-T Recommendation. He had been awarded several Outstanding Leadership and Outstanding Service Awards by IEEE Communications Society and several best papers awards. Prof. Rodrigues is a member of the Internet Society, a senior member ACM, and Fellow of AAIA and IEEE.

Dr. A. K. Verma is currently working as a Professor in the Department of Computer Science and Engineering at Thapar Institute of Engineering & Technology, Patiala in Punjab (India). He received his B.E., M.E., and Ph.D. in 1991, 2001, and 2008, respectively, majoring in Computer Science and Engineering. He has worked as a Lecturer at M.M.M. Engg. College, Gorakhpur (now, M.M.M. University of Technology) from 1991 to 1996. Since 1996, he is associated with Thapar Institute of Engineering & Technology. He is leading the research group on Mobile Computing and Communication (MC2) at Thapar Institute of Engineering & Technology. He has published over 150 papers in refereed journals and conferences (India and Abroad). He is a member of various program committees for different international/national conferences and is on the review board of various international/national journals. He has visited the USA (2005), South Korea (2012), Japan (2013), Ireland (2015), and Bahrain (2017) for academic purposes. He is a MACM (USA), MISCI (Turkey), LMCSI (Mumbai), and GMAIMA (New Delhi). He is a certified software quality auditor by MoCIT, Govt. of India.

Contributors

Aman Arora
Electrical and Computer Engineering
University of Texas, Austin
Austin, USA

Anjali Kataria
Chitkara University Institute of
  Engineering and Technology
Chitkara University
Rajpura, India

Archana Mantri
Chitkara University Institute of
  Engineering and Technology
Chitkara University
Rajpura, India

Arun Chokkalingam
Department of Electronics and
  Communication Engineering
RMK College of Engineering and
  Technology
Thiruvallur, India

Ashish Kumar
School of Computer Science
  Engineering and Technology
Bennett University
Greater Noida, India

Dhivya Kesavan
Department of Electronics and
  Communication Engineering
RMK College of Engineering and
  Technology
Thiruvallur, India

Gopal Chaudhary
Department of Computer Science
Bharati Vidyapeeth's College of
  Engineering
New Delhi, India

Gurinderjit Kaur
Department of Applied Science
Chandigarh Group of Colleges
Landran, Punjab

Gurjinder Singh
Chitkara University Institute of
  Engineering and Technology
Chitkara University
Rajpura, India

Jai Ganesh Sekar
Department of Electronics and
  Communication Engineering
RMK College of Engineering and
  Technology
Thiruvallur, India

Jasminder Kaur Sandhu
Department of Computer Science and
  Engineering
Chandigarh University
Mohali, India

Jishnu Bhardwaj
Department of Computer Science and
  Engineering
Bharati Vidyapeeth's College of
  Engineering
New Delhi, India

Joao Alexandre Lobo Marques
Department of Applied Neurosciences
University of Saint Joseph
Macao, China

Joginder Singh
Department of Applied Science
Chandigarh Group of Colleges
Landran, India

Kuldeep Sharma
Department of ECE
Chandigarh Engineering College
Landran, India

Manvinder Sharma
Department of CSE
CGC—College of Engineering
Landran, India

Monika Kiroriwal
Department of Electronics and
    Communication Engineering
Deenbandhu Chhotu Ram University of
    Science & Technology
Sonepat, India

Muhammad Fazal ljaz
School of Intelligent Mechatronics
    Engineering
Sejong University
Seoul, South Korea

Pankaj Palta
Department of CSE
CGC—College of Engineering
Landran, India

Poonam Singal
Deenbandhu Chhotu Ram University of
    Science & Technology
Sonepat, India

Praveen Singh
Department of Electronics and
    Communication
Bharati Vidyapeeth's College of
    Engineering
New Delhi, India

Prince Sareen
Department of Electronics and
    Communication Engineering
Bharati Vidyapeeth's College of
    Engineering
New Delhi, India

Rahul Kakkar
Department of CSE
CGC—College of Engineering
Landran, India

Raja
Department of Electronics and
    Communication Engineering
Bharati Vidyapeeth's College of
    Engineering
New Delhi, India

Raunak Negi
Department of Computer Science and
    Engineering
Bharati Vidyapeeth's College of
    Engineering
New Delhi, India

Rinkesh Mittal
Department of ECE
Chandigarh Engineering College
Landran, India

Rubina Dutta
Chitkara University Institute of
    Engineering and Technology
Chitkara University
Rajpura, India

Shyam Bihari Goyal
Faculty of Information Technology
City University
Selagor, Malaysia

Shinnu Jangra
Chitkara University Institute of
    Engineering and Technology
Chitkara University
Rajpura, India

Shiva Tushir
Department of Pharmacy
Panipat Institute of Engineering and
    Technology (PIET)
Panipat, India

Sukhdeep Kaur
Department of ECE
Chandigarh Engineering College
Landran, India

Sumeet Goyal
Department of CSE
CGC—College of Engineering
Landran, India

Tapash Rudra
Amity Institute of Biotechnology
Amity University
Kolkata, India

Thennarasan Sabapathy
Advanced Communication Engineering
    (ACE) Centre of Excellence
Faculty of Electronic Engineering
    Technology
Universiti Malaysia Perlis
Perlis, Malaysia

1 Healthcare Engineering Using AI and Distributed Technologies

Ashish Kumar
Bennett University

Prince Sareen
Bharati Vidyapeeth's College of Engineering

Aman Arora
University of Texas, Austin

CONTENTS

1.1 INTRODUCTION

Recent developments in technology and connectivity have led to the origin of the Internet of Things (IoT) and artificial intelligence (AI). AI plays a significant role in advancing the healthcare industry and robotics technology with the help of IoT. In addition, AI also plays a critical role in data observation. The healthcare industry depends on AI for data analysis. A survey indicated that most Indians stay in villages and depend on primary health centers (PHC) for their health-related issues [1]. As rural PHCs face numerous problems, residents in those areas have limited options for healthcare-related services and advice. Currently, rural healthcare providers are struggling to address day-to-day challenges.

AI technology acts as a lifesaver to those healthcare service providers. AI is nothing but a machine with traits similar to the human mind, such as adapting and

DOI: 10.1201/9781003254119-1

1

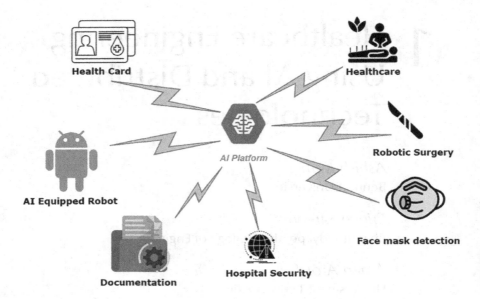

FIGURE 1.1 Application of AI in the healthcare industry.

solution thinking. It helps in multitasking and reduces the workload of a person. Figure 1.1 shows the integration of AI with the healthcare industry. AI helps in documentation, security purposes, complex surgeries, and drug development [2]. Also, it helps in setting up a robotic doctor and has impacted many areas of the medical field.

The application of AI is broadly classified as Narrow AI, General AI, and Super AI. Narrow AI is the machine's ability to perform a single task with a high success ratio, such as browsing web pages or playing chess. Narrow AI finds its application in image and facial recognition systems, chatbots and conversational assistants, self-driving vehicles, predictive maintenance models, and recommendation engines. On the other hand, General AI represents overall human cognitive abilities. Furthermore, Super AI is imaginary AI that does not just mimic or respond to human intelligence and behavior [3]. It is a technology where machines are already aware and have the ability of human-like intelligence. It is a software-based system with cognitive powers beyond humans across an almost comprehensive range of categories and fields of endeavor. In healthcare, AI has introduced some latest trends that help medical personnel to improve their work and provide benefits to the patients. In addition, Natural Language Processing (NLP) tools that can understand and classify clinical documents are a prominent aspect of AI in healthcare. NLP systems aid in examining clinical notes on sick persons, providing invaluable insight on quality, technique improvement, and improved outcomes. The AI-based smartwatch has all health-tracking facilities, exercise modes, health reminders, sleep monitoring, stress management, and many other essential features that benefit health [4]. The present-day trends in AI are increasingly oriented toward use in the healthcare sector.

The primary objective is to enhance the availability of better medical information and services at the lowest cost [5]. In sum, it has been well accepted that machine learning, distributed technologies, and AI play a dominant role in the healthcare sector. The world is changing at a very fast pace. The primary concern is to connect all the villages and metro cities with a strong medium. In the past decades, the government and many communication companies have made many efforts to make a strong connection between rural and urban areas. In the next section, we have reviewed the recent work and briefly described the latest trends in the domain.

1.2 RELATED WORK

This section has critically analyzed the potential work in smart healthcare. To explore the transformation in healthcare, we have reviewed the work in AI, distributed computing, machine learning, and IoT. AI with robotics offers several advantages and transforms healthcare globally [6]. Distributed computing has improved the accessibility of health records and changed how healthcare is delivered to the patient. Machine learning with IoT offers healthcare devices that can provide intensive care and monitoring, which cannot be done by humans efficiently. In hospitals, robots also help in proper cleaning and sanitization. In the future, we shall see robots doing many other works as training and testing in this regard have started [1].

AI has contributed to the healthcare industry by understanding a disease better with the appropriate cure for patients [6]. It provides a prediction model, which helps in the early detection of disease. Better radiology tools are developed with the help of AI, which helps treat cancer. AI plays a vital role in drug development. The complex process for specific drugs has been simplified using AI [1]. In addition, it helps in saving a lot of effort, time, and money. It also helps in structure-based drug discovery by appropriately predicting the protein structures. AI can distinguish between hit and lead compounds, confirming the drug target and improving the drug building more quickly with high efficiency [7]. The details of representative work in the healthcare industry exploiting recent technologies are tabulated in Table 1.1.

TABLE 1.1
Representative Work in the Domain of Healthcare Industry

Authors	Methods	Summary
Shailaja et al. (2018) [1]	AI and ML algorithms	Treatment of Covid patients takes place with the help of ML algorithms and they help predict lung infection via X-ray images.
Wiens and Shenoy (2018) [2]	Machine learning and neural network	Prediction in drug development using KNN and decision tree algorithms. Drug development process has been elaborated with ML benefits.
Escamilla-Ambrosio et al. (2018) [4]	Distributed computing, IoT, AI	Use of distributed computing, IoT, and AI in the healthcare sector leads to better monitoring and helps in the early diagnosis of diseases.

(Continued)

TABLE 1.1 (*Continued*)
Representative Work in the Domain of Healthcare Industry

Authors	Methods	Summary
Yoon and Lee (2018) [6]	IoT, distributed technology	Integrate IoT with medical equipments for health monitoring of patients for better clinical procedure.
Chowdhury et al. (2018) [5]	Data analytics,	AI helps in disease prediction via various algorithms like decision tree and naïve base.
Mirzaei et al. (2012) [8]	Machine vision, AI	Enumerates the importance of AI in healthcare industries and discusses the benefits of narrow artificial intelligence. Patient's medical history tracking and disease prediction using machine learning algorithms.
Villemagne et al. (2012) [7]	AI and IoT	Emphasis on the utility of AI in drug development and its clinical process to reduce computational efforts.
Davenport and Kalakota (2019) [9]	AI-based algorithm	Integration of various medical devices with AI also tells about the advancement of AI in modern days.
Liu et al. (2018) [10]	Distributed technologies and AI	Data transfer without human intervention and making the documentation process easy.
Fraley and Cannady (2017) [11]	Distributed technologies & cybersecurity	Distributing computing helps maintain health records and can be accessed from anywhere with high encryption.
Boulanger and Deroussent (2008) [12]	Machine learning	Elaborates on the advantage of AI in healthcare to link various healthcare devices with IoT.
Cieslak et al. (2006) [3]	Distributing computing, NLP	Explains the complications behind the documentation process and tells how NLP system makes it a little easier.
Esmaeilzadeh (2020) [13]	AI-based algorithms	AI-enabled robots help in surgery and support as an assistant in many medical-related works.
Lee and Yoon (2021) [14]	AI, IoT	Proposed AI gadgets with IoT-based solutions.
Zeadally et al. (2020) [15]	AI-based tools, ML	Explains the use of decision tree and KNN in disease prediction and the use of new radio technologies in the treatment of cancer.
Yeole and Kalbande (2016) [16]	IOT	Integrated medical devices with IOT hardware to provide real-time data.
Tyagi (2016) [17]	AI	Highlights the limitations of AI in the healthcare industry.

In another line of work, IoT with the help of distributed technologies has provided efficient healthcare services. IoT can share data without human support. IoT can provide continuous accessibility to hardware devices and gadgets anytime anywhere. IoT offers a framework for users to link various gadgets and operate them via big data distributed technologies. IoT can provide vital information in the pharmaceutical industry by connecting the patient, medical equipment, and supply chain into one structure. It helps in increasing safety, reducing cost, and improving time efficiency. IoT makes patient monitoring more manageable and efficient by incorporating sensors like fall detection and remote glucometers.

AI, IoT, and distributed technologies have a vital role in healthcare. These technologies benefit the industry and act as a boon to patients and healthcare staff. With the advent of technology, healthcare organizations can adopt the idea of digital health cards. The complete health information of the patient can be embedded in the card. With this, doctors can quickly know about the primary health condition of an individual. This will reduce the documentation work and help the doctors provide better diagnoses based on their health history.

In sum, AI with distributed technologies has provided numerous benefits to the healthcare industry. A variety of information can be made available that can ease a patient's monitoring, diagnosis, and treatment. Advancement in technology, i.e., robot-assisted surgery, online availability of patient health history, and reduced documentation work, has minimized the chances of error and enhanced the probability of survival. Despite these benefits, the recent technologies have their limitations. Online availability of data increases the chances of cyberattack. The security of patient's critical information is of prime concern. However, AI has improved the healthcare industry by increasing the survival rate in cases of critical diseases. In the next section, we will discuss the impact of AI in the healthcare industry with its benefits and limitations.

1.3 IMPACT OF AI IN THE HEALTHCARE INDUSTRY

To make the healthcare industry strong, many efforts are being made and work on interconnects of various medical resources using IoT. AI provides modern and advanced treatment to old-aged patients and patients with serious illnesses. We can take the example of AI assisting robots in making complex surgery easy with a high accuracy rate within less time [9]. Nowadays, many hospitals utilize AI strategies to provide better services to patients. AI systems improve the prediction rate and analyze the patient's details with better consistency. Figure 1.2 describes the connection of various hardware devices and the interconnection to provide services for the healthcare industry. In this, the integration of medical services with a person has been elaborated. When a person is not feeling well, a smartwatch, mobile, or personal digital assistance (PDA) indicates a notification on the server. From the server, this notification is sent to the nearest clinical staff, and after that, according to severity, the best possible medical services will be provided to the patient.

AI helps minimize testing errors and misdiagnosis while improving treatment accuracy with more detailed results. This will reduce the treatment cost and improve the survival rate in acute diseases like cancer, tumors, and COVID-19. In addition, AI provides many benefits, including robot-assisted surgeries, faster laboratory results, high success rate of surgery, early prediction, and better understanding of disease [10].

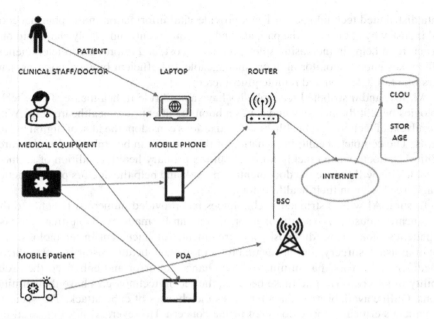

FIGURE 1.2   Communication process between various layers.

1.3.1   CHALLENGES IN AI IMPLEMENTATION IN HEALTHCARE

In many cases, the lack of proper infrastructure and funds is the leading impedi-ment in applying AI to existing applications. Doctors and other health staff take time to adapt to AI. If a person adapts easily and at a fast pace, they will quickly take advantage of AI. The challenges include immense pressure on healthcare systems and equipment growth of healthcare data, augmented intelligence for clinicians' inte-gration, and legal challenges [3].

Due to the current pandemic, factories can't work at the full pace, leading to chip shortages. Some companies also follow unfair means to produce chips or develop a low-quality chip. Due to lack of supply, the price will also increase, impacting device cost. In healthcare, AI helps to increase the speed of a specific work, develop advanced radiology tools, facilitate a better understanding that helps in seamless exe-cution, reduce the paper workload, and ensure better treatment of serious diseases.

1.3.2   AI TOOLS FOR PREDICTION OF CRITICAL DISEASES

AI tools play an essential role in the healthcare industry. It helps to increase the efficiency of doctors and helps in getting results more accurately and faster. With AI's help, disease diagnosis becomes easy and treatment speed increases with no compromises. No doubt that AI tools can predict acute diseases accurately and in a timely manner. Apple watch is the best example of an AI-equipped tool. This watch analyzes our health based on our daily routine and warns against any health risks in our body, but these AI-based tools are pretty expensive and require maintenance [14].

In developed countries, many efforts are made to make a doctor robot using AI to solve minor health issues. Here the robot visits the patient's home [18]. The increase in wrist wearables such as smart bands, watches, and other medical resources integrated with AI helps doctors to better monitor and helps in determining life-threatening diseases. AI can help improve surgical performance. There is no doubt in the context that AI is a boon for the patient. AI can analyze big data sets. AI plays a significant role in a patient's life. AI helps to improve health conditions and make daily tasks easier.

1.3.3　BENEFITS AND LIMITATIONS OF AI IN HEALTHCARE INDUSTRY

AI has the ability to examine records in a better way with a high rate of success and helps in better and fast laboratory results. It helps in better understanding of a particular topic at a good pace. It helps to perform normal or routine tasks with relative ease and better and faster results. It also helps to schedule our daily tasks and examine our health and stress condition. With the help of these AI-assembled technologies, we can easily achieve our fitness goals. These technologies help in examining various parameters like calorie burn, steps calculation, stress measurement, Spo2, and blood pressure measurements, and make our life easier [19].

One of the major disadvantages of AI is cost, that is, implementing AI even in a small part requires a huge budget. Moreover, since AI is new for all, it takes time to adapt. Acceptance of AI is very difficult as no one would want that their loved ones to be treated by robots instead of doctors in hospitals. Figure 1.3 shows the limitations of AI, restricting the people skills and developing them as machine dependent. Implementing AI is very expensive, it requires more training, adaptation is also difficult, and there is lack of creativity in AI. Errors and injuries: AI systems are susceptible to errors, which eventually results in patient injury or other significant problems. Likewise, AI-driven radiological scan may miss a tumor

> **Expensive**: No doubt AI plays a very important role in the healthcare industry. But, implementing or adapting to AI is a difficult task. For implementing AI, a huge investment in thousands of crores is required. Even if we are able to arrange this amount, adapting to AI is a challenge.

1.4　TRANSFORMING HEALTHCARE WITH DISTRIBUTED COMPUTING

Distributed computing system is a model in which data are shared among multiple computers, which means something is shared among multiple systems. There is no concern of location, that is, geographical location does not matter. Client-server, three tier, and N tier are the most famous designs for distributed computing. Client-server configurations are those in which smart clients request data from the server, which are subsequently formatted and shown to the users [19]. When a client input constitutes a permanent change, it is committed back to the server. Three-tier designs transfer client intelligence to a middle tier, allowing for the usage of stateless clients.

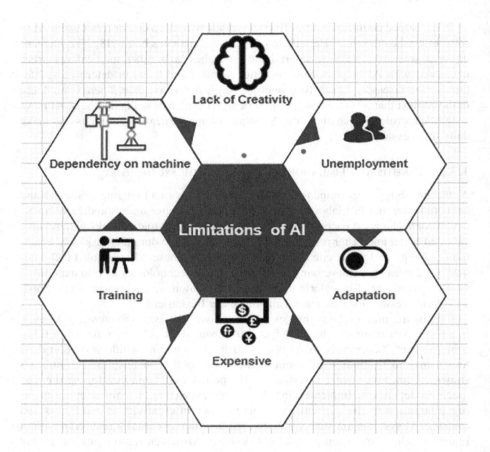

FIGURE 1.3   Limitations of AI impacting various domains.

This makes application deployment easier. N-Tier designs are often used to describe online apps that route requests to other corporate services. This is the sort of application that is primarily responsible for application server success.

Figure 1.4 shows the details of essential hardware elements in distributing computing system works. Network plays an important role, as this helps in mapping various workstations along with data servers.

In this terminology, if we upload data on a particular server, then we can access that data on any system at any time. Distributed systems are a group of independent computers. They are a group of separate computers that seem to consumers as a single coherent computing system. They are employed for high-performance computing tasks. Cluster computing systems consist of a number of workstations that all run the same operating system. Distributed computing plays a very important role in the healthcare industry. With the help of this technology, doctors can easily be familiar with our basic health condition. It helps to save time in case

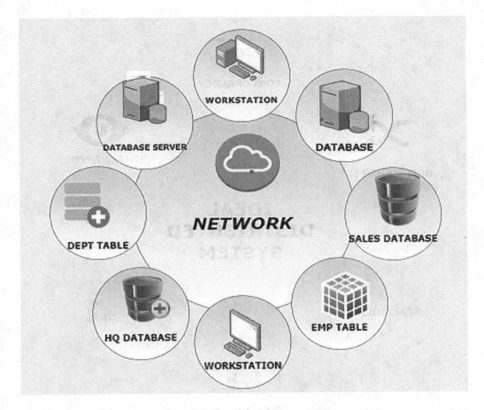

FIGURE 1.4 Details of various hardware systems in distributed computing.

of emergency. Basic health information includes our blood group, any persisting disease, allergies, and some other personal information. This information is uploaded on a particular server through which we can access it when required [15]. Figure 1.5 depicts how a distributed system should be. It should be concurrent, transparent, open, and secure.

Advantages of Distributed Systems
- In a distributed system, all the nodes are connected with each other.
- If one node is not working, it does not mean that all other nodes are not working. This is why the system does not fail.
- Addition of nodes is easily done in distributed computing.

Disadvantages of Distributed Computing
- Difficulty in troubleshooting.
- Less software supports.
- High network infrastructure costs.
- Security issues.

FIGURE 1.5   Details of advantages of the distributed system.

1.5   AI-BASED ROBOTS IN THE HEALTHCARE ECOSYSTEM

AI-based robots play a crucial role in the healthcare industry, not only in the patient's life but also in healthcare. They help in achieving great success in a complicated surgery. These robots can be operated 24×7 without any hassles. Robots perform their work as expected without fatigue. There have been several cases when AI robotics has been a boon to the healthcare business. Helper Robots: These are used in hospitals when several patients require the same medicine or help simultaneously. In these situations, the health provider is generally rushing to help the patient rather than perform other responsibilities. As a result, supplementary robots are rapidly taking care of duties like replenishing, collecting garbage, and cleaning. We utilize these supplementary robots as an automatic UV disinfectant that will also aid hospital co-workers. These robots will also assist in remote therapy since much research is being conducted to make it possible. Routine Activities: Robots can perform daily tasks and carry out various functions that humans previously managed. They aid in the maintenance of cleanliness and social distance. They examine patient's health status regularly. Simple routine check-ups may involve assessing the patient's blood pressure, blood sugar, and many other tasks. AI is new to surgery, with a strong foundation in imaging and navigation and early techniques. Robots play an essential role in surgery because they perform back-to-back surgeries, reducing the stress on doctors and increasing the success rate. The following are some of the operations in which robots are used: Robotic surgery through AI is now prevalent in developed countries and the success percentage is increasing day by day. Another example is that of laser operation; its cost is a little bit high, but success percentage is high, and recovery is significantly faster as compared to operations by doctors. AI diagnoses disease faster and helps in better cures. It also warns if there are any complications in our body, i.e., lowering of Spo2 level or any disorder in heartbeat rate. It also helps in stress management. It reminds our health activity according to our schedule [15]. As we know, everything has two sides. Similarly, robotic surgery too has a positive side and a negative side. To explore both sides, we present the pros and cons of AI.

Also, the robots are trained to assist the doctors and medical staff during the course of the treatment. There are specialized robots that can diagnose the problem and help enhance the success rate of the treatment. Figure 1.6 illustrates the tasks that robots can perform with the help of AI. This figure shows how robots help in various functions like explosive handling, health industry, and test and training purposes. They can work 24×7 without any complaint with a high accuracy rate.

There are certain benefits associated with robotic-assisted surgery. Cut marks are significantly minor during surgery than in traditional surgery. If a robot performs the surgery, the incisions are smaller, resulting in less blood loss and pain than the conventional method. Also, it ensures minimal tissue damage and fewer chances of getting any infection. This will lead to quick healing of the wounds, and the patient will get discharged from the hospital earlier. Only few medical staff are required during the procedure. Hence, the expense of staying in the hospital is lower, and the chances of complications are also reduced [16]. If a patient has any contagious disease, it can endanger the doctor's health. But, in robot-based surgery there is no such risk. The robot can perform surgeries one after another, as it does not get tired. It can operate 24×7 with little maintenance. Compared to humans, robots take less time during surgery, and the success rate is also high if the robots are appropriately trained. Surgery robots are emotionless, so it helps to achieve better results. Also, decision-making capacity does not involve any human intervention; and hence, it ensures more accuracy in outcome. On the other hand, there are certain limitations associated with robotic-assisted surgery. The main disadvantage of robotic surgery is its high cost. Even a tiny, microscopic surgery is costly. Much expensive research is being done, but a positive outcome is still awaited. Any maintenance of the robot incurs a considerable cost because different parts have to be sourced from other countries. No one wants to be treated by a robot, and it would be difficult for doctors to convince patients to accept robotic surgery [17]. Also, there are chances of mechanical failure, which could lead to patient death or cause fatal injuries. Sometimes episodes of breathing difficulties also occur, which can cause significant complications. In sum, robot-assisted surgery is an upcoming trend in the healthcare industry. It incorporates

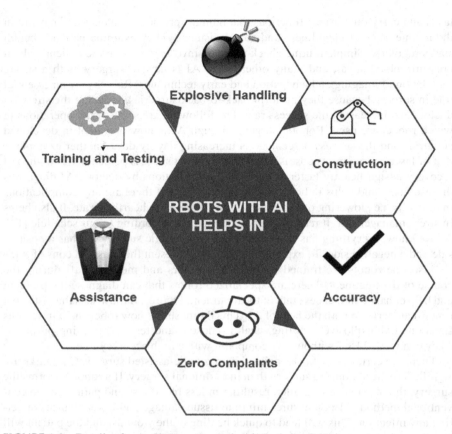

FIGURE 1.6   Details of areas/tasks automated with the help of robots.

many benefits. However, many areas require further research to address patient concerns and generate their interest in this innovative treatment.

1.6   CONCLUSION AND FUTURE SCOPE

AI and distributed technologies play a significant role in the healthcare industry. They not only help reduce the workload of healthcare professionals but also result in better efficiency. In addition, AI also plays a vital role in the patient's life. It helps in faster patient recovery and maintains a positive environment by assisting with a robot-like human being. It also ensures that the basic medical check-up of the patient is done continuously. AI makes difficult work easy and increases various medical procedures' success rate and accuracy. Robot-assisted surgery is a new trend in the healthcare industry. Due to this, surgery becomes a little easy, and the healing process is faster. Also, distributed computing helps maintain health records quickly and is accessible anywhere. It makes it easy for hospitals and doctors to access the patient's medical history and provide treatment accordingly. However, all of this is possible in developed countries only. AI requires massive funding, skilled doctors and engineers, and a good infrastructure for its implementation. Few developing countries are still struggling for better medical facilities. Nevertheless, with recent technology and distributed computing, AI can ensure massive development in the healthcare industry, which directly benefits the users. Across many sectors, AI and Distributed Technologies are changing the way people communicate, share consumer information, and receive goods and services. AI is already transforming the patient experience, how physicians practice medicine, and how pharmaceutical companies function in the healthcare industry. The expedition has only just begun. Everything from answering the phone to medical record review, population health trending and analytics, therapeutic drug and device creation, interpreting radiological images, establishing a clinical diagnosis and treatment plans, and even chatting with patients might be part of AI's future in healthcare. The future of AI and distributed technology in the healthcare industry also helps achieve patient self-service benefits. It will act as a boon for both patients and hospitals. In addition, it allows hospitals to reduce costs, reduce wait times, commit fewer errors, provide more accessible payment options, and increase patient satisfaction. For patients, it helps in faster, easier appointment scheduling, convenient bill payment, and lesser time spent for updating medical forms.

REFERENCES

[1] Shailaja, K., Seetharamulu, B., and Jabbar, M. A. (2018), Machine learning in healthcare: A review. In *2018 Second International Conference on Electronics, Communication and Aerospace Technology (ICECA)* (pp. 910–914). IEEE.

[2] Wiens, J. and Shenoy, E. S. (2018), Machine learning for healthcare: On the verge of a major shift in healthcare epidemiology. *Clinical Infectious Diseases*, 66(1), 149–153.

[3] Cieslak, D.A., Thain, D., and Chawla, N.V. (2006), Short paper: Troubleshooting distributed system via data mining. In *High Performance Distributed Computing, 2006 15th IEEE International Symposium on* (pp. 309–312).

[4] Escamilla-Ambrosio, P.J., Rodríguez-Mota, A., Aguirre-Anaya, E., Acosta-Bermejo, R., and Salinas-Rosales, M. (2018), Distributing computing in the internet of things: Cloud, fog and edge computing overview. In: Maldonado, Y., Trujillo, L., Schütze, O., Riccardi, A., Vasile, M. (eds) *NEO 2016.* Studies in Computational Intelligence (pp. 87–115, vol. 731), Springer, Cham.

[5] Chowdhury, M., Jahan, S., Islam, R., and Gao, J. (2018), Malware detection for healthcare data security. In *International Conference on Security and Privacy in Communication Systems* (pp. 407–416). Springer, Cham.

[6] Yoon, S. N. and Lee, D. (2018), Artificial intelligence and robots in healthcare: What are the success factors for technology-based service encounters? *International Journal of Healthcare Management*, 12, 218–225.

[7] Villemagne, B., Crauste, C., Flipo, M., Baulard, A. R., Déprez, B., and Willand, N. (2012), Tuberculosis: The drug development pipeline at a glance. *European Journal of Medicinal Chemistry*, 51, 1–16. doi:10.1016/j.ejmech.2012.02.03

[8] Mirzaei, M. R., Ghorshi, S., and Mortazavi, M. (2012), Combining augmented reality and speech technologies to help deaf and hard of hearing people. In *14th Symposium on Virtual and Augmented Reality* (pp. 174–181).

[9] Davenport, T. and Kalakota, R. (2019), The potential for artificial intelligence in healthcare. *Future Healthcare Journal*, 6(2), 94–98. doi:10.7861/futurehosp.6-2-94

[10] Liu, Q., Li, P., Zhao, W., Cai, W., Yu, S., and Leung, V. C. (2018), A survey on security threats and defensive techniques of machine learning: A data-driven view. *IEEE Access*, 6, 12103–12117.

[11] Fraley, J. B. and Cannady, J. (2017), The promise of machine learning in cybersecurity. In *SoutheastCon 2017* (pp. 1–6). IEEE, Concord, NC, USA.

[12] Boulanger, J. R. and Deroussent, C. (2008), Preliminary based service evaluation for elderly people and healthcare professionals in residential home care units. In *Second International Conference on the Digital Society* (pp. 93–101). IEEE.

[13] Esmaeilzadeh, P. (2020), Use of AI-based tools for healthcare purposes: A survey study from consumers perspectives. *BMC Medical Informatics and Decision Making*, 20(1), 1–19. doi:10.1186/s12911-020-01191-1

[14] Lee, D. and Yoon, S. N. (2021), Application of artificial intelligence-based technologies in the healthcare industry: Opportunities and challenges. *International Journal of Environmental Research and Public Health*, 18(1), 271. doi:10.3390/ijerph18010271

[15] Zeadally, S., Adi, E., Baig, Z., and Khan, I. A. (2020), Harnessing artificial intelligence capabilities to improve cybersecurity. *IEEE Access*, 8, 23817–23837.

[16] Yeole, A. S. and Kalbande, D. R. (2016), Use of internet of things (IoT) in healthcare: A survey. In *Proceedings of the ACM Symposium on Women in Research 2016* (pp. 71–76).

[17] Tyagi, A. (2016), "Artificial intelligence: Boon or bane?" *Available at SSRN 2836438*.

[18] Jalali, M. and Kaiser, J. (2018), Cybersecurity in hospitals: A systematic, organizational perspective. *Journal of Medical Internet Research*, 20(5), e10059.

[19] Ta, V. D., Liu, C. M., and Nkabinde, G. W. (2016), "Big data stream computing in healthcare real-time analytics. In *2016 IEEE International Conference on Cloud Computing and Big Data Analysis (ICCCBDA)* (pp. 37–42). DOI: 10.1109/ICCCBDA.2016.7529531.

2 Cloud Computing in Healthcare

A Systematic Study

Raunak Negi, Jishnu Bhardwaj, and Preeti Nagrath
Bharati Vidyapeeth's College of Engineering

CONTENTS

2.1   INTRODUCTION

The introduction of cloud services and associated revenue streams has significantly impacted the computer sector and several other industries. By the year 2025, it is expected that approximately 90% of today's firms will have shifted to the cloud. Organizations with insufficient resources for investment and creating platforms to launch their software can now use cloud services to meet their specific requirements [1]. Consumers can use the cloud's infrastructure to launch and run their products. They also provide a number of platforms that run on various operating systems and allow customers to develop; using virtual servers, one can test, scrutinize, and deploy apps.

In addition, the cloud provides a highly adaptable and versatile platform for effectively managing the load. Consumers and businesses can save a significant amount of money because the infrastructure and media are already constructed and available. Some larger companies are putting money into their own data centers, using the current platforms and resources. Since real-world companies and organizations develop applications in a dynamic environment involving networking, security, and millions of dollars in money transfers, they expect cloud providers and the cloud to offer a similar or better level of service to ensure that their data are secure and their businesses are not harmed [2]. On the Internet, a growing number of business-related technologies are being developed. Because of security and privacy issues, the healthcare industry has long been one of the industries that has resisted outsourcing. Private and medical records are susceptible, and the corporations expend millions of dollars protecting them while adhering to federally coordinated requirements [3].

2.2 LITERATURE REVIEW

Over the last few years, researchers have become increasingly interested in cloud computing technology. In both the government and industry, the volume of implementations has increased. Major firms are predicted to invest more than $150 billion in cloud computing by 2014, as per the United Kingdom's Department of Economics, Commerce, and Management. The ultimate total, though, is substantially higher than anticipated. Moreover, as per research on worldwide health information technology (IT) trends, the global smart healthcare sector's revenue would surely rise to $5.4 billion in 2017 as a result of its upwelling.

In addition, North America, the sector's largest contributor, is predicted to increase its market share to $6.5 billion in 2018 from $1.7 billion in 2013. To make data more transportable than before, most affluent countries build healthcare data clearinghouses. Canada, for example, is the first country to acknowledge diagnostic imaging repositories across the country in order to improve patients and save money. Continued investment in cloud computing by all governments will surely improve medical care. According to the survey, 37% of healthcare practitioners have plans and strategies for cloud adoption, 22% are in the planning stages, and 25% are actually implementing, showing that the sector will surely be driven by this [4].

It is uncommon for doctors, agencies, and even individuals to share patient data, and it is undoubtedly a difficult task. It's too expensive to perform untested data experiments if a business relies on vendors to link its numerous technologies. Various countries have dealt with this issue in a variety of ways, ranging from the United Kingdom's central national clearinghouse to regional health centers in Canada to more detailed health data, all of which have had varied degrees of success. In addition, countries that have progressed away from physical records and toward clinical information are expected to win in a limited sense. Though as of now, it is challenging to keep the record of inpatients and better tools and techniques are required. Most IT departments were previously used to conventional processes, which required licensing software platforms, hardware networks, and a large workforce. The demand for IT infrastructure grows as new technologies develop, stretching the bounds of the promised more efficient technologies.

Government incentives, although innovative in theory, do not cover the cost of replacing legacy technology or upgrading infrastructure. Current storage capacity must be enhanced as health records and sophisticated clinical systems grow [5]. Digital time pathologies ensure that backend technologies are properly developed and running, diverting effort off from medical criteria applications' attention. Reduced installation time poses a risk in terms of being able to adapt quickly to changing requirements and the introduction of new applications. Patients in this period are more vocal about their healthcare needs. One of the causes is that so many patients are well-informed about their illnesses or are concerned about them, which increases the demand for up-to-date technology. This leads to a desire to receive the best possible care at the lowest possible expense, as well as a desire to research the various possibilities.

2.3 MEDLINE

MEDLINE was searched in July 2013 and December 2014 for papers using the keywords "cloud technology" and "cloud-based." Before integrating their data, two researchers classified and evaluated each publication and conference publication individually. The review was broken down into four stages: (a) a MEDLINE network search to gather publications, (b) an initial relevancy screening to limit the results, (c) a study of the related documents, and (d) a text summarization [6].

2.3.1 DATA EXTRACTION AND FULL-TEXT SCREENING

The review procedure, as shown in Figure 2.1, comprised a data extraction form, explicit instructions, and inclusion/exclusion criteria. Closed questions collected data about the present state of the selected cloud computing system, the plan's users, and the cloud services provider. The five basic characteristics of cloud computing mentioned by the authors were checked against National Institute of Standards and Technology's definition. Aside from the advantages, there were several drawbacks highlighted, such as security problems and reliance on cloud providers [7].

In 2008, only one of 102 pieces was published, and in 2009, none. Seven reports were written in 2010, as shown in Figure 2.2.

The full list of articles was rescreened to see if there were any additional themes that may be included in the MEDLINE results page. Each of the two reviewers separately tagged the papers in the systematic review with the knowledge and relevance presented in the papers. The final list of themes was considered by all reviewers, and similar topics were merged into one core subject [8]. Ultimately, the following six cloud computing domains in healthcare were discovered (Figure 2.3), listed in order of the number of publications:

1. Telemedicine/teleconsultation
2. Imaging in medicine
3. Patient self-management and public health
4. Systems for hospital management and clinical information
5. Therapy
6. Secondary data use

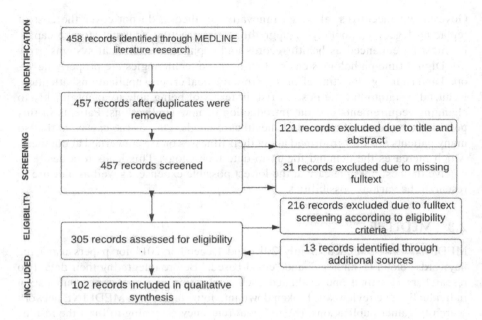

FIGURE 2.1   The method is depicted in a flowchart.

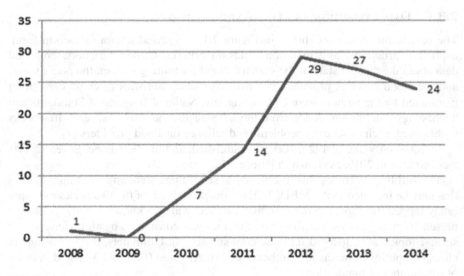

FIGURE 2.2   Distribution of published articles on a yearly basis.

The 102 studies looked at medical testing, global health, patients' self, hospital management, data management, treatment, and secondary information use. Broad communication network for exchanging and accessing data, as well as rapid flexibility to adapt to changing computing demands, are also frequent features. These

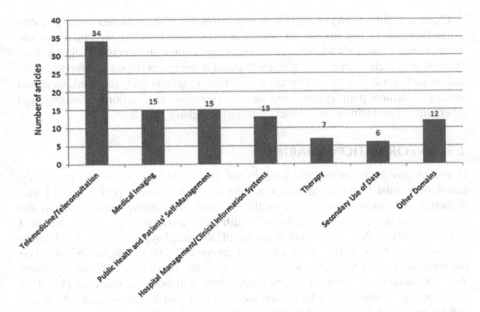

FIGURE 2.3   The primary domains of cloud computing in healthcare.

articles advocate for pay-per-use cloud-based services that eliminate upfront pay-ments. Just 14 articles report on effective implementation, despite the fact that 22 papers examine the wide prospects of cloud technology and 66 articles outline conceptual or prototype efforts [9].

The major hurdle to adoption in the healthcare sector is incorporating external cloud partners: numerous data security and prevention issues remain unaddressed. Until then, cloud computing is regarded as a cloud paradigm in and of itself, with features including flexibility, pay-per-use, and network access.

2.4   INFRASTRUCTURE AND DYNAMIC SCALABILITY

As the number of clients in the healthcare industry expands, so does the number of healthcare solution providers and their businesses. To accommodate the rising demand, businesses invest heavily in increased processing capacity and IT resources. These computational services are intended to work in a dynamic and complicated environment. Cloud computing has provided a solution to this challenge for businesses. Infrastructure-as-a-Service (IaaS) and Platform-as-a-Service (Platform-as-a-Service) are cloud-based revenue streams that allow corporations to make use of existing infrastructure or adapt it to suit unique requirements. In a short amount of time, more computers could be added or removed as needed. They can store information such as community and hospital settings, physician network, pharmaceuticals, and their locations in cloud-based data centers rather than on private on-site computers. The buyer will be responsible for maintaining the software up to date.

Cloud computing can greatly benefit small to medium-sized clinics that are unable to handle major IT investments and staff due to its price, effective structure, and low maintenance. Amazon's S3, which offers scalable storage architecture [10], is a good example of the claim above. The eHealth cloud is being developed to support applications and services such as "clinical application, judgment tools for assessment and therapy, treatment plan, commission tools, prescription medications, coaching, and other clinical and administrative services, as per Telstra" [11].

2.5 INFORMATION SHARING

Organizations in the healthcare field do not operate independently. As previously noted, they must maintain continual contact with other groups [12]. It could result in better and smoother service coordination and, ultimately, better productivity. Some patient data, such as Electronic Health Records (EHRs), Electronic Medical Records (EMRs), Personal Health Records (PHRs), and Payer Based Health Records (PBHRs), are shared with specific customer approval (PBHRs) [13], can be stored on the Internet, and shared with clinicians and hospitals in various states or countries. With the same knowledge across the board, there will be fewer mistakes [14]. This has a lot of potential to offer better service at a lower cost. Some of these advantages can be seen in Microsoft's HealthVault, which was created to build a centralized location to keep health information such as X-ray Images, client bills, doctors' notes, and convert them to digital formats.

HealthVault Connection Center allows clients to integrate their health and wellness equipment data, such as blood pressure and heart rate monitors, into their health records. Regional extension centers can use the software to manage communications with medical providers regarding selecting and deploying an EHR system. Accenture Medical Imaging Solution is a cloud-based medical imaging service developed by Accenture and American Telephone and Telegraph Company as part of a new product. This software will centralize picture management, enabling healthcare providers to examine, share, and send pictures more timely and safely.

2.6 AVAILABILITY

Cloud services with multiple servers and minimal downtime can only aid health businesses in providing continuous services with higher throughput. Near-real-time scalability possibilities can be accomplished by programmatically controlling the cloud. Clusters can be formed using many nodes [15]. Furthermore, because the resources are fixed at the start of the calculation, programs can be scaled up or down as the workload changes. It's also expected that storing and maintaining healthcare cloud applications will make them more universally available and accessible to the public. The cost of maintenance could be considerably reduced as a result. Understanding the security and privacy issues in healthcare could be the first step toward moving the industry forward. Understanding the security and privacy risks could be the first step toward moving healthcare apps to the cloud.

2.7   MONITORING SOFTWARE FOR THE CLOUD

In addition to the expansion of cloud computing, several third-party suppliers are producing tools to monitor cloud services. Healthcare companies collaborate with these vendors to tailor these technologies to their specific needs, including adding proper security elements. Cloudkick [16], LogicMonitor [17], Pandora Flexible Monitoring Solution [18], and other third-party companies that provide monitoring and cloud management technologies are on the rise. More crucially, numerous companies offer tools that just check the uptime of the server or service. On the EC2 instances that customers use, Amazon Web Services (AWS) provide its monitoring tools.

2.8   BIOMEDICINE AND HEALTHCARE BENEFIT
FROM CLOUD COMPUTING

Cloud computing has in recent research proved that it can enhance healthcare services and aid scientific research by opening up new possibilities. The need to lower healthcare delivery costs is a major driver of cloud migration in healthcare [19]. Because this price has grown to such vast dimensions, governments are facing tremendous budgetary issues. Governments are eager to assist the traditionally reluctant health sector to adopt technology more swiftly because they know that it can improve quality of care while cutting costs. They compared a cloud-based solution to a specific institutional cluster in terms of computational efficiency and cost-effectiveness. As the amount of digital data expands, this becomes increasingly challenging to manage [20]. Technologies have the potential to enable large-scale data integration and exchange. The work discusses elevated computer (HPC) approaches in informatics, Big Automated analysis frameworks for computational biology, and unsolved problems in the healthcare and medical domains. According to the scientists, cloud computing notably addresses Big Digital data and analysis difficulties in many areas of biology, due to virtualization, which prevents transporting too much data.

2.9   BIOTECH SOLUTIONS IN THE CLOUD

In the context of bioinformatics, cloud computing is a cost-effective alternative to the difficulties of data storage. The advancement of high-throughput sequencing technology has resulted in an exponential increase in biological data. As a result, traditional data processing computational infrastructure has become ineffective and onerous to maintain. Downloading public datasets, installing tools, and conducting analysis in-house are all part of classical bioinformatics analysis [21]. The supply of data as a service (DaaS) is essential due to this extraordinary data growth. DaaS enables data storage in a dynamic virtual environment hosted by the cloud, allowing for updated data to be accessed from various web-connected devices. The DaaS of AWS is an example. The AWS public dataset provides data from various scientific domains, including biology, astronomy, chemistry, climate, economics, etc. All datasets are available as AWS public services, making them simple to incorporate into cloud-based applications [22].

Examples of SaaS, PaaS, and IaaS for various tasks in the bioinformatics domain are provided in the subsections below.

2.9.1 Bioinformatics Software as a Service

Several attempts have been made to build cloud-based tools to do various bioinformatics tasks, such as genomic applications, sequence alignment, and gene expression analysis. The following are some more examples of SaaS bioinformatics software [23].

PeakRanger [24] is a software application that allows you to analyze Chromatin Immunoprecipitation Sequencing (ChIP-seq) data. This approach is connected to next-generation sequencing and will enable researchers to explore protein–DNA interactions. It may be utilized in a parallel cloud services environment to achieve extremely high throughput on large amounts of data.

VAT (Variant Annotation Tool) [25] was created to functionally annotate variations at the transcript level from different personal genomes and provide summary statistics across individuals. VAT also makes it easier to compare the effects of different variations on other groups of people by incorporating allele frequencies and genotyping data from the innate individuals and enables visualization of the impacts of multiple variations.

2.10 CLOUD-BASED MOLECULAR SIMULATION TOOLS

Molecular modeling operations, including molecular dynamics, quantum mechanical computations, and the creation of 3D users to access, are computationally intensive and produce or handle a vast amount of data. As a result, for molecular modeling workloads, the cloud infrastructure provides flexibility, reliability, and cost reductions [26]. Cloud technology for molecular modeling applications is still very much in adolescence since it requires the user to execute numerous technical chores, such as establishing the computer nodes, downloading the suitable technology, and starting, controlling, and terminating the calculation.

2.11 CLOUD-BASED MEDICAL IMAGING SOLUTIONS

Medical informatics has a basic difficulty in storing heterogeneous data in a unified searchable warehouse for scientific and clinical purposes. EHRs can be shared and merged more easily in the cloud, which saves money on equipment, technology, networks, and employees. As a result of these issues, the reliance on the cloud to keep sensitive health-related information is expected to increase dramatically. In a way to bolster the EHR, many researchers have recommended various cloud-based systems. A novel cloud computing access control mechanism that allows secure access to the patient's medical information including in cross systems has been proposed by Chen et al. [27]. Doukas et al. [28] described developing a mobile strategy that uses cloud computing to store, update, and retrieve eHealth data. There are various commercial systems established by firms that would serve medical record services, in addition to the works that have been exhibited thus far as the product of academic study.

Microsoft's HealthVault platform, for example, was created to manage the health information of its members. Users can use the system to obtain, save, and share relevant patient information with family members and healthcare professionals. It also allows third-party applications to control exercise and diet.

2.12 MEDICAL SOLUTIONS IN THE CLOUD

In several nations, increasing lifespan and decreasing birth rates have resulted in population aging and, as a result, an increase in the demand for medical care. Furthermore, because they reside in rural areas, a significant portion of the population does not have access to decent healthcare. Telemedicine enables those living in remote locations to get healthcare and save money by offering remote monitoring and medical assistance. Furthermore, cloud computing may make it possible to offer better telemedicine services. The cloud can assist delivering effective care and treatment for patients because of its features, such as on-demand access anywhere, at low pricing, and superior flexibility. Pandey et al. [29] offer an autonomous cloud system that captures health data of the clients, organizes it in a cloud-based platform, and allows market research via cloud-based software applications. Users (patients in this case) wear sensors on their body and use a smartphone to access an app. The sensors communicate with the app via Bluetooth. The client can receive graphs depicting the user's current health condition from the cloud, and the system also contains cloud-based middleware.

2.13 FOG COMPUTING

Many architectures have recently been introduced for fog computing [30], with the three-tier architecture being the most popular nowadays [31]. The three primary layers of the fundamental fog computing architecture are as follows:

1. **Device Layer**: This is the layer that has the most interaction with terminal users and gadgets. It is made up of a variety of devices, including smart objects and sensors. These devices are extensively dispersed around the globe and are in charge of sensing physical objects and transmitting data to the higher layer for processing and storage.
2. **Fog Layer**: This layer is placed at the network's edge and has many fog nodes, which are typically routers, gateways, and base stations. Tasks like scheduling, storing, and fog nodes handle managing distributed computers.
3. **Cloud Layer**: Cloud layer is in charge of long-term data storage and significant computational processing. Unlike standard cloud systems, fog computing accesses the cloud layer regularly and is controlled, resulting in inefficient use of all available resources.

Uses in Healthcare: An intelligent healthcare gateway for fog computing modules was released in 2017 [32]. The authors focused on establishing a link between household and hospital gateways. They demonstrated that fog computing is critical in enabling the intelligent gateway through several tests. Another study looked into the function of fog computing in implementing a healthcare monitoring system. They recommended a mediator layer that would accept raw data from sensor devices and then store it in the cloud. Finally, to illustrate the efficacy of adding the fog layer to the framework, early diagnosis of chronic disease systems was constructed via a program based on fog computing. HealthFog [33], a healthcare framework, was introduced in 2016. Fog computing technology connected the user's layer to the cloud layer in the suggested framework. They primarily focused on improving and resolving privacy issues in EMRs. The HealthFog was then enhanced with cloud-based security technologies to enhance system security. For a home and hospital management system, the proposed structure used edge computing. To support real-time systems, current fog computing systems were upgraded in 2015 by analyzing bio-signals on the fog server-side [34].

2.14   THREATS WITH CLOUD COMPUTING

Even while cloud computing has various advantages in the medical industry, there are some concerns about implementing this cutting-edge technology in such a complex field as healthcare [35]. The most pressing worry in this area is the security of patient data.

   I. **Privacy and Security Issues**: Cloud file sets might contain private or secret data regarding a patient's health history, which must be securely protected to avoid abuse and disclosure. Global concerns about data jurisdiction, data privacy, security, and compliance significantly impact healthcare businesses' adoption of cloud technologies.
  II. **Kind of Cloud**: The debate over which cloud model (public or private) is best for serving the needs of the healthcare industry has raged on for years. The major disadvantage of adopting a cloud service is that it misses the management and performance rules that a health institution requires; yet, a private cloud provides superior customization, security, and privacy, as well as a high degree of internal data handling. Private clouds, on the other hand, could have an advantage over public clouds, which are more vulnerable to data management due to their higher security measures.
 III. **Portability of Data**: Another important concern for some medical groups when using cloud services is the ability to switch cloud vendors or return to the healthcare organization without disrupting operations or creating rival data claims. Traditional IT technology gives the healthcare company physical control over its systems, services, and data. If a provider suspends services or rejects data access, a healthcare company may be incapable of

providing critical healthcare services to its clients (patients in this case), providing a challenge.

IV. **Trustability of Service**: The truth is that all cloud services and other corporate platforms might, at some point in the future, experience some amount of downtime. As a result, the applications must meet stringent performance, availability, and reliability requirements. In these dynamic conditions, the greater dependence on decentralized network-based services adds to the complexities and problems of data security and management.

The medical industry's reliance on the accessibility and accuracy of data can mean the difference between innocuous and life-threatening situations. Contingency planning stresses methods and strategies for resuming applications, data, technology, and other IT infrastructure in the case of a disaster, and it is an aspect of client satisfaction in the event of a disaster.

2.15 FUTURE RESEARCH

The use of cloud technology in healthcare is a relatively recent research subject. Medical data administration and EHRs focus on current cloud applications. On the other side, cloud computing can provide value-added healthcare services like screening and treatment, medicine, education, referrals, and recommendations. As a result, we might claim that the healthcare sector's successful use of cloud computing has not yet realized its full potential. Currently, data-driven cloud utilization is more prevalent than network-related services. Cloud services can offer judgment calls with access to a wide range of data. Nonetheless, cloud computing for healthcare management help has received little attention and requires more investigation. The medical industry may be disrupted by these value-added medical services. They can, however, be considered as a tool to help medical professionals, such as physicians and doctors, make better judgments. In the future, researchers may want to investigate these value-added cloud services in the healthcare industry, especially in the field of medical decision-making.

Furthermore, existing cloud applications are investigated mainly regarding their data processing capacity and availability [36]. Applications related to health monitoring, such as fitness tracking, have been extensively studied and implemented. On the other hand, cloud computing does not make it easy to track actions related to chronic patients and their treatment/care. Future research should focus on cloud-based health monitoring capabilities rather than data processing capabilities.

Future work could perhaps focus on the advantages and disadvantages of information exchange, as well as the compliance with laws of cloud service providers (CSPs) that offer similar services. For example, a study found that suitable privacy measures in cloud computing for the healthcare sector are a crucial subject for investigation in the coming years. CSPs are not yet required to be audited by a regulatory agency. As a result, a CSP is free to transfer data from one country to another [37]. Furthermore, despite the fact that these are marketed as distribution of responsibilities between service providers and medical centers, CSPs do not currently offer specialized data capabilities. Future research should focus on user's confidentiality restrictions, service standards, and CSP requirements.

2.16 CONCLUSION

The present trend of implementing cloud computing in the medical area has the potential to improve and solve a variety of collaborative information difficulties in healthcare companies and cost savings. When exchanging information among medical institutions, standardized cloud-based applications will benefit patients, physicians, insurance companies, pharmacies, imaging centers, etc. Issues like security and portability arise as a result of the cloud computing model. Therefore, as a consequence, cloud adoption is moving at a slower pace. Despite the hurdles, applying industry standards in the development, implementation, and use of cloud-based systems will ideally result in the adoption of cloud-based systems being more widespread in the future.

Cloud computing's promise for delivering 21st-century healthcare opens up a world of possibilities for healthcare professionals and organizations. However, to become a reliable IT service paradigm, the cloud must overcome the obstacles that are now preventing many businesses from embracing it. Contrary to popular belief, research shows that small local cloud providers are seen as more credible and trustworthy by companies than large, well-established cloud providers. Choosing the correct cloud provider will be the main issue for healthcare providers who recognize the value of adopting a cloud solution.

REFERENCES

1. Allen, S. (2011). Cloud computing and healthcare security. *Cloud Computing Journal.* Retrieved from http://cloudcomputing.sys-con.com/node/1796151
2. Barry, J., & Napatech. (2011). Testing the Cloud: Assuring Availability. Retrieved from http://www.hpcinthecloud.com/hpccloud/2011-08-16/testing_the_cloud:_assuring_availability.htm
3. Blaisdell, R. (2012). Cloud benefits in the health Industry. Retrieved from http://www.cloudtweaks.com/2012/02/cloud-benefits-in-the-health-industry/
4. Devadass, L., Sekaran, S. S., & Thinakaran, R. (2017). Cloud computing in healthcare. *International Journal of Students Research in Technology & Management,* 5(1), 25–31.
5. Kuttikrishnan, D. (2011). Cloud computing: The road ahead. Accessed on 15 September 2017.
6. Rostrom, T, & Teng, C. C. (2011). Secure communications for PACS in a cloud environment. In *2011 Annual International Conference of the IEEE Engineering in Medicine and Biology Society* (pp. 8219–8222). IEEE.
7. Mell, P., & Grance, T. (2011). *The NIST Definition of Cloud Computing.* NIST Special Publication 800-145.
8. Rosenthal, A., Mork, P., Li, M. H., Stanford, J., Koester, D., & Reynolds, P. (2010). Cloud computing: A new business paradigm for biomedical information sharing. *Journal of Biomedical Informatics;*43(2):342–53.
9. Yu, H. J., Lai, H. S., Chen, K. H., Chou, H. C., Wu, J. M., Dorjgochoo, S., et al. (2013). A sharable cloud-based pancreaticoduodenectomy collaborative database for physicians: Emphasis on security and clinical rule supporting. *Computer Methods and Programs in Biomedicine,* 111(2), 488–497.

10. Kuo, A. M. (2011). Opportunities and challenges of cloud computing to improve health care services. *Journal of Medical Internet Research*, 13(3), e67. http://dx.doi. org/10.2196/jmir.1867

11. Korea IT Times. (2010). Telstra Plans Launch of E-Health Cloud Services, Tip of the Iceberg for Opportunity. Retrieved from http://www.koreaittimes.com/story/9826/ telstra-plans-launch-e-health-cloud-services-tip-iceberg-opportunity

12. Rui, Z., & Ling, L. (2010). Security models and requirements for healthcare application clouds. In *2010 IEEE 3rd International Conference on cloud Computing* (pp. 268–275). IEEE.

13. Shimrat, O. (2009). Cloud Computing and Healthcare. Technology Matters. Retrieved from http://www.himss.org/content/files/Code%2093_Shimrat_CloudComputingandHealth care_2009.pdf

14. Raut, V. (2011). Cloud computing and health care. *Cloud Computing Journal*. Retrieved from http://cloudcomputing.sys-con.com/node/2026409

15. Kupferman, J., Silverman, J., Jara, P., & Browne, J. (2009). Scaling Into the Cloud. Retrieved from http://cs.ucsb.edu/~jkupferman/docs/ScalingIntoTheClouds.pdf

16. Rackspace Hosting. (2011). High Availability Cloud Environments. Retrieved from http://www.codeproject.com/Articles/157992/High-Availability-Cloud-Environments

17. Logic Monitor. (2012). LogicMonitor: Architecture White Paper. Retrieved from http:// www.logicmonitor.com /downloads/Architecture.pdf?84cd58

18. Pandora. (2011). FMS-Virtualization and cloud computing monitoring. Retrieved from http://pandorafms.com/downloads/PandoraFMS_Virtual_Enviroment_Monitoring.pdf

19. Hsieh, J. & Hsu, M. W. (2012). A cloud computing based 12-lead ECG telemedicine service, *BMC Medical Informatics and Decision Making*, 12, 1–12.

20. Dudley, J. T., Pouliot, Y., Chen, J. R., Morgan, A. A. & Butte, A. J. (2010). Translational bioinformatics in the cloud: An affordable alternative, *Genome Medicine*, 2(8), 1–6.

21. Schadt, E. E, Linderman, M. D., Sorenson, J., Lee, L., & Nolan, G. P. (2011). Cloud and heterogeneous computing solutions exist today for the emerging big data problems in biology, *Nature Reviews Genetics*, 12(3), 224.

22. Grossmann, R. L., & White, K. P. (2011). A vision for a biomedical cloud, *Journal of Internal Medicine*, 271(2), 122–130.

23. Schatz, M. C. (2009). CloudBurst: Highly sensitive read mapping with MapReduce, *Bioinformatics*, 25(11), 1363–1369.

24. Feng, X., Grossman, R., & Stein, L. (2011). PeakRanger: A cloud-enabled peak caller for ChIP-seq data, *BMC Bioinformatics*, 12(1), 1–11.

25. Habegger, L., Balasubramanian, S., Chen, D. Z., Khurana, E., Sboner, A., Harmanci, A. et al. (2012). VAT: A computational framework to functionally annotate variants in personal genomes within a cloud-computing environment, *Bioinformatics*, 28(17), 2267–2269.

26. Xia, H., Asif, I., & Zhao, X. (2013). Cloud-ECG for real-time ECG monitoring and analysis, *Computer Methods and Programs in Biomedicine*, 110, 253–259.

27. Chen, T. S., Liu, C. H., Chen, T. L., Chen, C. S., Bau, J. G., & Lin, T. C. (2012). Secure dynamic access control scheme of PHR in cloud computing, *Journal of Medical Systems*, 36(6): 4005–4020.

28. Doukas, C., Pliakas, T., & Maglogiannis, I. (2010). Mobile healthcare information man-agement utilizing Cloud Computing and Android OS. In *2010 Annual International Conference of the IEEE Engineering in Medicine and Biology* (pp. 1037–1040). IEEE.

29. Pandey, S., Voorsluys, W., Niu, S., Doker, A., & Buyya, R. (2012). An autonomic cloud environment for hosting ECG data analysis services, *Future Generation Computer Systems*, 28, 147–154.

30. Azam, M., & Huh, E. (2014) Fog computing and smart gateway based communication for the cloud of things. In: *Proceedings of the 2nd International Conference on the Future Internet of Things and Cloud (FiCloud-2014)*, Barcelona.

31. Hu, P., Dhelim, S., Ning, H., & Qiu, T. (2017). Survey on fog computing: architecture, key technologies, applications, and open issues. *Journal of Network and Computer Applications*, 98, 27–42.
32. Dang, L. M., Piran, M. J., Han, D., Min, K., & Moon, H. (2019). A survey on internet of things and cloud computing for healthcare. *Electronics*, 8(7), 768.
33. Ahmad, M., Amin, M. B., Hussain, S., Kang, B. H., Cheong, T., & Lee, S. (2016). Health fog: A novel framework for health and wellness applications. *The Journal of Supercomputing*, 72(10), 3677–3695.
34. Nandyala, C. S., & Kim, H. K. (2016). From cloud to fog and IoT-based real-time U-healthcare monitoring for smart homes and hospitals. *International Journal of Smart Home*, 10(2), 187–196.
35. Reddy, G. N., & Reddy, G. J. (2014). Study of cloud computing in healthcare industry. *arXiv preprint arXiv:1402.1841*.
36. He, C., Fan, X., & Li, Y. (2013). Toward ubiquitous healthcare services with a novel efficient cloud platform. *IEEE Transaction of Biomedical Engineering*, 60(1), 230–234.
37. Sun, Y., Zhang, J., Xiong, Y., & Zhu, G. (2014). Data security and privacy in cloud computing. *International Journal of Distributed Sensor Networks*, 10(7), 190903.

3 Medical Information Extraction of Clinical Notes and Pictorial Visualisation of Electronic Medical Records Summary Interface

Praveen Singh and Gopal Chaudhary
Bharati Vidyapeeth's College of Engineering

Joao Alexandre Lobo Marques
University of Saint Joseph

CONTENTS

DOI: 10.1201/9781003254119-3

3.1   INTRODUCTION

All the medical history of patients is stored in medical records and it also plays a vital role in patient supervision. About 80% of hospitals and more than 50% of doctors have adopted EMRs according to a report from Centers for Medicare & Medicaid Services. EMRs are still facing difficulties in getting accepted in clinical practices irrespective of their huge potential because the delivered data of the EMRs are usually extensive, convoluted, not properly organised, and difficult to manage [1,2]. Important information is becoming constantly arduous to retrieve due to the huge increase in medical record bulks; hence, it is majorly restraining a physician's efficiency and diagnostics reasoning with which they function. Since the time for response is limited in the field of healthcare, professionals have only a couple of minutes to retrieve, review, and extract the necessary records and it's a very challenging task [3,4].

Ongoing EMR systems have not fully fulfilled their promise as a source of digital data where clinical information can be arranged to enhance the ease of extracting required data. The incorporation and retrieval of various types of data, such as treatments, tests, diagnostics, medications, symptoms, etc. should be made fast using EMR systems. The merit of medical data which are available online can be intensified with the help of information visualisation (InfoVis) [5,6]. Since the InfoVis provides medical records in instinctive, comprehensible, perceptible, and reasonable formats, users can quickly acknowledge and retrieve important data from huge amount of records.

Well-known EMR systems, such as eClinicalWorks [7], Allscripts [8], and EpicCare [9], offer features for allergy checks, list of problems, online prescriptions, order management, billing, and medication control. Flowsheet is mostly preferred for visualisation in EMR systems. It is widely occupied in intensive care units (ICUs). It emphasises trends and abnormal values since it comprises essential data of a single patient over a given period. Various other systems, like IBM Watson Health [10] and Oracle Health Sciences [11], often contain autonomous techniques for analysis based on Machine Learning and data mining. It takes time to analyse patients' history since clinical data are organised in ways that are unable to fulfil physicians' requisites. At present, EMR systems facilitate the inclusion and accumulation of medical information but are deprived of the functionalities for exploratory analysis tasks and temporal queries completely [12].

In this chapter, the authors convey a system of medical history synopsis that enables users to access the medical data, which are then analysed. The representation of the system is exhibited in Figure 3.1.

Section 3.1 includes the introduction to this chapter. Section 3.2 includes the related work, which is done by the authors such as retrieval and processing of the data. Section 3.3 includes pictorial visualisation of the data based on different interfaces. Methodology for information extraction is included in Section 3.4. Section 3.5 includes the result, and Section 3.6 includes conclusion and future work.

3.2   RELATED WORKS

3.2.1   RETRIEVAL OF MEDICAL INFORMATION

Medical history of patients contains prized and personal information. It is necessary for diagnosis processing to extract, visualise, and present these crucial medical data.

Firstly, an important step of data extraction is performed. Zeng et al. [13] extract medical data of doctor's interest using regression models. Sabra et al. [14] were entrenched on semantic retrieval from text-based history. In addition, to realise medical data visualisation and presentation [15], a 3D medical graphical avatar (MGA) was designed by Michael et al., which can facilitate the conveyance of various medical data comprising texts, videos, and images.

3.2.2 METAMAP AND UNIFIED MEDICAL LANGUAGE SYSTEM

In the biomedical sciences, the Unified Medical Language System [16,17] (UMLS) is a synopsis of many administered vocabularies. UMLS contains three tools (Semantic Network, Metathesaurus, and Specialist). The Metathesaurus is a huge multilingual data of vocabulary that accommodates data associated with health and clinical concepts, their numerous terms, and the relationships between them [18]. It goes beyond the specific terms, classifications, and thesauri. It associates different views and names of the identical ideas and are connected by them, and it also identifies useful interconnection that exists between various ideas. Dr. Alan (Lan) Aronson developed Metamap at the National Library of Medicine (NLM) [19]. It is a powerful tool to acknowledge UMLS concepts in medical data [20]. It has the capacity to link UMLS Metathesaurus to medical and biological text or, correspondingly, to discover Metathesaurus conceptualisation mentioned in data. In the structure presented, the authors use Metamap 2014AA and its related Java API to proceed with the retrieval of information.

3.3 PICTORIAL VISUALISATION OF DATA

Medical histories are divided into several categories and overlaid using two different interfaces: one is for spatial representation and the other for temporal depiction of medical data.

3.3.1 SPATIAL REPRESENTATION BASED ON POSITION

In a spatial medical record, the location of an illness or disease is arranged according to its physiological systems. We divided physiological data into six categories and combined pertinent photographs with text.

- Circulatory/respiratory
- Immune/endocrine
- Dermatological/rheumatological
- Gastrointestinal
- Neurological
- Urogenital

The information would be mundanely exhibited over its corresponding position with a marking on its relevant physiological data image if the sickness and information of the human body parts were collected.

The colours denote the physiological system to which it belongs. Symptoms with black circles indicate that physiological data are currently unclear. Furthermore, if the ailment has no defined site, such as Myasthenia Gravis, a whole-body problem picture would be employed.

3.3.2 REPRESENTATIONS BASED ON TEMPORAL-TIME

Medical histories are shown like a data sheet in temporal medical records, allowing visualisation of information and the change of health through time. A temporal summary can replace the whole medical record, but specifics must be obtained separately. Visits, medical imaging, medication, lab tests, and treatment are among the categories. They're represented on the timeline with various icons.

3.4 METHODOLOGY FOR INFORMATION EXTRACTION

Medical information visualisation uses spatial and temporal interfaces to summarise medical notes. As a result, we need to present our classified information retrieved from an existing medical data on our system.

In this paper, the authors convey a system of medical history synopsis that enables users to access the medical data, which are then analysed. The representation of the system is exhibited in Figure 3.1.

Metamap is used to extract medical information. Front and back views of physiological system is shown in Figure 3.2. As a pre-processing step, we transform the plain data to XML format. With 1,305 medical notes from i2b2, Apache OpenNLP [22] is used to train the model. The system's operation is depicted in Figure 3.1. The majority of clinical notes in many clinics and hospitals are organised in a regular and general style in forms with names. A structured clinical note is shown in Figure 3.3. Our system is now focused on structured data extraction.

3.4.1 FORMAT CONVERSION PRE-PROCESSING

We implemented the methodical keywords detection as shown in Table 3.1. The text is then further processed to transform them into XML annotation. An XML format is shown in Figure 3.4.

3.4.2 TOKENISATION

It plays a crucial part in natural language processing (NLP). It is used to transform an arrangement of characters into an arrangement of sentences and words independently. It can be achieved by Apache OpenNLP, which accommodates several tokeniser models [23,24]. For tokenisation of words and sentences, we employ en-token.bin [25] and en-sent.bin, respectively, in our system.

3.4.3 REMOVAL OF STOP WORDS

These are words that are taken out of natural language data before or after they are processed in computing [26–28]. Stop words relate to the most often used function words in the English language, such as the, am, is, a, etc. On the Internet, you may

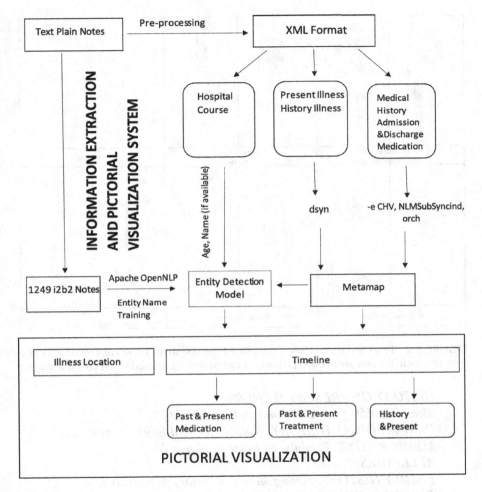

FIGURE 3.1   Retrieval of medical data and system of pictorial visualisation.

get a complete list of English stop words [29], which we utilise to filter the medical data for the next step.

3.4.4 METAMAP SETTING

For collecting medical information, such as admission drugs and discharge, previous and present sickness, upcoming medications, and even tests, we used the Metamap with the 2014AA knowledge source. Metamap includes numerous setup choices for different medical data extractions, as illustrated in Table 3.2.

The extracted specific semantic kinds in the medicine extraction section are Clinical Drug and orcs [30], which is represented by Organic Chemical. In the meantime, the CHV and NLMSubsyn sources are not included in this section.

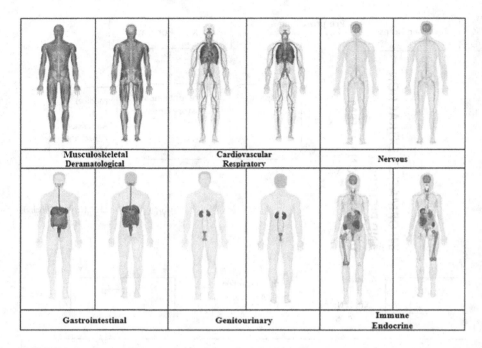

| Musculoskeletal Deramatological | Cardiovascular Respiratory | Nervous |

| Gastrointestinal | Genitourinary | Immune Endocrine |

FIGURE 3.2   Front and back views of the physiological system. There are a total of six systems in which diseases are divided [21], which can be easily retrieved based on the ailment.

HISTORY OF PRESENT ILLNESS:
Mrs. A is a 50-year-old woman with multiple ......
PAST MEDICAL HISTORY: Notable for multiple cavernous ......
MEDICATIONS: Prednisone taper as above.
ALLERGIES: None.
FAMILY HISTORY: Strong maternal history of psoriasis.
PHYSICAL EXAMINATION: Temperature 99.8 ......

FIGURE 3.3   Sample of constructed medical notes.

3.4.5   RECOGNITION OF TIME-ENTITY EXPRESSION

Named-entity recognition (NER) is a subtask of information extraction that aims to locate and categorise named entities in text into pre-defined categories (also known as entity identification, entity chunking, and entity extraction). Time knowledge is critical for caregivers to understand the patient's history and present circumstances. We trained a Time-Entity Expression model to recognise time information using Apache OpenNLP and manually marked phrases from 1,294 clinical notes from i2b2. The labelled data are shown below.

- On <START:time> 12/18 <END> the patient was seen with a laceration and a bruise

TABLE 3.1
XML Annotations and Keywords of Title Detection

Annotation	Description	Keywords
PMH	History of Past Medications	("HISTORY"|"PAST")&("MEDICATIONS")
DGN	Discharge & Main Diagnoses	"DIAGNOSES"
HOP	Family History	"FAMILY"&"HISTORY"
MED	Admission & Discharge Medications	("ADMISSION"|"DISCHARGE")& ("MEDICATIONS")
LAB	Laboratory	"LABORATORIES"|"LAB"|"LABORATORY"
PE	Physical Examination	("PHYSICAL"&"EXAMINATIONS")
HPC	Hospital Course	"COURSE"
HPI	History of Past Illness	("HISTORY"|"PAST")&("ILLNESS"|"DISEASE")

| represents OR operator and & represents AND operator.

```
<HPI> Mrs. A is a 50-year-old woman with multiple …… </HPI>
<PMH> Notable for multiple cavernous hemangiomas …… </PMH>
<MED> Prednisone taper as above. </MED>
<ALR> None. </ALR>
<HOF> A strong maternal history of psoriasis. </HOF>
<PE>  Temperature 99.8 …… </PE>
```

FIGURE 3.4 XML format notes from Figure 3.3.

TABLE 3.2
Metamap Setup Options of the Medical Information

Medical Information	Metamap Setups
Disease and illness	"-J dsyn"
Human body location	"-J blor,bpoc"
Physical Exams	"-J diap"
Medication	"-J clnd,orch"&"-e CHV ,NLMSubsyn"

- The patient had many cannulation and admitted into the hospital from <START:time> June <END> to <START:time> August 2020 <END> due to
- He was sent to Coopers Hospital by EMS on <START:time> 8/7/22 <END>, and the patient

The extracted data can be stored on cloud, and they can be used to train machine learning models in Python libraries such as TensorFlow. This will further increase the efficiency of extraction of medical information and will make the accessing and comprehension of the patient's medical history and current information quicker.

3.5   RESULTS

We manually labelled 1,880 phrases from 1,305 medical notes using time expressions. The Time-Entity Detection model was trained using 1,405 phrases. The data are split and transformed to XML format with stratified information by recognising title boundaries. Metamap is quite good at recognising the UMLS idea for retrieving clinical data. The following is an example of the findings obtained using Metamap. Input data are illustrated in Figure 3.5, and output data are illustrated in Figure 3.6.

Input data:

Mrs. Axxxx is a 50-year-old woman with multiple cavernous psoriasis. She is right- handed. She was in her usual state of health until two weeks prior to admission. She developed sore skin, for which she saw her primary care physician, Anamika was prescribed Celebrex drops. A few days later she complained of red, scaly patches on body. This was mostly described as swollen and stiff joints. She stated that she had trouble getting up from bed. She was seen again by primary care physician, Ram since she had complaints of swollen joints, as well as a new complaint of itching burning and soreness, eczema disease was considered. She was given an oral acitretin taper. This unsteady gait progressed, and then she subsequently started to develop thickened, ridged nails. Her condition got progressively worse and red patches increased. Some parts of the skin were bleeding. At an outside hospital, skin biopsy revealed that the skin cells are getting replaced more quickly than usual. She was transferred here for further care.

FIGURE 3.5   The input clinical data.

Output data:

Diagnostic Procedure:
MRS (magnetic resonance spectroscopic imaging) Body Part, Organ, or Organ Component:
right handed (Structure of right hand)
Body Part, Organ, or Organ Component:
Legs, Knees
Disease or Syndrome:
Red patches on skin and swollen joints
Sign or Symptom: Blister, swollen joints
Disease or Syndrome: Psoriasis
Body Location or Region: FACE (Face) Diagnostic Procedure:
Skin biopsy
Body Part, Organ, or Organ Component:
Pons (Pontine structure)

FIGURE 3.6   Output clinical data obtained using Metamap.

As illustrated in Figure 3.7, time information is also retrieved, and all retrieved data are communicated to the graphical visualisation system for presentation of data.

A time-based temporal representation is shown in Figure 3.8.

The above representation is stored in the form of a table to be used as a database for future reference. These data can be used for the training of the model. The tabular representation of the data depicted in Figure 3.8 is shown in Table 3.3.

The trained model was set into test with 192 records. Around 93% of the records used for testing were similar to the data used for training the model and the rest of the records were intentionally taken somewhat different from the training dataset to

```
<PHYEXAM>Fasciotomy<DATETIME>01/19</DATETIME></PHYEXAM>
<MEDICATION>Atorvastatin<DATETIME>09/17</DATETIME></MEDICATION>
<MEDICATION>Clopidogrel<DATETIME>02/16</DATETIME></MEDICATION>
<MEDICATION>Metformin<DATETIME>07/14</DATETIME></MEDICATION>
<PHYEXAM>Valvuloplasty<DATETIME>03/22</DATETIME></PHYEXAM>
<PHYEXAM>Adrenalectomy<DATETIME>4/5/02</DATETIME></PHYEXAM>
```

FIGURE 3.7 Relevant time and the retrieved output medical data.

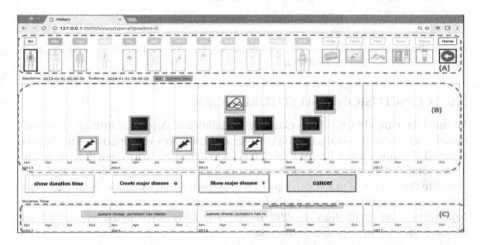

FIGURE 3.8 Timeline display of information. Time is denoted on the horizontal line and the icons show several events.

TABLE 3.3
Tabular Display of Events with Respect to Date Fetched from Figure 3.8

Date	Event
1 October 2013	Vaccination for Rubella
11 April 2014	Diagnosis of cold and flu
27 April 2014	Diagnosis of allergy
23 October 2014	Vaccination for Hepatitis B
18 March 2015	Diagnosis of mononucleosis
29 May 2015	Diagnosis of dengue
2 June 2015	Medication for dengue
22 August 2015	Vaccination for tetanus
3 October 2015	Diagnosis of anthrax
4 March 2016	Diagnosis of influenza
18 April 2016	Diagnosis of diabetes
20 June 2016	Diagnosis of indigestion

TABLE 3.4

Analysed Result after Testing the Trained Model

Type of Input data	Number of Tests	Totally Correct	Partially Correct	Incorrect
Similar to the data used for training	178	169	7	2
Not similar to the data used for training	14	3	5	6

ensure the reliability of the model. An accuracy of 96% was achieved and the analysed result is depicted in Table 3.4.

3.6 CONCLUSION AND FUTURE WORK

Medical data are obtained from plain medical data and described through a picture-based interface in a visualisation system for clinical notes information. The Apache OpenNLP-trained Time-Entity model aids us in detecting time-related material and its associated date. Illnesses are displayed on their respective physiological system image in the section of graphical depiction of extracted medical data. Simultaneously, time-related information is compiled on a timeline in chronological sequence. To summarise, our technology enables users to quickly fetch and comprehend the patient's medical history and current data.

There are several poorly laid out clinical data containing vital information about the patient. Unstructured notes are difficult to comprehend by software programs for subsequent processing since they do not follow any predetermined structure. Specific aspects are still described in other sections. One part, for example, has many clinical medications and substances, and we refer to it as the medication section. The physical examination section also includes names of different body parts of humans. Our continuing research is focused on using deep learning to analyse unstructured clinical notes. Furthermore, the analysed data could be stored on the cloud and a machine learning model can be trained using the stored data to increase the efficiency of extraction of medical information.

REFERENCES

[1] R. Smith, "What clinical information do doctors need?" *BMJ*, vol. 313, no. 7064, pp. 1062–1068, Oct. 1996, doi: 10.1136/BMJ.313.7064.1062.

[2] J. Wyatt, "Medical informatics, artefacts or science?," *Methods of Information in Medicine*, vol. 35, no. 3, pp. 197–200, Feb. 1996, doi: 10.1055/S-0038-1634665/ID/JR4665-25.

[3] I. Keshta and A. Odeh, "Security and privacy of electronic health records: Concerns and challenges," *Egyptian Informatics Journal*, vol. 22, no. 2, pp. 177–183, Jul. 2021, doi: 10.1016/J.EIJ.2020.07.003.

[4] "Problems With Electronic Health Records (EHRs)." https://www.dittotranscripts.com/blog/problems-with-electronic-health-records/ (accessed May 20, 2022).

[5] L. Chittaro, "Information visualization and its application to medicine," *Artificial Intelligence in Medicine*, vol. 22, no. 2, pp. 81–88, 2001, doi: 10.1016/S0933-3657(00)00101-9.

[6] S. Card, J. Mackinlay, and B. Shneiderman, *Readings in Information Visualisation: Using Vision to Think*, Morgan Kaufmann, p. 686, 1999. [Online]. Available: http://www.amazon.de/Readings-Information-Visualisation-Vision-Think/dp/1558605339/ref=sr_1_2?ie=UTF8&qid=1407927051&sr=82&keywords=Readings+in+Information+visualization (accessed May 20, 2022).

[7] "Top EHR Vendors for 2015." https://www.bizbrain.org/top-ehr-vendors/ (accessed May 14, 2022).

[8] "Allscripts Professional EHR Reviews, Demo & Pricing -2022." https://www.softwareadvice.com/medical/allscripts-professional-ehr-profile/ (accessed May 20, 2022).

[9] "eClinicalWorks Reviews, Demo & Pricing -2022." https://www.softwareadvice.com/medical/eclinicalworks-profile/ (accessed May 14, 2022).

[10] "IBM Watson Health | AI Healthcare Solutions - India | IBM." https://www.ibm.com/in-en/watson-health (accessed May 14, 2022).

[11] "Health Sciences Support | Oracle India." https://www.oracle.com/in/industries/health-sciences/support/ (accessed May 20, 2022).

[12] O. Półchłopek, N. R. Koning, F. L. Büchner, M. R. Crone, M. E. Numans, and M. Hoogendoorn, "Quantitative and temporal approach to utilising electronic medical records from general practices in mental health prediction," *Computers in Biology and Medicine*, vol. 125, Oct. 2020, doi: 10.1016/J.COMPBIOMED.2020.103973.

[13] Q. Zeng, X. Zhang, Z. Li, L. Liu, and W. Zhang, "Extracting clinical information from free-text of pathology and operation notes via Chinese natural language processing," in *2010 IEEE International Conference on Bioinformatics and Biomedicine Workshops, BIBMW 2010*, pp. 593–597, 2010, doi: 10.1109/BIBMW.2010.5703867.

[14] S. Sabra, K. Mahmood, and M. Alobaidi, "A semantic extraction and sentimental assessment of risk factors (SESARF): An NLP approach for precision medicine: A medical decision support tool for early diagnosis from clinical notes," in *Proceedings - International Computer Software and Applications Conference*, vol. 2, pp. 131–136, Sep. 2017, doi: 10.1109/COMPSAC.2017.34.

[15] M. de Ridder et al., "A web-based medical multimedia visualisation interface for personal health records," in *Proceedings of CBMS 2013–26th IEEE International Symposium on Computer-Based Medical Systems*, pp. 191–196, 2013, doi: 10.1109/CBMS.2013.6627787.

[16] O. Bodenreider, "The unified medical language system (UMLS): Integrating biomedical terminology," *Nucleic Acids Research*, vol. 32, no. suppl_1, Jan. 2004, doi: 10.1093/nar/gkh061.

[17] D. A. B. Lindberg, B. L. Humphreys, and A. T. McCray, "The unified medical language system," *Yearbook of Medical Informatics*, vol. 02, no. 01, pp. 41–51, Mar. 2018, doi: 10.1055/S-0038-1637976.

[18] B. L. Humphreys, D. A. B. Lindberg, H. M. Schoolman, and G. O. Barnett, "The unified medical language system: An informatics research collaboration," *Journal of the American Medical Informatics Association*, vol. 5, no. 1, pp. 1–11, Jan. 1998, doi: 10.1136/JAMIA.1998.0050001.

[19] "UMLS - MetaMap." https://www.nlm.nih.gov/research/umls/implementationresources/metamap.html (accessed May 20, 2022).

[20] A. R. Aronson and alansnlm nih gov, "Effective mapping of biomedical text to the UMLS Metathesaurus: the MetaMap program," in *Proceedings of the AMIA Symposium*, p. 17, 2001, [Online]. Available: https://pubmed.ncbi.nlm.nih.gov/11825149/ (accessed May 20, 2022).

[21] "Explore Human Anatomy, Physiology, and Genetics | Innerbody." https://www.innerbody.com/htm/body.html (accessed May 14, 2022).

[22] "Apache OpenNLP." https://opennlp.apache.org/ (accessed May 20, 2022).

[23] "What is Tokenization | Tokenization in NLP." https://www.analyticsvidhya.com/blog/2020/05/what-is-tokenization-nlp/ (accessed May 20, 2022).

[24] "Tokenization in NLP: Types, Challenges, Examples, Tools - neptune.ai." https://neptune.ai/blog/tokenization-in-nlp (accessed May 20, 2022).

[25] "OpenNLP - Browse /models-1.5 at SourceForge.net." https://sourceforge.net/projects/opennlp/files/models-1.5/ (accessed May 20, 2022).

[26] O. Maimon and L. Rokach, "Introduction to knowledge discovery and data mining," in *Data Mining and Knowledge Discovery Handbook*, pp. 1–15, 2009, doi: 10.1007/978-0-387-09823-4_1.

[27] O. Maimon and L. Rokach, eds, *Data Mining and Knowledge Discovery Handbook*, 2010, doi: 10.1007/978-0-387-09823-4.

[28] A. Rajaraman and J. D. Ullman, "Data mining," in *Mining of Massive Datasets*, pp. 1–17, 2011, doi: 10.1017/CBO9781139058452.002.

[29] "Stopwords." https://www.ranks.nl/stopwords (accessed May 14, 2022).

[30] "Semantic Types and Groups - MetaMap documentation." https://lhncbc.nlm.nih.gov/ii/tools/MetaMap/documentation/SemanticTypesAndGroups.html (accessed May 20, 2022).

4 Investigations on RFID-Enabled Healthcare Usage and Adoption Issues

Pankaj Palta, Rahul Kakkar,
Sumeet Goyal, and Manvinder Sharma
CGC – College of Engineering

Joginder Singh
Chandigarh Group of Colleges

CONTENTS

DOI: 10.1201/9781003254119-4

41

Healthcare is constantly evolving. Patient safety, nurse efficiency, and treatment quality all improve productivity in different healthcare procedures. Healthcare has turned to IT and its applications to achieve this, since these have been shown to increase efficiency for healthcare personnel [1]. Over the last 10 years, hospitals have seen a rise in critical care monitored beds, medical devices, emergency visits, and postsurgical cases [2–4]. With the decline of family members, many patients are depending on hospital emergency rooms as their primary source for general healthcare, affecting volume, throughput, and patient flow. At the same time, hospitals are also deploying a variety of data systems to support clinical procedures, such as electronic medical records (EMR), alert notification systems, and administration platforms for medication purpose, which provides data in a new format with more information and in easy-to-read format. This confluence of challenges has a direct influence on care professionals' workloads, requiring them to handle a large number of patients along with larger amounts of data. One of the most important aspects of healthcare is identification. It plays a key part in patient identification and even the identification of different devices, components, equipment, items, instruments, and pharmaceuticals. There is a large number of targets in healthcare, which must be identified for purposes of registration, tracking, and monitoring. Unidentified patients/medications result in some serious issues, even deadly. This is why it's critical to investigate and identify how radio frequency identification (RFID) technology is employed and what kinds of results have been discovered in the healthcare system.

RFID is a technology that employs radio waves to automate identification. It consists of three major components: RFID identification, RFID reader, and a data processing system. RFID tags consist of an antenna and a data chip for storing information, and are typically used to identify targets. RIFD reader, which is often mobile/fixed and coupled to a data system, can read/write the contents of the chip. The technology is similar to bar code technology, in which information is read from a bar code by a reader. When compared to bar code technology, RFID offers various advantages, such as the reader's ability to read/write tag data without requiring a line of sight, the ability to rewrite tag information where a bar code cannot, and the RFID reader's ability to read many RFID tags at once. RFID technology also has other advantages, such as a long-distance reading range, re-usability, data security, and simple data transmission between the tag and the reader [5,6].

4.1   BACKGROUND

4.1.1   RFID System

RFID is a technology that is successful in many industries like agriculture, supply chain, transportation, warehousing, construction, library, tolls on highway, etc. [7–9]. RFID has the potential for monitoring, tracking, and storing read data in real time. This technology is better than bar code reader as there is no line of sight as in bar code and RFIDs are also used with collaboration of internet of things (IoT) and Wireless Sensor Network (WSN). RFID system consists of RFID tags and RFID reader. RFID tags are of three types: Passive tags, Active tags, and Semi-passive tags.

4.1.2 RFID READER

RFID readers are also known as RFID interrogators, as they communicate with tags and collect information and store that information in the computer or some middleware (middleware processes and stores the information received from tags if network is large or no computer is connected with readers) [9].

4.1.3 RFID TAGS

Tags are of three types:

- Active.
- Passive.
- Semi-passive.

Active RFID tags have internal power source and these types of tags read readers' frequency and send revert signals on their own, i.e., no external power is required for sending signal back to reader/interrogator. As active tags have their own power, their range of communication is more than other tags, approximately 10–15 m. Active tags have a storage capacity of 128 Kbytes [7]. Passive tags are those tags that do not have internal power source, so passive tags receive power from an interrogator radio frequency to revert back the signals to the reader. Passive tags contain capacitors that are charged inductively by readers' radio frequency. Semi-passive tags are those tags that have their own power source but still they use readers' radio signals power for sending signal back to the reader. The range of semi-passive and passive tags is few meters, approximately 1 m [7,10,11]. Passive tags and semi- passive tags have a storage capacity of less than 128 Kbytes [7]. RFID systems use low frequencies for low cost and for short range is from 30 to 500 KHz, short range tags use inductive coupling. High-cost devices and longer range 900 MHz–2.5 GHz are used [10]. For long range, electromagnetic coupling is used. These RIFD tags reply with fixed frequency, which is different for each tag, which will help in identification of item to which tag is attached. RFID technology is not new as the first RFID tag was invented by Mario W. Cardullo [12] but used later when organizations started using these tags for different applications.

4.2 RFID IN HEALTHCARE SYSTEM

Each year, approximately 1.5 million patients in the United States are affected by pharmaceutical errors, resulting in additional healthcare expenses of $ 2.3 billion in 1993 and $ 3.5 billion in 2006 [13]. So, to avoid such a big loss, RFID system has various potential benefits in the field of healthcare, as listed in Figure 4.1.

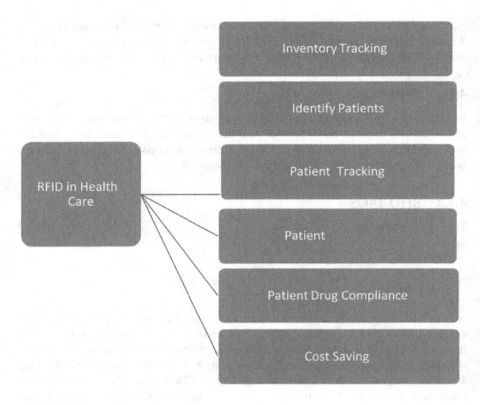

FIGURE 4.1   Field of health care.

4.2.1 INVENTORY TRACKING

By implanting RFID tags on medical devices that are not used most often, we can easily retrieve their location, which, in turn, saves time of nursing staff. Ultimately, they give more attention to patients and the healthcare center can utilize their equipment more efficiently, which will reduce the cost of renting these devices or losing customers [14]. Intel, Autentica, Cisco Systems, and San Raffaele Hospital in Milan, Italy, have been testing RFID to improve blood transfusion safety. Patients and healthcare workers were identified in the system via RFID-enabled wristbands, while blood bags were identifiable with re-useable RFID tags. The system's goal was to keep track of blood donors and transfusions. Data were sent between the transfusion center and RFID readers via wireless access points in various wards of the hospital [15].

4.2.2 IDENTIFY PATIENTS

Most of the medical errors occur due to misidentification of patients in hospital, i.e., wrong treatment given to misidentified patient. RFID tags are used for identification of the correct patient. We can use RFID tag enabled smart band that can be scanned to identify patients before giving any kind of treatment. These tags must have stored the basic information about patient name, sex, blood group, allergies, treatment in process, and medical history, if any [9,16,17]. RFID wireless networks and portable devices were utilized to scan patients' RFID wristbands for identification in a trial conducted at the University College Hospital Galway in Ireland. After establishing patient identity, the handheld device and the system sent the patient information across the wireless network for data processing. This simplified the patient identification process and expedited the retrieval of patient data [18].

4.2.3 PATIENT TRACKING

RFIDs were initially used for tracking objects, animals, vehicles, etc., but with the usage of tags in healthcare, now we can track old-aged patients, disabled patients, and new-born children by which newborns can be protected from theft, and old-aged and disabled persons can be easily located and provided the required treatment. These RFID tags are highly useful to track psychiatric patients [19,20].

4.2.4 PATIENT MONITORING

Accurate identification of patients while operating, proper tracking of patients, especially for senior citizens and persons with certain specified disability, reducing errors in adverse drug effect, keeping track of medication and dosage, getting medical treatment on time, which is possible for patients at home or at remote locations with the help of active RFID tags, sensors, especially used for medical devices like heart rate monitor sensor and IoT will improve patient safety [9,21]. Similarly, the use of RFID-enabled smart bandages will help to get the status of patients after surgery [22]. RFID technology was used as part of a project in Taiwan combined with bar code technology; it was used during medication delivery to patients. At the hospital's drug storage facility, there is a drug dispenser, which is a device that was used to package drugs into doses that were ready to use. Every dose is different. The bar code that referred to the data in regard to drugs Patients used RFID tags on the ward. For patient information and medicines, the nurse used a handheld PDA. Data comparison was performed by the PDA to see if the appropriate drugs were administered to the appropriate patient. PDA demonstrated that it is possible to increase medical quality while also lowering mistakes [23].

4.2.5 PATIENT DRUG COMPLIANCE

Combination of RFID tags on patients and bar code on medicine packages will limit medication errors. It is very common that patients take wrong medicine or incorrect sequence of medicine at home. These types of issues are also traced by using RFID tags; these tags are attached to the medicine container. Every time a container is opened, it sends a signal to healthcare center, which is traced by either system or staff of the hospital. If any issues find then an alert will be send to the patient via internet or SMS. The system also sends notifications if the medicine is expired [9,17].

4.2.6 Cost Saving

An RFID deployment's total cost includes not just the initial investment but also ongoing operating expenses and effects. RFID systems are a large investment that yields a significant financial return on investment (ROI) through the deployment of a diverse collection of applications and use cases. The increased use of technology in any field will definitely reduce man power as most of the data are automatically stored and managed. Data, which we store in the form of records on paper and files, now can be stored directly to the computer, which will reduce paper work, and they are easily manageable too. With inventory tracking, we save the cost of renting medical devices. We save man power, clerical work, and other cost benefits, which will help in improving budget issues in healthcare.

4.3 RFID ADOPTION ISSUES

Although RFID tags have many advantages in the field of healthcare, they still have many adoption issues like:

- Communication range limitation.
- Lifetime of active tags.
- Electromagnetic interference.
- Technological challenges.
- Privacy, security, and data management challenges.
- Financial and organizational challenges.

4.3.1 Communication Range

RFID tags have a limited range, which is an issue in using this technology. To increase the range of data transmission, RFID is used in collaboration with other technologies like WSN and Zigbee. For the collaboration with the IEEE 802.15.4 Zigbee, researchers from Refs. [24–28] collaborate RFID tags with Zigbee network. RFID is used as front-end user and for end user Zigbee technology is used. After collaboration of the two technologies, the range has increased to the extent that data transmission is even possible for multiple floors. Zigbee has a special feature of connecting with other readers automatically.

4.3.2 Lifetime of Active Tags

RFID active tags have to send/receive signals by using their own power, but battery used in active tags is too small, so there is a lifetime issue of these tags. In order to save power, tags are used with sleep and wake-up modes which will save power. As active tags have to monitor and send signal to middle ware all the time, energy loss is still a problem for these types of tags. A solution is to make tags that generate their own power. Two leading techniques used for generation of power within tags are:

- Microelectromechanical system.
- Thermoelectric Generator.

4.3.3 Microelectromechanical System (MEMS)

MEMS generates power from mechanical vibrations that are produced from electrostatic and electromagnetic to electric power. To regenerate power, movement is needed. But, in healthcare system, movement is limited for patients, so this approach will not work [7,11,29].

4.3.4 Thermoelectric Generator

Thermoelectric technology works on the concept of transducers, wherein two different ends of two different materials are set to different temperatures that produce output voltage. This concept can be used for healthcare issues as we can get two different temperatures from human body too [7,30,31].

4.3.5 Electromagnetic Interference

Radio signals from RFID tags may produce electromagnetic interference with biomedical devices; this interference will produce an adverse effect on the working of biomedical devices. EMI generated from tags could be the reason to switch off the biomedical devices, which could lead to risk of a patient's life.

4.3.6 Technological Challenges

There are few technical issues with RFID tags as they are not as reliable as barcode readers as RFID tags' reading depends on read distance, angle of rotation, and RFID tags are also difficult to read if tags/readers are near dielectric sources, water, etc. (5). Lack of wireless infrastructure in healthcare to support this technology will also be an issue [7].

4.3.7 Security, Privacy, and Data Management Challenges

They cover various issues like security and privacy of data. Huge amount of data generated by RFID tags are not secure as these data are transmitted through radio waves to middleware, which can be easily accessed. RFID tags also store information like insurance, blood group, allergies, medication, etc., which can also easily be intercepted as there is no encryption on RFID tags and data stored in these tags. Government restrictions also prohibit the storage of unencrypted data in tags [3,9,32].

4.3.7.1 Spoofing

Using properly designed data on rewritable or blank RFID tags, an attacker can create "authentic" RFID tags.

4.3.7.2 Denial of Service

The RFID systems are unable to work correctly as a result of a Denial of Service assault.

4.3.7.3 Sniffing

There is a possibility that tags can be read without the knowledge of the tag bearer [33].

4.3.8 ORGANIZATIONAL AND FINANCIAL CHALLENGES

RFID tags' price reduced significantly but still to implement RFID tags and RFID readers in collaboration with other technologies like WSN, IoT, etc. in healthcare requires a huge investment. As tags are required for patients, doctors, nursing staff, other staff, visitors, etc. along with passive tags and active tags, RFID readers, middleware software, database for data collection, and high-speed internet are required too. Study [34] in an American hospital shows the rate of interest through 5 years of 2%, with a payback period of 4 years approximately.

Along with financial expenses, there are also some organizational challenges like training of nursing staff, doctors, etc. As they all are already overburdened with their routine tasks, it's difficult for them to learn about all this technology and its working principles. Also, as there is also a lack of organizational support, few organizations give training to their employees with extra working hours.

4.4 CONCLUSION

Researchers in different domains, such as medical informatics, computer science, industrial engineering, and electrical engineering, are all interested in RFID applications. In hospitals and laboratories, useful and novel applications have been developed and tested. When RFID is linked with current hospital infrastructure, its true value is achieved. It can provide valuable process-integrated decision support based on current medical knowledge. It can also use patient data for research and healthcare reporting in a variety of ways. Several studies anticipate an RFID-enabled smart hospital in the future, which will combine RFID and wireless technology to provide a variety of services. It is proven that RFID tags technology is useful for the healthcare and hospitals, especially for those people who are bed-ridden, senior citizens, psychiatric patients, and others too. In spite of having many advantages like error reduction in medical health care, patient tracking, and improving patient safety, there are many adoption issues like communication range, and technological, organizational, and financial challenges. To help healthcare stakeholders adopt RFID systems successfully, we provide the following recommendations. First, before executing an RFID project, the stakeholder should undergo a comprehensive ROI analysis. The major challenge is to weigh the whole cost of deploying an RFID system against the total savings realized by using it. The cost savings might come from a variety of places, including enhanced service quality, improved productivity, and reduced medical errors. It's also a good idea to assess patient happiness and employee productivity. Second, medical staff, patients, and caretaker should be informed on RFID technology so that they are aware of the benefits and potential privacy concerns. When consumers learn that RFID can help improve their safety and minimize medical errors, they will be more inclined to wear RFID tags and care less about their privacy.

REFERENCES

[1] Perrin R, Simpson N, "RFID and bar codes – critical importance in enhancing safe patient care," *J Health Manag* 2004; 18(4):33–39.

[2] DeGroot H, "Patient classification system evaluation, Part I: Essential system elements," *J Nurs Adm* 1989; 19(6):30–5.

[3] Van Slyck A, Johnson KR, "Using patient acuity data to manage patient care outcomes and patient care costs," *Outcomes Manage* 2001; 5(1):36–40.

[4] Arvantes, J, "Emergency Room Visits Climb Amid Primary Care Shortages, Study Results Show," AAFP News. 2008: 27.

[5] RFID Journal, 2002–2008, referred 2.5.2009, available http://www.rfidjournal.com.

[6] Cheng-Ju L, Li L, Shi-Zong C, Chi Chen W, Chun- Huang H, Xin-Mei C, "Mobile healthcare service system using RFID," in *Proceedings of the 2004 IEEE International Conference on Networking, Sensing and Control*, 2004.

[7] Gulcharan NF, Daud H, Nor NM, Ibrahim T, Nyamasvisva ET, "Limitation and solution for healthcare network using RFID technology: A review," *Proc Technol* 2013; 11:565–71.

[8] Anny Leema A, Hemalatha M, "Proposed prediction algorithm based on hybrid approach to deal with anomalies of RFID data in healthcare," *Egypt Inform J* 2013; 14(2):135–45.

[9] Haddara M, Staaby A, "RFID applications and adoptions in healthcare: A review on patient safety," *Proc Comp Sci* 2018; 138:80–8.

[10] Reynolds DR, Riley JR, "Remote-sensing, telemetric and computer-based technologies for investigating insect movement: A survey of existing and potential techniques," *Comput Electron Agric* 2002; 35(2–3):271–307.

[11] Chu H, Wu G, Chen J, Zhao Y, "Study and simulation of semi-active RFID tags using piezoelectric power supply for mobile process temperature sensing," in *2011 IEEE International Conference on Cyber Technology in Automation, Control, and Intelligent Systems*, 2011 Mar 20 (pp. 38–42). IEEE.

[12] Roberti M, "The history of RFID technology," *RFID J* 2005; 16(1):8–11.

[13] Bates DW, "Preventing medication errors: a summary". *Am J Health-System Pharm* 2007; 64(14_Supplement_9):S3–S9.

[14] Fisher JA, Monahan T, "Tracking the social dimensions of RFID systems in hospitals," *Int J Med Inform* 2008; 77(3):176–83.

[15] Dalton J, Rossini S, "Using RFID technologies to reduce blood transfusion errors," white Paper by Intel Corporation, Autentica, Cisco Systems and San Raffaele Hospital, 2005.

[16] Tzeng S-F, Chen W-H, Pai F-Y, "Evaluating the business value of RFID: Evidence from five case studies", *Int J Prod Econ* 2008; 112(2):601–13.

[17] Panagiotis K, Ria B, "Radio frequency identification (RFID) in a hospital environment", *J Inf Technol Healthc* 2006; 4(2):83–91.

[18] Aguilar A, van der Putten W, Kirrane F, "Positive patient identification using RFID and wireless networks," in *HISI 11th Annual Conference and Scientific Symposium*, November 2003.

[19] Pérez MM, Cabrero-Canosa M, Hermida JV, García LC, Gómez DL, González GV, "Application of RFID technology in patient tracking and medication traceability in emergency care," *J Med Syst* 2012; 36(6):3983–93.

[20] Liao Y-T, Chen T-L, Chen T-S, Zhong Z-H, Hwang J-H, "The Application of RFID to healthcare management of nursing house," *Wirel Pers Commun* 2016; 91(3):1237–57.

[21] Atkins AS, Alharbe N, "Sensor technologies using ZigBee and RFID within the cloud of internet of things in healthcare applications", *Technia* 2014; 6(2):923.

[22] Podaima BW, Friesen M, McLeod RD, "A review of emerging smart RFID in healthcare", *CMBES Proc* 2018; 33. https://proceedings.cmbes.ca/index.php/proceedings/article/view/559

[23] Wu F, Kuo F, Liu L-W, "The application of RFID on drug safety of inpatient nursing healthcare," in *ICEC '05: Proceedings of the 7th International Conference on Electronic commerce.* New York, NY, USA: ACM, pp. 85–92, 2005.

[24] Seetharam D, Fletcher, R, "Battery-powered RFID," in *1st ACM Workshop on Convergence of RFID and Wireless Sensor Networks and their Applications*, 2007.

[25] Ruiz-Garcia L, Lunadei L, Barreiro P, Robla JI, "A review of wireless sensor technologies and applications in agriculture and food industry: State of the art and current trends," *Sensors* 2009; 9(6):4728–50.

[26] Ruan Q, Xu W, Wang G, "RFID and ZigBee based manufacturing monitoring system," in *2011 International Conference on Electric Information and Control Engineering* 2011 Apr 15 (pp. 1672–1675). IEEE.

[27] Sumi M, Soujeri EA, Rajan R, Harikrishnan AI, "Design of a zigbee-based RFID network for industry applications," *SIN* 2009; 9:111–6.

[28] Castaño B, Rodriguez-Moreno M, "A ZigBee and RFID hybrid system for people monitoring and helping inside large buildings," in *2010 IEEE Symposium on Industrial Electronics and Applications (ISIEA)* 2010 Oct 3 (pp. 16–21). IEEE.

[29] Kaya T, Koser H, "A new batteryless active RFID system: smart RFID," in *2007 1st Annual RFID Eurasia* 2007 Sep 5 (pp. 1–4). IEEE.

[30] Leonov V, Fiorini P, Sedky S, Torfs T, Van Hoof C, "Thermoelectric MEMS generators as a power supply for a body area network," in *The 13th International Conference on Solid-State Sensors, Actuators and Microsystems*, 2005.

[31] Snyder GJ, "Small thermoelectric generators," *Electrochem Soc Interface* 2008; 17(3), 54.

[32] Wamba SF, Anand A, Carter L, "A Literature review of RFID enabled healthcare applications and issues," *Int J Inf Manage* 2013; 33(5):875–91.

[33] Rieback M, Crispo B, Tanenbaum A, "Is your cat infected with a computer virus?" in *Fourth Annual IEEE International Conference on Pervasive Computing and Communications, 2006. PerCom 2006*, p. 10, March 2006.

[34] Coustasse A, Cunningham B, Deslich S, Wilson E, Meadows P, *Management of RFID Systems in Hospital Transfusion Services.* Marshall University, Huntington, WV, 2015.

5 Photonic Crystal Fiber Plasmonic Sensor for Applications in Medicine

Monika Kiroriwal and Poonam Singal
Deenbandhu Chhotu Ram University
of Science & Technology

CONTENTS

5.1 INTRODUCTION

Light is a medium to communicate information in an effective way with security. To transmit light over long distances with less attenuation, light has been encapsulated with a glass medium known as optical fiber (OF) [1]. For more than three decades, this thinnest fiber has been playing a crucial role in multiple real-time applications from artificial to human life. After inventing the low-loss optical fiber, experiments have been performed for sensing systems, and research proved that the OFs are effective for sensing applications [2]. OFs marked their presence in the field of science and technology due to their appealing properties such as compact size, lightweight, flexibility, remote area working, high sensitivity, and working potential in harsh environmental conditions, including high voltage, atmospheric turbulences, explosive media, and strong electromagnetic field [3–5]. With their supporting characteristics, optical fiber sensors (OFSs) can measure in such difficult situations. Conventional OFSs have limitations such as the need for two glass materials with different refractive indices

DOI: 10.1201/9781003254119-5

for light guiding, fixed geometry dimensions, less birefringence, and low sensitivity [6]. After introducing the photonic bandgap concept, a simple microstructured optical fiber came into the limelight in the 1990s [7]. This fiber is getting famous as the name of the photonic crystal fiber (PCF) first introduced by Russel. Light would now able to be directed and controlled in ways that were just unrealistic, nor even visualized, in conventional optical fiber and all on account of that bunch of fine air holes longitudinal to fiber length [8–10]. The PCF can guide the light in a single mode through photonic bandgap impacts with less optical nonlinearity. On the other hand, nonlinearity can be enhanced with the help of a small core area. The dispersion can be controlled by tuning the zero-dispersion wavelength (ZDW). ZDW can be moved to smaller or higher wavelengths by altering the waveguide design, which provides the dispersion region for soliton dynamics and its related effects unattainable in traditional existing fiber [11]. Various alterable or tunable design parameters like lattice period, air holes' shape and size, and number and arrangement of air hole rings around the core region make it a promising contender for different application areas such as biomedical imaging, supercontinuum (SC) generation, optical imaging, advanced laser sources, optical parametric amplification, optical gating, filtering, frequency metrology, and medical diagnostics [12–15]. The remarkable properties of PCF make it suitable for advanced applications in the sensing field [16]. The working principle of fiber optic–based surface plasmon resonance (SPR), sensor structure, and applications were reviewed by Gupta and Verma [17]. A qualitative overview of PCF for sensing application has been provided by Pinto and Amo [18]. In this review, different types of sensors based on physical and chemical quantities were discussed [19]. Rifat et al. presented a study that discusses the operating methodology and various fabrication techniques, including plasmonic material (PM) selection, to design, optimize, and construct plasmonic sensors [20]. PCF's air holes can be invaded with solids, fluids, and gases, giving remarkable freedoms for applications. This technique shows the pattern and the capability of penetrated PCF sensor to foster all-fiber sensors sooner rather than later in a few vital innovative fields [21]. An extensive range of physical, biochemical, and biomedical sensors are discussed for different sensing elements such as blood, fuel, glucose, food, DNA hybridization, magnetic field, etc. [22]. To understand the fiber behavior, PCF geometry and its light guiding phenomenon will be overviewed in the second section, followed by the third section to understand the sensor's working principle and different PCF sensor structures. The future scope is ended with a conclusion in the remaining part of the chapter.

5.2   BACKGROUND AND DEVELOPMENT OF PHOTONIC CRYSTAL FIBER

Conventional optical fibers (COFs) are gaining importance in the telecommunication field due to their high performance. However, there are some drawbacks that lessen the glory of these fibers when compared with the performance of the PCF [23]. The most crucial property of PCF is single-mode operation over a long distance, whereas multimode propagation is unavoidable in COF. Light confines inside the core area than COF because of high refractive index (RI) difference between inner (core) and outer (cladding) areas [12]. Dispersion engineering can be done with the help of dimension, location, and the numbered air holes in the outer area. The adjustable dispersion profile and endlessly single-mode propagation of light make it feasible for dispersion shifting and compensating fiber devices and nonlinear applications [24]. Defects can be inserted to break the symmetry of the design, which leads to high birefringence. Polarization-maintaining fibers can be designed with the help of the high birefringence property of PCF [25]. To solve the signals multiplexing issues like cross talks, interference, etc., multicore PCFs can be used [26]. The selected air holes situated over a large pitch are eliminated from the cladding region; this feature is helpful for sensing to confine the light in the desired region. This single-material-based fiber is more thermal stable than fibers made from two different materials. Thus, light propagation depends not only on RI contrast, but light modeling can also be achieved with the variation in geometrical parameters of PCF [27,28]. Apart from the above advantages, one other merit is that the air holes can be filled with liquids, solids, and gases to alter the material's effective RI; this feature is more suitable for sensing and monitoring applications [29–31].

PCF's unique optical characteristics can be defined by some key elements: (a) background material of PCF, (b) dimensions of core and cladding air holes, and (c) air holes' manner. These elements are responsible for controlling and maintaining the optical behavior of the fiber [32]. An electromagnetic wave is guided through the geometry of PCF and can be categorized into four forms: index guiding, photonic bandgap guiding (PBG), all-solid PBG guiding, and hybrid (total internal reflection [TIR] +PBG) guiding [21], as shown in Figure 5.1. When a solid core PCF is considered, due to air holes cladding, RI is lower than the solid core, and light is propagated through modified total internal reflection (MTIR). This PCF is expressed as index guiding PCF [33]. Two-dimensional PCF structure is created due to the periodic pattern of air holes, which produce PBG effect around the defected core. This effect is applicable to confine the light into the core for limited frequency range (LFR); otherwise, signal refraction occurs. When air holes are filled with high-index solid materials to induce high-index cladding around the low-index solid core, the structure is called the all-solid PBG PCF. An anti-resonant reflecting waveguide model (ARROW) is demonstrated to determine the optical behavior of the all-solid PBG PCF. In hybrid PCF, light is guided by the mutual interaction of TIR and PBG, as the first hybrid PCF was introduced in Ref. [34]. Table 5.1 presents the historical development of PCF from 1995 to 2021.

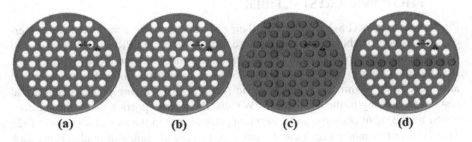

FIGURE 5.1 (a) Index-guiding PCF, (b) photonic band-gap guiding PCF, (c) all-solid PCF, and (d) hybrid guiding PCF.

TABLE 5.1

Development of PCF

Year	Development	Ref.
1995	2D band-gaps can exist in silica/air PCF for $n_{ax} < 1$	[35]
1996	First solid-core PCF	[36]
1997	Concept of single mode operation	[37]
1998	Ultra-large effective mode area	[38]
1999	Hollow core PBG PCF	[39]
2000	Multicore PCF, PM PCF, and Rare earth Doped PCF laser	[40]
2001	CO_2-based Laser PCF, FWM in PCF, Polymer PCF	[41]
2002	Long-period gratings in PCF	[42]
2003	Filters using PCF	[43]
2004	Double photon creation in PCF	[44]
2005	High energy pulse transmission in PCF	[45]
2006	PCF long-period grating for biochemical sensing	[46]
2007	SBS characterization in PCF	[47]
2008	Phase matched double and triple frequency generation in PCF	[48]
2009	Quantum dot nanocoated PCF for temperature sensing	[49]
2010	PCF with superlattice structure	[50]
2011	Micro-displacement sensor based on PCF	[51]
2012	PCF for temperature sensing	[52]
2013	PCF ultrafast fiber laser for amplification	[32]
2014	Higher order mode excitation in PCF	[53]
2015	Hi-Bi PCF sensor for liquid analyte sensing	[54]
2016	Performance comparison of SF57 over silica for dispersion compensation	[55]
2017	PCF parameter estimation using Fussy Logic	[56]
2018	High birefringent Hexa sectored PCF	[57]
2019	PCF for Orbital angular momentum mode division multiplexing system	[58]
2020	Multi-parameters characteristics of PCF sensor	[59]
2021	Single mode multicore PCF for crosstalk reduction	[26]

5.3 PLASMONIC SENSOR BASED ON PHOTONIC CRYSTAL FIBER

Plasmonic sensors (PSs) are marking their presence as a key component for numerous applications in the sensing field. These sensors work on SPR effect that occurred on the metal-dielectric meeting place when the confined mode matches with the surface plasmon polariton (SPP) mode [60]. SPPs can penetrate about 10 nm into metal and more than 100 nm into the dielectric medium [61]. During phase matching, at resonant wavelength, the SP wave (SPW) adsorbs a large portion of the power conveyed by the input photons, and a maxima peak occurs in the modal loss curve [62]. This type of resonance effect can be employed in a wide range of applications such as modulators [63], filters [64], optical sensing [65], nano-film thickness monitoring [66], and label-free monitoring [67]. In 1907, Zenneck investigated the resonance effect due to stimulated plasmons [68]. It was perceived that surface waves (SWs) could be generated at the matching point of the lossless and lossy medium. Further SWs' exponential behavior was discovered by Sommerfeld in 1909 [69]. The actual generation of SPs was introduced in the literature by Ritchie in 1957 [70]. After this theoretical investigation, an Otto configuration was explained by Otto for the SPR effect [71]; in this configuration, the sensing medium was sandwiched between the prism and plasmonic layer. The detecting strategy was refined as a defined gap that was needed between these layers [72]. This design was updated by Kretschmann arrangement, where there is no distance between the prism and plasmonic coating [73]. Until this point, Kretschmann and Otto's setups were top well-known methods for creating the SPR effect [74]. As the analyte RI has been changed, the engendering consistency of the SP mode is adjusted, which changes the interacting behavior of the incident and the plasmon waves [75]. Albeit the exhibition of Kretschmann set up is vigorous and costly, due to cumbersome necessary optical and physical parts. These necessities limit these systems' optimization and real-life use in point-of-care settings [76]. These massive parts needed for the precise interrogation in these gadgets are an additional significant expense. The regular sensors are not reasonable for real-time applications as an after-effect of dynamic optical and physical parts [77].

The extraordinary capacities of PCFs have offered a phase to defeat the issues related to Otto and Kretschmann setups. PCF sensors are likewise compact and can be integrated easily. By enjoying the benefit of adaptability in structure, PCFs can be streamlined to accomplish the required evanescent field. For example, various sorts of PCF design, such as hexagonal, circular, decagonal, octagonal, square, pentagonal, and hybrid, can be utilized in guiding the core-confined mode, and geometrical parameters can be varied to improve the guiding optical properties [78,79]. PCFs with endless propagation present the maximum peak outcomes in improving the sensitivity [80]. Wavelength and amplitude interrogation procedures are employed as primary components for investigating the detecting ability of plasmonic sensors. To upgrade the sensor potential, the PM layer must be covered to enhance the mutual coupling between modes [81].

According to the deposition of PM, PCF sensors are categorized into two classes: internal and external sensors. In the internal coating approach, PM is coated inside the selected air hole, and complex techniques are used for analyte infiltration [82–85]. Practically, implementation of such a type of approach is a challenge. In addition, specific fluid penetration and inclusion of metal nanowires in micron-sized air-holes would likewise be a muddled assignment [86]. Significant loss occurred due to inserted metal wires, and light will be lost. In this situation, it is unimaginable to expect to produce an output for sample detection. This loss restricts the fiber length. Because of the short length of the PCF, it has to be adjusted with the conventional single-mode fiber (SMF) for proper sample detection [87].

An external coating approach has been introduced to conquer the drawbacks of the internal coating approach. The plasmonic layer and detecting medium are set on the external layer of the fiber making the detecting phenomenon more advantageous. In this chapter, these SPR-PCF sensors are divided into categories: single-coated SPR-PCF sensors, double-coated SPR-PCF sensors, slotted SPR-PCF sensors, and miscellaneous SPR-PCF sensors. Before reviewing the divided categories, we have given a brief idea about PMs and the need for sensors in medicine in subsections (a) and (b), respectively.

a. **Choice of Plasmonic Materials**

Typically, Gold PM is a superb decision for SPR because of its chemical inertness and biocompatibility [88]. Yet, it has somewhat moderate optical damping and has expanded resonant wavelength, resulting in false RI detection. Silver might be viewed as one of the expected possibilities for PM [89]. The positive ascribes are narrow-band peak, low value of plasma frequency covering ultra violet range with low damping. Nonetheless, it makes fragile oxide layers reducing its inescapable uses as plasmonic sensors. Albeit this drawback might be emphatically forestalled by coating another metallic layer on the silver [90], this extra coating will reduce the sensor's feasibility. Copper has the additional possibility of being utilized as PM, yet it is inclined to oxidation [91]. Aluminum has not drawn in much consideration because of its high transition loss, high optical damping, and oxidation feature [92]. Graphene is synthetically dormant solid that keeps it detached from reaching with fluid arrangement [93]. Then again, analysts are working on other materials with solid mechanical, compound, and optical properties [94].

b. **Need of PCF-Based Sensor in Medicine**

Optical fibers are broadly utilized to perceive inside body parts and tissue that are open through regular openings. A new technique, optical coherence tomography (OCT), has been utilized for biomedical imaging [95]. Light pulse delay and backward power intensity are measured using an interferometer. Presently, OCT is a planned innovation that is utilized not just for ophthalmology but also for dermatology and dental, just as for the identification of cancer cell growth in stomach-related organs [96]. Broadband high-resolution optical imaging can be achieved using SC sources [97]. PCFs are exceptionally alluring and effective in delivering high-force light sources in the OCT framework. PCFs can produce SC range because of their design flexibility, making them conceivable to improve nonlinearity by diminishing the fundamental mode area and tailoring chromatic dispersion [98]. The PCF-based sensor is also applicable for individual molecule detection of DNA, protein, etc. PCF offers the opportunity to realize an optical endoscopy with high resolution [19–21].

Sensors have vital applications in ecological science, well-being review, illness determination, biomedical imaging, and pharmaceuticals. Medical instruments have been researched depending on a wide scope of advancements, including electrochemistry, fluorescence transmission, optical resonators, optical modulators, utilizing an assortment of nanowires and PCF sensors [18–20]. A large portion of these biosensors depend on recognizing the RI of bio-elements, however, changing their fixation instigated by the molecular collaboration at the interacting point. Hence, any one technique is used to make an effective biosensor, the principal objective of which is to upgrade the detecting ability of the sensor [12,20–23].

5.3.1 SINGLE-COATED PLASMONIC SENSORS

As observed from the literature, the real-time implementation of internally coated sensors is difficult, decreasing the overall performance of the sensor. Single-coated plasmonic sensors came into the limelight to improve the efficiency of the sensors [99]. The arrangement of layers in the sensor structure follows a pattern starting from the core, cladding zone, one or more layers of PM, sensing layer, and the outermost layer is a perfectly matched layer (PML), as presented in Figure 5.2. All the external sensing-based sensors follow the same structure format. Most of the sensors are designed and simulated by employing the finite element solver-based COMSOL software.

Haider et al. [100] reported that a single gold layer and sensing layer are coated outside the PCF boundary. The air holes scaled-down approach has a great effect on the resonance. The highest wavelength sensitivity (WS) of 30,000 nm/RIU and amplitude sensitivity (AS) of 1,212 RIU^{-1} were observed. Due to very small-size air holes, the practical implementation is difficult. There is some cross-talk interference between the adjacent analyte channels, so Liu et al. proposed a gold-coated solid-core sensor with an array of four air holes in the PCF [101]. This uniform structure can be easily fabricated, but the sensitivity is lower than other reported sensors [102–107].

A single gold-coated structure has been proposed by Chakma et al. [108]. Only one ring of air holes is placed in the cladding area, and three other air holes are inserted in the middle horizontal direction. The air holes' size is chosen to get a strong coupling at the interface. Islam et al. proposed a gold-plated sensor to attain the WS of 62,000 nm/RIU and 1,293/RIU of AS. Although WS is very high, very small-sized air holes and rectangular core make the fabrication process complex [109]. The specific arrangement of air holes such as spiral pattern [110], vertical bow with two large size air holes near the boundary in the horizontal direction [111], circular [112], and hexagonal arrangement with some missing air holes [113] also plays a crucial part in enhancing the overall sensing ability.

Effects of changing the orientation of air holes have been discussed by the author with the help of three PCF structures in which air holes are displaced at particular angles [114]. The effect of three different coating materials (Au, niobium, and niobium+Al$_2$O$_3$) with the same PCF design parameters on the sensor performance has been investigated by Khalek et al. [115]. This investigation reveals that the sensitivities can be improved by depositing the doping material.

A single titanium nitride (TiN) coating can be effective in stimulating the SPR mechanism explored by Kaur and Singh [102]. This SPR sensor comprises two air

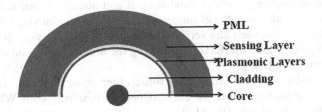

FIGURE 5.2 Structural layers' arrangement for external sensing approach.

hole rings with different diameters, and two air holes are vertically arranged for light confinement. Externally coated TiN material is helpful to get high WS, but due to fewer lattices matching with glass, this structure is not suitable for high AS. Khalil et al. illustrated a TiN-coated PCF sensor to get the maximum RI sensitivity of 7,700 nm/RIU [103]. Indium tin oxide (ITO) might be an effective coating material in achieving the WS of 35,000 nm/RIU [104]. Au-coated ring shape PCF senor has been studied by Zhou et al. [105]. The second air hole layer was missing to get the light confinement, and two air holes were diagonally eliminated from the third air hole ring to generate the resonance effect.

Air holes' size and lattice period are the key parameters in enhancing the sensor performance. Besides, the number of cores is also getting attraction to get the high sensitivity. Yang et al. simulated a gold-coated PCF sensor with three cores arranged at 120°. Air holes are fashioned in a hexagonal manner with a defective central core. This center defect is responsible for phase-matching condition between confined and resonance mode to get the highest WS of 30,600 nm RIU^{-1} with figure of merit (FOM) of 300 [116]. Fan displayed a gold-plated plasmonic sensor with six air holes capable of attaining a sensitivity of 15,180 nm/RIU [117]. Also demonstrated is the coupling between second-order, fifth-order, and sixth-order plasmonic mode and the confined core mode, which offers a range of sensors with different spans of analyte RI. An analyte with a wide RI range (1.33–1.44) can be detected through a dual-core gold-covered PCF sensor with a resolution of 8.92×10^{-6} RIU^{-1} [118].

Silver-plated PCF sensor was proposed by Momota et al. [119] to acquire 300 RIU^{-1} AS. Furthermore, Hossain et al. present the numerical modeling of silver-coated hollow-core SPR-PCF sensor. With a WS of 21,000 nm/RIU, this sensor can be suitable for sensing the proteins and liquids in the sensing medium [120].

Paul et al. numerically investigated graphene-covered high-sensitive PCF sensor to achieve the highest AS of 14,847.03/RIU [121]. Three air hole rings are patterned in an octagonal manner. Different dimensions of air holes in all three rings have a combined effect of getting the desired coupling between fundamental mode and resonance mode. Other graphene-coated SPR-PCF sensor can be used for monitoring the condition of transformer oil [106]. Another external sensing sensor utilized four cores near the fiber boundary, which enhances the stimulation of free electrons. Four cores are able to detect the analyte refractive index (ARI) with a wide detection area [122]. The proposed sensor has WS of 10,000 nm/RIU with a resolution of 1×10^{-5} RIU.

In 2021, research on the outside detecting approach with single coating is still going on [107,123]; toward this, Sakib et al. show a gold-coated sensor with two air hole rings. Four air holes have been eliminated from the last ring to acquire a strong mutual coupling between fundamental and plasmon mode responsible for high sensitivities with low value of linearity fit [124]. Phase-matching condition with a sharp value of confinement loss verifies the resonance phenomenon. Sensitivity can be improved up to 29,500 nm/RIU by removing the middle horizontal air holes with defective center core [125].

Apart from these above structures, some other structures are also available in the literature such as butterfly core shaped PCF sensor with WS of 56,000 nm/RIU [126], alphabetic (R, M, S)-core PCF sensor with maximum AS of 12,000/RIU [127], asymmetric PCF sensor with highest WS of 22,000 nm/RIU

[128], elliptical core PCF sensor with AS of 1,443/RIU [129], H-shape PCF sensor with WS of 25,900 nm/RIU [130], and eye-shaped PCF sensor with AS of 4,779.7 RIU[-1] [131]. Table 5.2 presents the sensor performance parameters and their structure's advantages and drawbacks.

TABLE 5.2
Comparison of Existing Single-Coated Plasmonic Sensors' Performance

Plasmonic Sensor Design	Amplitude Sensitivity (/RIU)	Wavelength Sensitivity (nm/RIU)	Advantages	Drawbacks
Circular PCF sensor [99]	266	2,200	Simple structure from fabrication point of view	Sensor performance is lower than other existing sensors
Gold-plated PCF sensor [100]	1,212	30,000	Different sensitivities can be obtained for both polarization states	Scaled-down approach of air holes creates deformation during fabrication
Circular PCF with dual core sensor [108]	318	9,000	It can be used for biological analyte detection	Due to central defect, feasibility is difficult
Spiral PCF sensor [110]	371.5	4,600	Cost effective sensing approach	Spiral orientation is difficult to realize
TiN-coated PCF sensor [102]	70	10,000	It can be used in visible and infrared spectrum due to TiN coating	Lower amplitude sensitivity
ITO-coated PCF sensor [104]	1,120.73	35,000	Sensor performance is high with fabrication feasibility	Different dimensions of air holes produce splicing loss
Three-core PCF sensor [116]	–	30,600	High sensitivity with less air holes	Less stable confinement mode due to three cores
Dual-core PCF sensor [118]	505.037	11,200	Simple structure with high linearity	Lower amplitude sensitivity
Silver-coated PCF sensor [120]	2,456	21,000	Cost effective due to silver coating	Oxidation issue due to silver plasmonic material
Asymmetric PCF sensor [128]	–	22,000	High sensitivity, high linearity, and birefringence	Fabrication is difficult due to asymmetric nature
PCF sensor with elliptical core [129]	1,443	8,000	More confined area with acceptable sensitivities	Elliptical core makes the fabrication complex
H-shaped PCF sensor [130]	–	25,000	Large detection range of refractive index (1.33–1.49)	Metal deposition in H-groove is challenging
Eye-shaped PCF sensor [131]	4,779.7	14,000	Novel concept with high sensitivities	Gold deposition over a specified area is challenging

5.3.2 DOUBLE-COATED PLASMONIC SENSORS

Conventional PMs have some limitations because of their properties. Gold (Au) presents poor attachment with glass, although it is inert and chemically stable. Silver (Ag), copper (Cu), and aluminum (Al) raise the oxidizing issue and present a lower detection ability. So, to stimulate the resonance phenomenon, these materials are covered with nano-films of oxides, nitrides, and other mixtures having the protection property [132].

To increase the adhesive force between gold and glass substrate, gold is covered with a thin graphene layer, as suggested by Liu et al. [133]. This seven air holes PCF sensor investigation shows the influence of air-hole dimensions, single (Au), and bimetallic (Au+graphene) layer on the sensor's sensitivity. Au-graphene covering can be employed on the flat surface to improve the sensor sensing ability by increasing the volume ratio of the analyte. Although the structure is simple to fabricate, the confinement loss is more due to lower core radiation [134]. An et al. [135] investigated a graphene-coated ITO to present the sensor performance in terms of sensitivity with easy fabrication for identifying biomolecules.

To solve the oxidation problem of the conductive materials, these materials are covered with other protective materials. Dash and Jha demonstrated a silver-graphene-coated SPR-PCF sensor to solve the problem of silver oxidation [87]. In this design, air holes with different dimensions are patterned in two different manners; the inner air hole ring is in hexagonal manner and the outer ring is in circular manner. This arrangement has the capability to produce a high AS of 860 RIU^{-1} with good resolution. This sensor has three different air hole diameters making it complex during fabrication. In the same way, Rifat et al. reported an externally Cu-graphene covered SPR-PCF sensor with uniform air holes. Due to hexagonal lattice structure, this graphene coating increases the surface-to-volume ratio and creates excellent plasmonic properties for high sensitivity. Although the WS is not high for this structure, the more chemically stable copper makes it cheaper than other sensors [136].

Confinement loss can be decreased with the help of bimetallic coating and by varying the cladding air-hole pattern [137]. In this context, Mahfuz et al. displayed a spiral SPR-PCF sensor structure with Au-TiO$_2$ covering, which is able to attain the maximum Ws of 23,000 nm/RIU over a wide detecting range from 1.32 to 1.40. This sensor exhibits 2.87 dB/cm loss at RI of 1.40, resulting in low splicing loss [138]. The same coating has been utilized to obtain the WS of 20,000nm/RIU with a moderate value of AS covering a broad RI range from 1.0 to 1.37 RI, by Haque et al. [139]. The bimetallic deposition over a flat surface creates a fabrication challenge. Niobium+Al$_2$O$_3$ layer can be utilized to improve the coupling strength during the SPR effect. This improvement has been demonstrated by Hasan et al. by placing two small air holes near the cladding boundary of defected core PCF [140].

In 2019, an ultrasensitive SPR-PCF sensor with high birefringence has been proposed by Islam et al. [141]. Four groups of four air holes are placed with 90° angle from each group, and five air holes are inserted in the vicinity of the core to attain the high birefringence. To stimulate the SPR, TiO$_2$ covered gold is plated at the outer side of the fiber. This sensor unveils the highest WS of 25,000 nm/RIU. The same double coating has been utilized by Mahfuz et al. to enhance the WS up to 28,000 nm/RIU. This reported structure has four very small size air holes with defective core, which create complications during fabrication [142].

Lou et al. presented a novel concept of double coating SPR-PCF sensor [143]. In this design, graphene covered gold metal layer is deposited on less than half part of the PCF circumference. Uniform air holes are fashioned in a hexagonal manner, and the core is created by eliminating the one air hole in the vertical direction near the cladding boundary. This design is capable of estimating a WS of 8,600 nm/RIU and also presents the effect of the graphene layer's presence on the sensor potential. Sensitivity can be improved by filling the analyte in the selective air holes, which are placed near to plasmonic layer; this concept has been presented by Ahmad et al. [144]. The MgF_2 layer is plated on Au for controlling the corrosion and is also helpful in achieving the double resonance mode at the same time, respectively. Along with a high WS of 27,959 nm/RIU, this sensor also shows a high birefringence of 3.9×10^{-4}.

Das and Singh [145] proposed an $Au-Ta_2O_5$ covered plasmonic sensor to get the WS of 16,354 nm/RIU. Furthermore, this sensitivity has been increased up to 50,000 nm/RIU after utilizing silver in place of gold and also shows that the ARI range might be tuned by varying the Ta_2O_5 film thickness [146]. Silver-coated sensor performance has been assessed with graphene and zinc oxide layer by Liang et al. [147]. An elliptical core was used to decrease the effective RI for light confinement. Sensitivity of 4,485 nm/RIU has been acquired with Ag-ZnO coating higher than the Ag-graphene coating. A performance overview of all discussed double-coated sensors is given in Table 5.3.

5.3.3 SLOTTED PLASMONIC SENSORS

Slotted SPR-PCF sensors are created by different investigations in order to find out the location of different analytes. Using the scaled-down method of air holes in the core adjacent ring, birefringent impacts could be figured out. Birefringent conduct prompted the more grounded light proliferation in both polarization states for the location of mixed analytes [148]. Two bimetallic (Ag+Au)-coated slots with a single air-hole ring SPR-PCF sensor were introduced by Akowuah et al., where the air holes with two different diameters are placed for guiding the light [149]. Otupiri et al. suggested a slotted PCF sensor comprising four elliptical air holes. The gold plated boundary was divided into four slots for multi-analyte detection. In horizontal slots, Au is covered with Ta_2O_5 in order to achieve the self-referencing mode (resonance peak can be moved towards higher wavelength by varying the RI in one channel over fixed RI in the other channel) [150].

Elliptical shape air holes give less fabrication feasibility; therefore, to resolve the fabrication issue with high sensing ability, Azzam et al. numerically analyzed a PCF design with uniform circular air holes [151]. The horizontally placed two air holes are shifted to get the birefringence behavior, and the center air hole is employed to reduce the cladding's RI leading to the phase-matching condition. In 2017, a single slotted hexagonal SPR-PCF sensor was investigated by Chen et al. [152]. This gold-coated sensor could recognize low ARI from 1.20 to 1.29. The structure also evaluated the effect of plane inclination on the loss spectra along with the effect of varying geometrical parameters.

TABLE 5.3
Comparison of Existing Double-Coated Plasmonic Sensors in Terms of Sensitivities

Plasmonic Sensor Design	Amplitude Sensitivity (/RIU)	Wavelength Sensitivity (nm/RIU)	Advantages	Drawbacks
Seven air holes PCF sensor [133]	375	7,500	Simple structure	Bi-metallic coating creates complex structure
Au-graphene plated PCF sensor [134]	450	4,200	Low loss transmission with birefringence property	Radiation losses due to lower core
Graphene-coated ITO PCF sensor [135]	95	10,693	High stability due to graphene coating	Very lower amplitude sensitivity
Cu-graphene covered PCF sensor [136]	140	2,000	Cost effective with fabrication feasibility	Both sensitivities are very low
Spiral PCF sensor [138]	–	23,000	Low confinement loss over a large detection range (1.32–1.40)	Missing amplitude sensitivity
Au-TiO$_2$ covered PCF sensor [139]	811	20,000	High sensitivity with simple structure	Flat surface deposition is complex
Niobium+Al$_2$O$_3$ deposited PCF sensor [140]	1,560	8,000	Less oxidation due to alumina coating	Oxidation problem is here
Au-TiO$_2$ plated PCF sensor [141]	1,411	25,000	High stability due to plasmonic material properties	Fabrication issue due to vertically arranged core structure
Au-TiO$_2$ coated PCF sensor [142]	6,829	28,000	High sensor performance	Splicing loss with SMF due to very small-sized air holes
Au-graphene-coated PCF sensor [143]	–	8,600	Cost effective	Plasmonic layers deposition over a specified curved area is complicated
Silver-Graphene-/ZnO-coated PCF sensor [147]	–	6,000	Less oxidation, moderate sensitivity, and high linearity	No discussion about amplitude sensitivity

Further single slot PCF sensor has been explored to get 20,000 nm/RIU WS with resolution of 10^{-6} RIU for a wide RI range (1.18–1.36) [153]. Deposition of PM over the slotted area creates difficulty during realization, Haque et al. illustrated a noble design of single slot PCF sensor, in which the bimetallic layer was coated on flat surface to observe the maximum WS of 1,16,000 nm/RIU over the recognition range from 1.29 to 1.39 [154]. In 2018, Haque et al. numerically studied an Au-TiO$_2$-covered slotted PCF sensor to detect the analyte's unknown RI. It gives the confinement loss of 26.44 dB/cm for RI of 1.36 with WS of 51,000 nm/RIU. This sensor has the ability to be applicable for pharmaceutical inspection and leakage monitoring [155]. The other advantage of the slotted sensor is that the slotted channels can be coated with different PMs simultaneously for detecting multiple analytes. Yasli et al. [156] present a novel sensor's structure with four slots (two channels). Channels are filled with different analytes, and resonance peaks are observed for calculating the sensitivities. The orientation of slots creates a complex irregular structure. Therefore, the same author team reported a slotted circular PCF sensor with two channels. The left channel is coated with gold and the right with silver for identifying the unknown analytes simultaneously [157]. Another reported slotted sensor has two large gold-coated slots, which improve the coupling strength. The author also illustrated the influence of PML thickness on model loss spectra and sensor's AS [158].

In 2020, to get the high-performance sensor, the cladding part of the fiber can be circular slotted and deposited with gold metal. This novel concept with only two air rings has been introduced by Sakib et al. [159]. Large volume of analyte is in direct contact with this slotted region and an AS of 780/RIU can be acquired. The double metal coating is effective to attain high sensor sensitivity. Anik et al. introduced a Gold-TiO_2-coated slotted sensor structure [160]. This structure has a square arrangement of air holes with bimetallic milled micro-channel, and open D channel is inserted to make it slotted to get the WS of 53,800 nm/RIU. After 1 year, the same team investigated a novel structure of PCF sensor with four gold-coated slots. These slots are further covered with Si_3N_4 and TiO_2 for analyzing the effect of these materials on sensor ability and observed the highest WS of 21,000 nm/RIU with AS of 914 RIU^{-1} for TiO_2 covering [161].

To reduce the interference between analytes and increase the analyte volume, Bing et al. present a new concept of PCF sensor design [162]. Two semi-circular slots are inserted in the upward and downward directions, and the flat part inside is coated with gold. In the lower slotted section, dielectric layer is placed between Au-film and analyte layer for simultaneous recognition of ARI. Author also shows the effect of removing the upper slot, and one analyte solution is in direct contact with modified D-shape PCF.

The large amount of SPR can be produced by reducing the gap between the main core and sensing layer. Towards this, Ahmed et al. [163] illustrated a gold-coated U-shape slotted PCF sensor to acquire the highest AS of 2,940/RIU with WS of 66,000 nm/RIU. Half-circular U-shaped curves are inserted at the PCF cladding surface to enhance the SPs stimulation. The resonance phenomenon can be tuned through a scaled-down approach [164].

Eight rectangular slots in the group of two-two are placed in the cladding region to enhance the sensor sensitivity, as explored by Sarker et al. [165]. Gold film and biolayer are placed at fiber's outside in order to obtain the highest WS of 22,000 nm/RIU with AS of 1,782.56 RIU^{-1}. Fabrication of rectangular slots is a challenging part during real-time implementation. Fabrication difficulty can be resolved by employing the two open ring gold-plated channels in the x direction, as suggested by Liu et al. [166].

There are eight micron-sized circular slots in Ref. [159] that create fabrication difficulty; after 1 year, the same author reduced this problem by employing four large

TABLE 5.4

Existing Slotted Plasmonic Sensors Performance Comparison

Plasmonic Sensor Design	Amplitude Sensitivity (/RIU)	Wavelength Sensitivity (nm/RIU)	Advantages	Drawbacks
Dual-core PCF sensor [154]	–	1,16,000	Less confinement loss with high performance	No discussion about amplitude sensitivity
Bimetallic micro-channel PCF [155]	1,872	51,000	Multi-analyte sensing is possible	Dual coating makes fabrication difficult
Two-channel PCF [156]	–	2,500	Four analytes can be detected simultaneously	Irregular cladding zone due to slots orientation
Two-slot PCF [158]	396	5,000	Simple structure with high volume of detecting sample	Low amplitude sensitivity
Circularly slotted PCF [159]	780	16,000	Cost effective and holds large volume of analytes	Deposition of gold inside the slots is challenging
Dual-channel PCF [162]	–	11,600	Multi-sample detection is easy	No discussion about amplitude sensitivity
U-shaped micro-channel PCF [163]	2,940	66,000	Fabrication is easy due to uniform air-hole structure with low confinement loss	Small volume of analyte concentration
Rectangular-slotted PCF [165]	1,782.56	22,000	Novel design with high sensitivity	Fabrication is difficult
Dual-core four open channel PCF [167]	1,286	38,000	Large detection range, high linearity, and cost effective	Different air-hole diameters create manufacturing issues
Circular-slotted PCF [169]	1,897	25,000	Simple design with wide transmission range	Slotted fabrication is not feasible

size slots at the cladding boundary to achieve a high FOM [167]. Two air holes are missing to make it dual-core with birefringence. To get the light confinement into double core simultaneously, one air hole is inserted into the center. This sensor is successful in achieving WS of 38,000 nm/RIU. Single solid-core spiral PCF [168] and circular slotted PCF [169] with four Au-deposited slots have been investigated to get the WS of 41,000 and 25,000 nm/RIU, respectively. Performance parameters are listed in Table 5.4 for slotted sensors.

5.3.4 MISCELLANEOUS SPR-PCF SENSOR

Apart from the discussed sensors, some more sensor structures are explored in order to enhance the sensing potential. These structures have some complexity from a fabrication point of view. In 2019, Li et al. fabricated and analyzed two large air holes in Au-graphene-coated PCF sensor. A notch has been made in the upper side to collect the liquid, and the electron beam evaporation method was successful in getting a control on plasmonic layer thickness. The author also presented the microscopic image of transmitted and reflected light [170]. Sensitivity can be enhanced with a triangular pattern of cladding air holes compared to the hexagonal arrangement suggested by Bing et al. [171]. Three D-shaped holes are placed at 120° from each other surrounding the clad air holes, and the flat surface is coated with gold. The maximum WS of 10,100 nm/RIU has been acquired and also presents the effect of holes rotation on the WS. Two circular channels with two gold rings are helpful in detecting the multi-analyte, as suggested by Kaur and Singh [172]. This simple and easy to fabricate structure is capable of recognizing the unknown analyte with the highest WS of 1,000 and 3,750 nm/RIU for the first and second channel, respectively. In another PCF sensor, ITO is coated inside the square slot to acquire the maximum WS of 10,700 nm/RIU covering a vast range of ARI from 1.19 to 1.29 [173].

Highest WS of 80,000 nm/RIU is attained by employing the semi-hexagonal PCF with an analyte-filled D-shaped sensing part, as reported by Isti et al. [174]. Two orthogonal modes are induced due to asymmetric core leading to birefringence, and a 40 nm semi-circular gold layer has been deposited using famous coating methods. Yasli presents a three air-holes rings-based SPR-PCF sensor to detect a cancer cell. The first ring is designed to trap the light with the support of second and third rings. To get the resonance condition, some air holes are omitted and create a gold-coated crescent shape on PCF right side [175]. Although running fabrication and deposition methods need some improvement to realize this type of structure, the amended performance ensures that this sensor has the potential to detect the cancerous cell with WS of 7,142.86 nm/RIU.

5.4 FABRICATION TECHNIQUES

The manufacturing interaction of the PCF sensor is more difficult contrasted with the regular optical fiber [176]. Conventional fabrication procedures such as stack and draw method [177], extrusion method, insertion modeling [178], and modern methods like sol-gel [179], and mechanical drilling [180] are very famous. Solid and hollow capillaries are arranged in a periodic form to form air holes of different dimensions. After assembling the fiber framework, one or more layers of PM need to be deposited on it. Some popular deposition methods can be utilized for covering the fiber with selected metal; for example, chemical vapor deposition [181], wheel polishing, and atomic layer deposition (ALD) [182]. A significant range of working wavelengths make it more appealing for detection and broadcast communications inferable from their small sizes, simplicity of manufacture, and reduction in back-reflection.

5.5 FUTURE APPLICATIONS OF PLASMONIC SENSORS

SPR-PCF sensing is a promising and advanced detecting innovation. Be that as it may, these sensors are currently at the beginning phase. The majority of the research announced in the literature includes confirmation of mathematical, hypothetical, and computational models. The utilization of these hypothetical models to the real-time application is restricted as a result of manufacturing difficulties. Although some experimental setups are demonstrated, having limited applications due to costly and specific equipment. Notwithstanding, there are still some extreme issues for the plasmonic sensors. Moreover, the nature of the sensors relies upon the fabrication technology, which implies that juvenile advancements might cause a coupling loss between PCF and SMFs. Future applications will be conceivable thanks to the development of new glass fiber and advanced fabrication methods [183]. Devices' wavelength range can be expanded in order to improve PCF sensors and lasers' behavior. PSs can be integrated with other optical components such as filters, modulators, splitters, couplers, detectors, and lasers's to the ease of lab-on-a-chip technology [184,185].

The impacts of mechanical associations between the optical fiber and plasmonic layer on fiber strength should be explained. Mix usefulness and working capacity in more cruel conditions likewise should be clarified. Various promising patterns of PCFs can be recognized, particularly the improvement of a smart structure and implanted sensors. With the help of advanced technology, compact, user-friendly, intuitive, and appropriate sensors can be created for secured data transmission. Artificial intelligence can be a good option to enhance the sensor performance for signal processing and imaging [186]. Apart from these future directions, newly developed PMs/meta-materials can be a part of the overall development of sensing technology [187].

Albeit the plasmonic upgrade being viewed as valuable for photo-catalysis applications, extensive exertion is expected to foster the material and design for improvement. The chemical and mechanical strength of PMs is not up to the mark, especially when muddled morphologies with high underlying energies are required [188]. While many examinations have revealed more vigor of the PMs, the trade among insurance and effectiveness should be tended to. The restricted comprehension of the connection between PMs and analytes in plasmonic impacts ruins the advancement of the novel, viable materials.

5.6 CONCLUSION

The recent development in plasmonic sensors using different PCF structures has been reviewed. These are newly adopted optical fibers because of their unique properties. PCF sensors can likewise profit from the advancements and improvements in regular optical filaments, which can without much of a stretch incorporate with the current optical identifiers and viable detecting modalities. The impacts of mechanical associations between the fiber and covering layer on fiber strength should be explained [189]. Mutual functionality and working capacity in more brutal conditions additionally should be clarified. Several promising trends of PCFs can be distinguished, particularly the improvement of smart designs and installed sensors. The high-level optical sign handling and organization innovation will empower its applications in fiber-optic sensor networks. We accept that the upsides of these sensors will contribute in industrialized and market-dominant development [190].

In rundown, PCF sensors play a significant part that supplements other detecting innovations. These sensors present a few benefits when contrasted with conventional fiber sensors because of their design: they are adaptable and can accomplish a wide range of setups. The PCF's air holes assume a significant part since they can be filled with solids, liquids, and gases; in addition, the connection between directed light and analyte are improved, and subsequently, the sensing ability with high resolution. In future, with progress in fabrication strategies, these sensors might be used in different applications going from clinical diagnostics, biological, and food handling to security. The improvements in structure and fabrication techniques will probably drive future patterns in the innovative work of PCF sensors.

AUTHOR CONTRIBUTION

M. Kiroriwal and P. Singal designed the proposal and wrote the chapter.

ACKNOWLEDGEMENT

The authors thank Dr. M. Sharma, Assistant Professor, Department of Physics, Modi University, Laxamangargh, Sikar, Rajasthan, for his valuable discussions.

REFERENCES

[1] Grattan, K. T. V., and Sun, T. 2000. Fiber optic sensor technology: an overview. *Sensors and Actuators A: Physical* 82: 40–61.

[2] Correia, R., James, S., Lee, S. W., Morgan, S. P., and Korposh, S. 2018. Biomedical application of optical fibre sensors. *Journal of Optics* 20: 073003.

[3] Nylander, C., Liedberg, B., and Lind, T. 1982. Gas detection by means of surface plasmon resonance. *Sensors and Actuators* 3: 79–88.

[4] Dougherty, G. 1993. A compact optoelectronic instrument with a disposable sensor based on surface plasmon resonance. *Measurement Science and Technology* 4: 697.

[5] Argyros, A. 2009. Structure, properties and characteristics of optical fibres. In *Handbook of Textile Fibre Structure*. Echhorn, S. J. CRC Press, Washington DC.

[6] Yin S., 2008. *Fiber Optic Sensors*, 2nd Ed, Taylor & Francis Group, CRC Boca Raton.

[7] Russell, P. S. J. 2006. Photonic-crystal fibers. *Journal of Lightwave Technology* 24: 4729–49.

[8] Russell, P. 2007. Photonic crystal fiber: finding the holey grail. *Optics and Photonics News* 18: 26–31.

[9] Cregan, R. F., Mangan, B. J., Knight, J. C., et al. 1999. Single-mode photonic band gap guidance of light in air. *Science* 285: 1537–39.

[10] Korposh, S., Lee, S. W., James, S., et al. 2017. Biomedical application of optical fibre sensors. *Proc SPIE* 10111: 101112Y.

[11] Ebnali-Heidari, M., Dehghan, F., Saghaei, H., et al. 2012. Dispersion engineering of photonic crystal fibers by means of fluidic infiltration. *Journal of Modern Optics* 59: 1384–90.

[12] Cerqueira Jr, S. A. 2010. Recent progress and novel applications of photonic crystal fibers. *Reports on Progress in Physics* 73: 024401.

[13] De, M., Gangopadhyay, T. K., and Singh, V. K. 2020. Prospects of photonic crystal fiber for analyte sensing applications: an overview. *Measurement Science and Technology* 31: 042001.

[14] Dixit, A., Tiwari, S., Ramani, U., and Pandey, P. C. 2020. Refractive index sensor based on evanescent field effects in hollow core PCF for detection of analytes over extended E+ S+ C+ L+ U communication bands. *Optics & Laser Technology* 121: 105779.

[15] Monir, M. K., Hasan, M., Paul, B. K., et al. 2019. High birefringent, low loss and flattened dispersion asymmetric slotted core-based photonic crystal fiber in THz regime. *International Journal of Modern Physics B* 33: 1950218.

[16] Arif, M. F. H., Ahmed, K., Asaduzzaman, S., and Azad, M. A. K. 2016. Design and optimization of photonic crystal fiber for liquid sensing applications. *Photonic Sensors* 6: 279–88.

[17] Gupta, B. D., Shrivastav, A. M., and Usha, S. P. 2016. Surface plasmon resonance-based fiber optic sensors utilizing molecular imprinting. *Sensors* 16: 1381.

[18] Pinto, A. M., and Lopez-Amo, M. 2012. Photonic crystal fibers for sensing applications. *Journal of Sensors*, 2012: 598178.

[19] Zhang, T., Zheng, Y., Wang, C., et al. 2018. A review of photonic crystal fiber sensor applications for different physical quantities. *Applied Spectroscopy Reviews* 53: 486–502.

[20] Rifat, A. A., Ahmed, R., and Yetisen, A. K., 2017. Photonic crystal fiber based plasmonic sensors. *Sensors and Actuators B: Chemical* 243: 311–25.

[21] Algorri, J. F., Zografopoulos, D. C., Tapetado, A., et al. 2018. Infiltrated photonic crystal fibers for sensing applications. *Sensors* 18: 4263.

[22] Hemalatha, R., and Revathi, S. 2020. Photonic crystal fiber for sensing application. *The International Journal of Engineering and Advanced Technology* 9(5): 481–94.

[23] Zhao, Y., Deng, Z. Q., and Li, J. 2014. Photonic crystal fiber based surface plasmon resonance chemical sensors. *Sensors and Actuators B: Chemical* 202: 557–67.

[24] Bhattacharya, R., and Konar, S. 2012. Extremely large birefringence and shifting of zero dispersion wavelength of photonic crystal fibers. *Optics & Laser Technology* 44: 2210–16.

[25] Ortigosa-Blanch, A., Knight, J. C., Wadsworth, W. J., et al. 2000. Highly birefringent photonic crystal fibers. *Optics Letters* 25: 1325–27.

[26] Zhang, H., Wang, G., Zhang, J., et al. 2021. Design and optimization of a single-mode multi-core photonic crystal fiber with the nano rod assisted structure to suppress the crosstalk. *IEEE Photonics Journal* 13: 1–6.

[27] Tong, Z. R., Li, J. X., Zhang, W. H., and Liu, J. W. 2021. Research on repeatability and stability of sensors based on alcohol-filled photonic crystal fiber. *Journal of Modern Optics* 68: 276–83.

[28] Saghaei, H., Heidari, V., Ebnali-Heidari, M., and Yazdani, M. R. 2016. A systematic study of linear and nonlinear properties of photonic crystal fibers. *Optik* 127: 11938–47.

[29] Kiroriwal M., and Singal P. 2020. Analysis of optical properties of selectively filled photonic crystal fiber and its application: review. *Sensors Letters* 18: 595–603.

[30] Sonnenfeld, C., Sulejmani, S., Geernaert, T. et al. 2011. Microstructured optical fiber sensors embedded in a laminate composite for smart material applications. *Sensors* 11: 2566–79.

[31] Vieweg, M., Gissibl, T., Pricking, S., et al. 2010. Ultrafast nonlinear optofluidics in selectively liquid-filled photonic crystal fibers. *Optics Express* 18: 25232–40.

[32] Alkeskjold, T. T., Laurila, M., Weirich, J., et al. 2013. Photonic crystal fiber amplifiers for high power ultrafast fiber lasers. *Nanophotonics* 2: 369–81.

[33] Nandan, P., Mahanta, L., and Kumar, P. 2018. Index guiding photonic crystal fibers for optical sensing. In *2018 International Conference on Communication and Signal Processing (ICCSP)* (pp. 0327–0330). IEEE.

[34] Schmidt, M. A., Granzow, N., Da, N., et al. 2009. All-solid bandgap guiding in tellurite-filled silica photonic crystal fibers. *Optics Letters* 34: 1946–48.

[35] Birks, T. A., Roberts, P. J., Russell, P. S. J., et al. 1995. Full 2-D photonic bandgaps in silica/air structures. *Electronics Letters* 31: 1941–43.

[36] Knight, J. C., Birks, T. A., Russell, P. S. J. and Atkin, D. M. 1996. All-silica single-mode optical fiber with photonic crystal cladding. *Optics Letters* 21: 1547–49.

[37] Knight, J. C., Birks, T. A., Russell, P. S. J., and Atkin, D. M. 1997. All-silica single-mode optical fiber with photonic crystal cladding: errata. *Optics Letters* 22: 484–85.

[38] Knight, J. C., Birks, T. A., Cregan, R. F., et al. 1998. Large mode area photonic crystal fibre. *Electronics Letters* 34: 1347–48.

[39] Birks, T. A., Mogilevtsev, D., Knight, J. C., and Russell, P. S. J. 1999. Dispersion compensation using single-material fibers. *IEEE Photonics Technology Letters* 11: 674–76.

[40] Ranka, J. K., Windeler, R. S. and Stentz, A. J. 2000. Visible continuum generation in air–silica microstructure optical fibers with anomalous dispersion at 800 nm. *Optics Letters* 25: 25–27.

[41] Sharping, J. E., Fiorentino, M., and Coker, A., 2001. Four-wave mixing in microstructure fiber. *Optics Letters* 26: 1048–50.

[42] Kakarantzas, G., Birks, T. A., and Russell, P. S. J. 2002. Structural long-period gratings in photonic crystal fibers. *Optics Letters* 27: 1013–15.

[43] Skryabin, D. V., Luan, F., Knight, J. C., and Russell, P. S. J. 2003. Soliton self-frequency shift cancellation in photonic crystal fibers. *Science* 301: 1705–08.

[44] Sharping, J. E., Chen, J., and Li, X. 2004. Quantum-correlated twin photons from microstructure fiber. *Optics Express* 12: 3086–94.

[45] Al-Janabi, A. H. 2005. Transportation of nanosecond laser pulses by hollow core photonic crystal fiber for laser ignition. *Laser Physics Letters* 2: 529.

[46] Rindorf, L., Jensen, J. B., Dufva, M., et al. 2006. Photonic crystal fiber long-period gratings for biochemical sensing. *Optics Express* 14: 8224–31.

[47] Beugnot, J. C., Sylvestre, T., and Alasia, D. 2007. Complete experimental characterization of stimulated Brillouin scattering in photonic crystal fiber. *Optics Express* 15: 15517–22.

[48] Bétourné, A., Quiquempois, Y., Bouwmans, G., and Douay, M. 2008. Design of a photonic crystal fiber for phase-matched frequency doubling or tripling. *Optics Express* 16: 14255–62.

[49] Larrión, B., Hernáez, M., Arregui, F. J., et al. 2009. Photonic crystal fiber temperature sensor based on quantum dot nanocoatings. *Journal of Sensors* 2009: 932471.

[50] Chen, D., Vincent Tse, M. L., and Tam, H. Y. 2010. Super-lattice structure photonic crystal fiber. *Progress in Electromagnetics Research* 11: 53–64.

[51] Dong, B., and Hao, E. J. 2011. Temperature-insensitive and intensity-modulated embedded photonic-crystal-fiber modal-interferometer-based micro-displacement sensor. *JOSA B* 28: 2332–36.

[52] Qiu, S. J., Chen, Y., Xu, F., and Lu, Y. Q. 2012. Temperature sensor based on an isopropanol-sealed photonic crystal fiber in-line interferometer with enhanced refractive index sensitivity. *Optics Letters* 37: 863–65.

[53] Trabold, B. M., Novoa, D., Abdolvand, A., and Russell, P. S. J. 2014. Selective excitation of pure higher order modes in hollow-core PCF via side-coupling. In *2014 Conference on Lasers and Electro-Optics (CLEO)-Laser Science to Photonic Applications* (pp. 1–2). IEEE.

[54] Ademgil, H., and Haxha, S. 2015. PCF based sensor with high sensitivity, high birefringence and low confinement losses for liquid analyte sensing applications. *Sensors* 15: 31833–42.

[55] Mahmud, R. R., Khan, M. A. G., and Razzak, S. A. 2016. Design and comparison of SF57 over SiO_2 on same structured PCF for residual dispersion compensation. *IEEE Photonics Journal* 8: 1–10.

[56] Daoud, R. W. 2017. An innovative way to determine the PCF parameters for particular packet of data using fuzzy logic. In *2017 Second Al-Sadiq International Conference on Multidisciplinary in IT and Communication Science and Applications (AIC-MITCSA)* (pp. 102–106).

[57] Anas, M. T., Asaduzzaman, S., Ahmed, K., and Bhuiyan, T. 2018. Investigation of highly birefringent and highly nonlinear hexa sectored PCF with low confinement loss. *Results in Physics* 11: 1039–43.

[58] Zhang, H., Han, D., Xi, L., et al. 2019. Two-layer erbium-doped air-core circular photonic crystal fiber amplifier for orbital angular momentum mode division multiplexing system. *Crystals* 9: 156.

[59] Li, J., Tong, Z., Zhang, W., and Liu, J., 2020. Research on multi-parameter characteristics of a PCF sensor modified by GO composite films. *Applied Optics* 59: 9216–24.

[60] Butt, M. A., Khonina, S. N., and Kazanskiy, N. L. 2021 Plasmonics: a necessity in the field of sensing-a review. *Fiber and Integrated Optics* 40: 14–47.

[61] Achanta, V. G. 2020. Surface waves at metal-dielectric interfaces: material science perspective. *Reviews in Physics* 5: 100041.

[62] Ekgasit, S., Tangcharoenbumrungsuk, A., Yu, F., et al. 2005. Resonance shifts in SPR curves of non absorbing, weakly absorbing, and strongly absorbing dielectrics. *Sensors and Actuators B: Chemical* 105: 532–541.

[63] Tan, Z., Hao, X., and Shao, Y. 2014. Phase modulation and structural effects in a D-shaped all-solid photonic crystal fiber surface plasmon resonance sensor. *Optics Express* 22: 15049–63.

[64] Qu, Y., Yuan, J., and Zhou, X. 2019. A V-shape photonic crystal fiber polarization filter based on surface plasmon resonance effect. *Optics Communications* 452: 1–6.

[65] Frazao, O., Santos, J. L., Araujo, F. M., and Ferreira, L. A. 2008. Optical sensing with photonic crystal fibers. *Laser & Photonics Reviews* 2: 449–59.

[66] Chyou, J. J., Chu, C. S., Chien, F. C., et al. 2006. Precise determination of the dielectric constant and thickness of a nanolayer by use of surface plasmon resonance sensing and multiexperiment linear data analysis. *Applied Optics* 45: 6038–44.

[67] Shevchenko, Y., Camci-Unal, G., and Cuttica, D. F. 2014. Surface plasmon resonance fiber sensor for real-time and label-free monitoring of cellular behavior. *Biosensors and Bioelectronics* 56: 359–67.

[68] Grandidier, J., Des Francs, G. C., and Massenot, S. 2010. Leakage radiation microscopy of surface plasmon coupled emission: investigation of gain-assisted propagation in an integrated plasmonic waveguide. *Journal of Microscopy* 239: 167–72.

[69] Michalski, K. A., and Mosig, J. R. 2016. The Sommerfeld half-space problem revisited: from radio frequencies and Zenneck waves to visible light and Fano modes. *Journal of Electromagnetic Waves and Applications* 30: 1–42.

[70] Zhang, J., Zhang, L., and Xu, W. 2012. Surface plasmon polaritons: physics and applications. *Journal of Physics D: Applied Physics* 45: 113001.

[71] Sharma, A. K., Jha, R., and Gupta, B. D. 2007. Fiber-optic sensors based on surface plasmon resonance: a comprehensive review. *IEEE Sensors Journal* 7: 1118–29.

[72] Anwar, R. S., Ning, H., and Mao, L. 2018. Recent advancements in surface plasmon polaritons-plasmonics in subwavelength structures in microwave and terahertz regimes. *Digital Communications and Networks* 4: 244–57.

[73] Barchiesi, D., and Otto, A. 2013. Excitations of surface plasmon polaritons by attenuated total reflection, revisited. *La Rivista del Nuovo Cimento* 36: 173–209.

[74] Liedberg, B., Nylander, C., and Lunström, I. 1983. Surface plasmon resonance for gas detection and biosensing. *Sensors and Actuators* 4: 299–304.

[75] Culshaw, B. 2000. Fiber optics in sensing and measurement. *IEEE Journal of Selected Topics in Quantum Electronics* 6: 1014–21.

[76] Sohrabi, F., and Hamidi, S.M. 2016. Neuroplasmonics: from Kretschmann configuration to plasmonic crystals. *The European Physical Journal Plus* 131: 1–15.

[77] Kooyman, R. P. 2008. Physics of surface plasmon resonance. In *Handbook of Surface Plasmon Resonance* (p. 1), Schasfoort, R. B. M., Royal Society of Chemistry, Cambridge.

[78] Mittal, S., Sharma, T., and Tiwari, M. 2021. Surface plasmon resonance based photonic crystal fiber biosensors: a review. *Materials Today: Proceedings* 43:3071–74.

[79] Morshed, M., Hasan, M. I., and Razzak, S. A. 2015. Enhancement of the sensitivity of gas sensor based on microstructure optical fiber. *Photonic Sensors* 5: 312–20.

[80] Bender, W. J., and Dessy, R. E. 1994. Surface plasmon resonance sensor. Google Patents.

[81] Hu, D. J. J., and Ho, H. P. 2017. Recent advances in plasmonic photonic crystal fibers: design, fabrication and applications. *Advances in Optics and Photonics* 9: 257–314.

[82] Wei, Q., Shu-Guang, L., Jian-Rong, X., et al. 2013. Numerical analysis of a photonic crystal fiber based on two polarized modes for biosensing applications. *Chinese Physics B* 22: 074213.

[83] Tian, M., Lu, P., Chen, L., et al. 2012. All-solid D-shaped photonic fiber sensor based on surface plasmon resonance. *Optics Communications* 285: 1550–54.

[84] Dash, J. N., and Jha, R. 2014. Graphene-based birefringent photonic crystal fiber sensor using surface plasmon resonance. *IEEE Photonics Technology Letters* 26: 1092–95.

[85] Chowdhury, S., and Maity, A. 2017. Numerical analysis of photonic crystal fiber based hemoglobin sensor. *Optik* 130: 825–29.

[86] Yang, X. C., Lu, Y., Wang, M. T., and Yao, J. Q. 2016. A photonic crystal fiber glucose sensor filled with silver nanowires. *Optics Communications* 359: 279–84.

[87] Liu, C., Wang, F., Lv, J., et al. 2016. A highly temperature-sensitive photonic crystal fiber based on surface plasmon resonance. *Optics Communications* 359: 378–82.

[88] Garoli, D., Calandrini, E., Giovannini, G., et al. 2019. Nanoporous gold metamaterials for high sensitivity plasmonic sensing. *Nanoscale Horizons* 4: 1153–57.

[89] Loiseau, A., Asila, V., and Boitel-Aullen, G. 2019. Silver-based plasmonic nanoparticles for and their use in biosensing. *Biosensors* 9: 78.

[90] Baburin, A. S., Merzlikin, A. M., Baryshev, A. V., et al. 2019. Silver-based plasmonics: golden material platform and application challenges. *Optical Materials Express* 9: 611–42.

[91] Stebunov, Y. V., Yakubovsky, D. I., and Fedyanin, D. Y. 2018. Superior sensitivity of copper-based plasmonic biosensors. *Langmuir* 34: 4681–87.

[92] Lee, K. L., You, M. L., and Wei, P. K. 2019. Aluminum nanostructures for surface-plasmon-resonance-based sensing applications. *ACS Applied Nano Materials* 2: 1930–39.

[93] Kravets, V. G., Jalil, R., and Kim, Y. J. 2014. Graphene-protected copper and silver plasmonics. *Scientific Reports* 4: 1–8.

[94] Naik, G. V., Shalaev, V. M., and Boltasseva, A. 2013. Alternative plasmonic materials: beyond gold and silver. *Advanced Materials* 25: 3264–94.

[95] Hossain, M., and Maniruzzaman, M. 2013. Prospect of photonic crystal fiber (pcf) in medical science. In *Proceedings of 4th Global Engineering, Science and Technology Conference* (pp. 1–5), BIAM Foundation, Dhaka, Bangladesh.

[96] Sen, S., Abdullah-Al-Shafi, M., and Kabir, M. A. 2020. Hexagonal photonic crystal fiber (H-PCF) based optical sensor with high relative sensitivity and low confinement loss for terahertz (THz) regime. *Sensing and Bio-Sensing Research* 30: 100377.

[97] Nishizawa, N., Chen, Y., Hsiung, P., et al. 2004. Real-time, ultrahigh-resolution, optical coherence tomography with an all-fiber, femtosecond fiber laser continuum at 1.5 μm. *Optics Letters* 29: 2846–48.

[98] Agrawal, G. P. 2000. Nonlinear fiber optics. In *Nonlinear Science at the Dawn of the 21st Century*. Springer, Berlin, Heidelberg.

[99] Hasan, M., Akter, S., Rifat, A. A., et al. 2017. A highly sensitive gold-coated photonic crystal fiber biosensor based on surface plasmon resonance. *Photonics* 4(1): 18).

[100] Haider, F., Aoni, R. A., and Ahmed, R. 2018. Propagation controlled photonic crystal fiber-based plasmonic sensor via scaled-down approach. *IEEE Sensors Journal* 19: 962–69.

[101] Liu, M., Yang, X., and Zhao, B. 2017. Square array photonic crystal fiber-based surface plasmon resonance refractive index sensor. *Modern Physics Letters B* 31: 1750352.

[102] Kaur, V., and Singh, S. 2019. Design of titanium nitride coated PCF-SPR sensor for liquid sensing applications. *Optical Fiber Technology* 48: 159–64.

[103] Khalil, A. E., El-Saeed, A. H., Ibrahim, M. A., et al. 2018. Highly sensitive photonic crystal fiber biosensor based on titanium nitride. *Optical and Quantum Electronics* 50: 1–12.

[104] Liu, Q., Sun, J., Sun, Y., et al. 2020. Surface plasmon resonance sensor based on photonic crystal fiber with indium tin oxide film. *Optical Materials* 102: 109800.

[105] Zhou X., Cheng T., Li S., et al. 2018. Practical sensing approach based on surface plasmon resonance in a photonic crystal fiber. *OSA Continuum* 1: 1332–40.

[106] Paul, A. K. 2020. Design and analysis of photonic crystal fiber plasmonic refractive Index sensor for condition monitoring of transformer oil. *OSA Continuum* 3: 2253–63.

[107] Islam, M. R., Iftekher, A. N. M., and Hasan, K. R. 2021. Surface plasmon resonance based highly sensitive gold coated PCF biosensor. *Applied Physics A* 127: 1–12.

[108] Chakma, S., Khalek, M. A., and Paul, B. K. 2018. Gold-coated photonic crystal fiber biosensor based on surface plasmon resonance: design and analysis. *Sensing and Bio-Sensing Research* 18: 7–12.

[109] Islam, M. S., Sultana, J., and Rifat, A. A. 2018. Dual-polarized highly sensitive plasmonic sensor in the visible to near-IR spectrum. *Optics Express* 26: 30347–61.

[110] Hasan, M. R., Akter, S., and Rifat, A. A. 2017. Spiral photonic crystal fiber-based dual-polarized surface plasmon resonance biosensor. *IEEE Sensors Journal* 18: 133–40.

[111] Shafkat, A. 2020. Analysis of a gold coated plasmonic sensor based on a duplex core photonic crystal fiber. *Sensing and Bio-Sensing Research* 28: 100324.

[112] Mollah, M. A., Razzak, S. A., Paul, A. K., and Hasan, M. R. 2019. Microstructure optical fiber based plasmonic refractive index sensor. *Sensing and Bio-Sensing Research* 24: 100286.

[113] Haider, F., Aoni, R. A., Ahmed, R., and Miroshnichenko, A. E. 2018. Highly amplitude-sensitive photonic-crystal-fiber-based plasmonic sensor. *JOSA B* 35: 2816–21.

[114] Rafi, H. N., Kaysir, M. R., and Islam, M. J. 2020. Air-hole attributed performance of photonic crystal fiber-based SPR sensors. *Sensing and Bio-Sensing Research* 29: 100364.

[115] Khalek, M. A., Chakma, S., Ahmed, K., et al. 2019. Materials effect in sensing performance based on surface plasmon resonance using photonic crystal fiber. *Plasmonics* 14: 861–67.

[116] Yang, Y., Qin, Y., Lu, X., and Zeng, Y. 2021. High-sensitivity three-core photonic crystal fiber sensor based on surface plasmon resonance with gold film coatings. *Japanese Journal of Applied Physics* 60: 122002.

[117] Fan, Z. 2019. A tunable high-sensitivity refractive index of analyte biosensor based on metal-nanoscale covered photonic crystal fiber with surface plasmon resonance. *IEEE Photonics Journal* 11: 1–14.

[118] Kamrunnahar, Q. M., Mou, J. R., and Momtaj, M. 2020. Dual-core gold coated photonic crystal fiber plasmonic sensor: design and analysis. *Results in Physics* 18: 103319.

[119] Momota, M. R., and Hasan, M. R. 2018. Hollow-core silver coated photonic crystal fiber plasmonic sensor. *Optical Materials* 76: 287–94.

[120] Hossain, M. B., Islam, S. R., and Hossain, K. T. 2020. High sensitivity hollow core circular shaped PCF surface plasmonic biosensor employing silver coat: a numerical design and analysis with external sensing approach. *Results in Physics* 16: 102909.

[121] Paul, A.K., Mollah, M., and Hassan, M. 2021. Graphene-coated highly sensitive photonic crystal fiber surface plasmon resonance sensor for aqueous solution: design and numerical analysis. *Photonics* 8(5): 155.

[122] Rahman, M. M., Rana, M. M., and Anower, M. S. 2020. Design and analysis of photonic crystal fiber-based plasmonic microbiosensor: an external sensing scheme. *SN Applied Sciences* 2: 1–11.

[123] Kiroriwal, M., and Singal, P. 2021. Design and analysis of highly sensitive solid core gold-coated hexagonal photonic crystal fiber sensor based on surface plasmon resonance. *Journal of Nanophotonics* 15: 026008.

[124] Sakib, N., Hassan, W., and Rahman, T. 2021. Performance study of a highly sensitive plasmonic sensor based on microstructure photonics using an outside detecting method. *OSA Continuum* 4: 2615–29.

[125] Zhu, M., Yang, L., and Lv, J., 2021. Highly sensitive dual-core photonic crystal fiber based on a surface plasmon resonance sensor with gold film. *Plasmonics* 17: 543–50.

[126] Mashrafi, M., Kamrunnahar, Q. M., and Haider, F. 2021. Bio-inspired butterfly core-shaped photonic crystal fiber-based refractive index sensor. *OSA Continuum* 4: 1179–90.

[127] Haider, F., Aoni, R.A., Ahmed, R., et al. 2020. Alphabetic-core assisted microstructure fiber based plasmonic biosensor. *Plasmonics* 15: 1949–58.

[128] Al Mahfuz, M., Hasan, M.R., Momota, M.R. et al. 2019. Asymmetrical photonic crystal fiber based plasmonic sensor using the lower birefringence peak method. *OSA Continuum* 2: 1713–25.

[129] Zuhayer, A., and Shafkat, A. 2021. Design and analysis of a gold-coated dual-core photonic crystal fiber bio-sensor using surface plasmon resonance. *Sensing and Bio-Sensing Research* 33: 100432.

[130] Han, H., Hou, D., and Zhao, L., 2020. A large detection-range plasmonic sensor based on an H-shaped photonic crystal fiber. *Sensors* 20: 1009.

[131] Islam, M.R., Yasir, F., Antor, M., et al. 2021. An eye-shaped ultra-sensitive localized surface plasmon resonance–based biochemical sensor. *Plasmonics* 17: 131–41.

[132] Haes, A.J., Haynes, C.L., and McFarland, A.D. 2005. Plasmonic materials for surface-enhanced sensing and spectroscopy. *MRS Bulletin* 30: 368–75.

[133] Liu, C., Yang, L., Su, W. et al. 2017. Numerical analysis of a photonic crystal fiber based on a surface plasmon resonance sensor with an annular analyte channel. *Optics Communications* 382: 162–66.

[134] Yang, H., Liu, M., Chen, Y., et al. 2021. Highly sensitive graphene-Au coated plasmon resonance PCF sensor. *Sensors* 21: 818.

[135] An, G., Li, S., Wang, H., and Zhang, X. 2017. Metal oxide-graphene-based quasi-D-shaped optical fiber plasmonic biosensor. *IEEE Photonics Journal* 9: 1–9.

[136] Rifat, A. A., Mahdiraji, G. A., and Ahmed, R. 2015. Copper-graphene-based photonic crystal fiber plasmonic biosensor. *IEEE Photonics Journal* 8: 1–8.

[137] Hasan, M.R., Akter, S., Rahman, M.S. et al. 2017. Design of a surface plasmon resonance refractive index sensor with high sensitivity. *Optical Engineering* 56: 087101.

[138] Mahfuz, M.A., Hossain, M., Haque, E., et al. 2019. A bimetallic-coated, low propagation loss, photonic crystal fiber based plasmonic refractive index sensor. *Sensors* 19: 3794.

[139] Haque, E., Hossain, M.A., and Pham, T. 2019. Surface plasmonic resonance sensor for wider range of low refractive index detection. In *2019 26th International Conference on Telecommunications (ICT)* (pp. 479–84).

[140] Hasan, M.R., Akter, S., Ahmed, K. et al. 2017. Plasmonic refractive index sensor employing niobium nanofilm on photonic crystal fiber. *IEEE Photonics Technology Letters* 30: 315–18.

[141] Islam, M. S., Cordeiro, C. M., and Sultana, J. 2019. A Hi-Bi ultra-sensitive surface plasmon resonance fiber sensor. *IEEE Access* 7: 79085–94.

[142] Al Mahfuz, M., Hossain, M. A., and Haque, E. 2020. Dual-core photonic crystal fiber-based plasmonic RI sensor in the visible to near-IR operating band. *IEEE Sensors Journal* 20: 7692–7700.

[143] Lou, J., Cheng, T., Li, S. et al. 2019. Surface plasmon resonance photonic crystal fiber biosensor based on gold-graphene layers. *Optical Fiber Technology* 50: 206–11.

[144] Ahmed, K., AlZain, M.A., and Abdullah, H. 2021. Highly sensitive twin resonance coupling refractive index sensor based on gold-and MgF_2-coated nano metal films. *Biosensors* 11: 104.

[145] Das, S., and Singh, V. K. 2021. Design and analysis of a tunable refractive index sensor by using a Ta_2O_5-coated photonic crystal fiber. *Journal of Nanophotonics* 15: 016006.

[146] Das, S. 2021. The role of Ta_2O_5 thin film on a plasmonic refractive index sensor based on photonic crystal fiber. *Photonics and Nanostructures-Fundamentals and Applications* 44: 100904.

[147] Liang, H., Shen, T., Feng, Y., et al. 2021. A D-Shaped photonic crystal fiber refractive index sensor coated with graphene and zinc oxide. *Sensors* 21: 71.

[148] Zynio, S. A., Samoylov, A. V., Surovtseva, E. R. et al. 2002. Bimetallic layers increase sensitivity of affinity sensors based on surface plasmon resonance. *Sensors* 2: 62–70.

[149] Akowuah, E. K., Gorman, T., and Ademgil, H. 2012. A novel compact photonic crystal fibre surface plasmon resonance biosensor for an aqueous environment. In *Photonic Crystals—Innovative Systems, Lasers and Waveguides*. Massaro, A. InTech, Janeza Trdine 9,51000 Rijeka, Croatia.

[150] Otupiri, R., Akowuah, E. K., and Haxha, S. 2015. Multi-channel SPR biosensor based on PCF for multi-analyte sensing applications. *Optics Express* 23: 15716–27.

[151] Azzam, S. I., Hameed, M. F. O., Shehata, R. E. A., Heikal, A. M., and Obayya, S. S. 2016. Multichannel photonic crystal fiber surface plasmon resonance based sensor. *Optical and Quantum Electronics* 48: 142.

[152] Chen, X., Xia, L., and Li, C. 2018. Surface plasmon resonance sensor based on a novel D-shaped photonic crystal fiber for low refractive index detection. *IEEE Photonics Journal* 10: 1–9.

[153] Haque, E., Hossain, M. A., Ahmed, F., and Namihira, Y. 2018. Surface plasmon resonance sensor based on modified D-shaped photonic crystal fiber for wider range of refractive index detection. *IEEE Sensors Journal* 18: 8287–93.

[154] Haque, E., Mahmuda, S., Hossain, M. A., Hai, N. H., Namihira, Y., and Ahmed, F. 2019. Highly sensitive dual-core PCF based plasmonic refractive index sensor for low refractive index detection. *IEEE Photonics Journal* 11: 1–9.

[155] Haque, E., Hossain, M. A., Namihira, Y., and Ahmed, F. 2019. Microchannel-based plasmonic refractive index sensor for low refractive index detection. *Applied Optics* 58: 1547–54.

[156] Yasli, A., Ademgil, H., Haxha, S., and Aggoun, A. 2019. Multi-channel photonic crystal fiber based surface plasmon resonance sensor for multi-analyte sensing. *IEEE Photonics Journal* 12: 1–15.

[157] Yasli, A., and Ademgil, H. 2020. Multianalyte sensing analysis with multilayer photonic crystal fiber-based surface plasmon resonance sensor. *Modern Physics Letters B* 34: 2050375.

[158] Akter, S., Rahman, M. Z., and Mahmud, S. 2019. Highly sensitive open-channels based plasmonic biosensor in visible to near-infrared wavelength. *Results in Physics* 13: 102328.

[159] Sakib, M. N., Islam, S. R., Mahendiran, T. V., et al. 2020. Numerical study of circularly slotted highly sensitive plasmonic biosensor: a novel approach. *Results in Physics* 17: 103130.

[160] Anik, M. H. K., Isti, M. I. A., Islam, S. R., et al. 2020. Milled microchannel-assisted open D-channel photonic crystal fiber plasmonic biosensor. *IEEE Access* 9: 2924–33.

[161] Anik, M. H. K., Islam, S. R., Talukder, H., et al. 2021. A highly sensitive quadruple D-shaped open channel photonic crystal fiber plasmonic sensor: a comparative study on materials effect. *Results in Physics* 23: 104050.

[162] Bing, P., Sui, J., Wu, G., et al. 2020. Analysis of dual-channel simultaneous detection of photonic crystal fiber sensors. *Plasmonics* 15: 1071–76.

[163] Ahmed, T., Haider, F., Aoni, R.A., and Ahmed, R. 2021. Highly sensitive U-shaped micro-channel photonic crystal fiber–based plasmonic biosensor. *Plasmonics* 16(6): 2215–23.

[164] Islam, A., Haider, F., Aoni, R.A., Hossen, M., Begum, F., and Ahmed, R. 2021. U-grooved dual-channel plasmonic sensor for simultaneous multi-analyte detection. *JOSA B* 38: 3055–63.

[165] Sarker, H., Faisal, M., and Mollah, M. A. 2021. Slotted photonic crystal fiber-based plasmonic biosensor. *Applied Optics* 60(2): 358–366.

[166] Liu, C., Yang, L., Lu, X., et al. 2017. Mid-infrared surface plasmon resonance sensor based on photonic crystal fibers. *Optics Express* 25: 14227–37.

[167] Sakib, N., Hassan, W., Kamrunnahar, Q. M., Momtaj, M., and Rahman, T. 2021. Dual core four open channel circularly slotted gold coated plasmonic biosensor. *Optical Materials Express* 11: 273–88.

[168] Rahman, Z., Hassan, W., Rahman, T., Sakib, N., and Mahmud, S. 2020. Highly sensitive tetra-slotted gold-coated spiral plasmonic biosensor with a large detection range. *OSA Continuum* 3: 3445–59.

[169] Rahman, M. T., Datto, S., and Sakib, M. N. 2021. Highly sensitive circular slotted gold-coated micro channel photonic crystal fiber based plasmonic biosensor. *OSA Continuum* 4: 1808–26.

[170] Li, B., Cheng, T., Chen, J., and Yan, X. 2019. Graphene-enhanced surface plasmon resonance liquid refractive index sensor based on photonic crystal fiber. *Sensors* 19: 3666.

[171] Bing, P., Sui, J., Huang, S., et al. 2019. A novel photonic crystal fiber sensor with three D-shaped holes based on surface plasmon resonance. *Current Optics and Photonics* 3: 541–47.

[172] Kaur, V. and Singh, S. 2019. A dual-channel surface plasmon resonance biosensor based on a photonic crystal fiber for multianalyte sensing. *Journal of Computational Electronics* 18: 319–28.

[173] Yang, Z., Xia, L., Li, C., Chen, X., and Liu, D. 2019. A surface plasmon resonance sensor based on concave-shaped photonic crystal fiber for low refractive index detection. *Optics Communications* 430: 195–203.

[174] Isti, M. I. A., Talukder, H., Islam, S. R., et al. 2020. Asymmetrical D-channel photonic crystal fiber-based plasmonic sensor using the wavelength interrogation and lower birefringence peak method. *Results in Physics* 19: 103372.

[175] Yasli, A. 2021. Cancer detection with surface plasmon resonance-based photonic crystal fiber biosensor. *Plasmonics* 16: 1605–12.

[176] Amouzad Mahdiraji, G., Chow, D. M., Sandoghchi, S. R., et al. 2014. Challenges and solutions in fabrication of silica-based photonic crystal fibers: an experimental study. *Fiber and Integrated Optics* 33: 85–104.

[177] Issa, N.A., van Eijkelenborg, M. A., Fellew, M, Cox, F, Henry, G., and Large, M. C. 2004. Fabrication and study of microstructured optical fibers with elliptical holes. *Optics Letters* 29: 1336–38.

[178] Chow, D. M., Sandoghchi, S. R., and Adikan, F. M. 2012. Fabrication of photonic crystal fibers. In *2012 IEEE 3rd International Conference on Photonics* (pp. 227–230).

[179] Bise, R. T., and Trevor, D. J. 2005. Sol-gel derived micro-structured fiber: fabrication and characterization. *In Optical Fiber Communication Conference* (p. OWL6). Optical Society of America.

[180] Zhang, P., Zhang, J., Yang, P., Dai, S., Wang, X., and Zhang, W. 2015. Fabrication of chalcogenide glass photonic crystal fibers with mechanical drilling. *Optical Fiber Technology* 26: 176–79.

[181] Wack, S., Lunca Popa, P., Adjeroud, N., Vergne, C., and Leturcq, R. 2020. Two-step approach for conformal chemical vapor-phase deposition of ultra-thin conductive silver films. *ACS Applied Materials & Interfaces* 12: 36329–38.

[182] Im, H., Wittenberg, N. J., Lindquist, N. C., and Oh, S. H. 2012. Atomic layer deposition: a versatile technique for plasmonics and nanobiotechnology. *Journal of Materials Research* 27: 663–71.

[183] Cordeiro, C. M., Ng, A. K., and Ebendorff-Heidepriem, H. 2020. Ultra-simplified single-step fabrication of microstructured optical fiber. *Scientific Reports* 10: 1–12.

[184] Jiang, Y., Ling, T., Gu, L., Jiang, W., Chen, X., and Chen, R. T. 2006. Highly dispersive photonic crystal waveguides and their applications in optical modulators and true-time delay lines. *Proc SPIE* 6128: 61280Y.

[185] F Carvalho, W. O., and Mejía-Salazar, J. R. 2020. Plasmonics for telecommunication applications. *Sensors* 20: 2488.

[186] Li, X., Shu, J., Gu, W., and Gao, L. 2019. Deep neural network for plasmonic sensor modeling. *Optical Materials Express* 9: 3857–62.

[187] Zheludev, N. I. 2011. A roadmap for metamaterials. *Optics and Photonics News* 22: 30–35.

[188] Duan, Q., Liu, Y., Chang, S., Chen, H., and Chen, J. H. 2021. Surface plasmonic sensors: sensing mechanism and recent applications. *Sensors* 21: 5262.

[189] Lv, J., Leong, E. S. P., Jiang, X., Kou, S., Dai, H., Lin, J., Liu, Y. J., and Si, G. 2015. Plasmon-enhanced sensing: current status and prospects. *Journal of Nanomaterials* 2015: 474730.

[190] Stockman, M. I., Kneipp, K., Bozhevolnyi, S. I., et al. 2018. Roadmap on plasmonics. *Journal of Optics* 20: 043001.

6 Augmented Reality as a Boon to Disability

Ashish Kumar
Bennett University

Raja
Bharati Vidyapeeth's College of Engineering

Muhammad Fazal Ijaz
Sejong University

CONTENTS

6.1 INTRODUCTION: AIM AND REAL-USE CASES OF AUGMENTED REALITY

In this modern era, AR is a very useful and innovative technology. It makes the whole world more powerful by adding digital data in the form of illusion of higher realities in the actual world. Basically, AR integrates the virtual knowledge with the real-time data of nature. This technology was developed in 1968, with the development of Ivan Sutherland's program [1].

AR technology is a boon to the society and makes people's life easy. People can easily learn social skills and safety measures from augmented reality (AR). This technology can act as a mode of accessibility between teacher and students.

DOI: 10.1201/9781003254119-6

It can add value to the learning systems by enabling online learning. It can open doors to cultural events and experiences. In addition, AR is touching the lives of everyone including specially abled persons by offering a spacious experience. People can participate in the virtual world with the help of AR and can make their life better [2,3]. Generally, there are three areas in which AR has incorporated innovations. This includes visualization, annotation, and storytelling. These areas are helpful for better learning of physically challenged students. They can become independent and can understand concepts very easily. For the disabled people, AR gives back the confidence that they had lost due to their disability [4]. In another line of innovation, AR has provided many important benefits to products and organizations. AR can provide a rich user experience. Studies have shown that AR can also increase the value of products by incorporating innovation and visualization. In sum, this technology provides a new path to communicate with the reality and can build some interesting gadgets with virtual experience that would never have happened in the real world. This technology has the enough potential to build up huge learning environments, which mix up real and tangible data [5].

6.1.1 AIM OF AUGMENTED REALITY

AR aims to simplify the user's life by not only bringing virtual information into their immediate surroundings but also any indirect visualization of the real-world environment, such as in a live-video stream. AR enhances user perception and interaction with the real world, whereas virtual reality (VR) technology or virtual environment completely immerses users in the artificial world without seeing the real world. AR technology superimposes virtual objects and signals onto the real world in real time. It enhances the sense of reality and the common architecture of AR for disabilities, as described in Figure 6.1. It illustrates how various elements are linked to each other. AR connects the user to devices that are linked to AR technology. Once the processing is done, the specially abled person can take advantage of this technology [6].

AR technology is very vast, and it can help disabled people in many ways. There are so many opportunities where a person with disability can take the help of AR. This technology offers several possibilities to change the perception of life of people with disabilities. There are many areas where AR has provided support aimed at bettering the lives of specially abled persons. Person can be physically, mentally, or visually impaired; the AR technology has limitless possibilities to enhance their lifetime experience.

6.1.2 REAL-USE CASES FOR AR FOR PEOPLE WITH DISABILITIES

- **Medical Training:** AR can not only be used for more accurate and less risky surgery, but it can also help surgeons save time during emergency surgery. And for people with disabilities, it is the most effective technology.

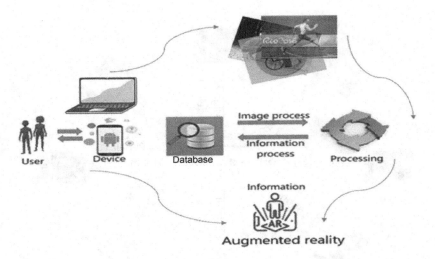

FIGURE 6.1 Overview of the procedure of augmented reality for disabled people.

Instead of searching between papers or electronic medical records, surgeons can find all that information on their AR screen in seconds

- **Repair & Maintenance:** The AR process of using good technology to model and train conservation professionals on how to perform the necessary maintenance procedures.
- **Design & Modeling:** From interior design to construction, AR helps professionals identify their final products during the creative process. Use of headsets enables architects, engineers, and design professionals step directly into their buildings and spaces to see how their designs might look, and even make virtual on the spot changes. Every person who has some disorders can benefit from this technology.
- **Retail:** One of the most appealing applications is trying to provide a more friendly shopping experience for consumers with disabilities. This is important, as the shopping experience is usually not designed for people with mental disabilities.
- **Business Logistics:** Another AR is used in businesses with 3D modeling. This is often used during the design process for items such as homes and cars. AR can also be used as an aid in the design and development of a first-class product, giving designers a clear idea of the product's form and function.
- **Tourism Industry:** AR transforms the perceptions of travellers and provides additional tourism activities and networking opportunities. AR-enabled glasses offer an immersion experience that can add fun and eliminate the need for a tour guide
- **Classroom Education:** The most interesting thing about AR in schools is the use of AR applications directly in the classroom. In this case, they can

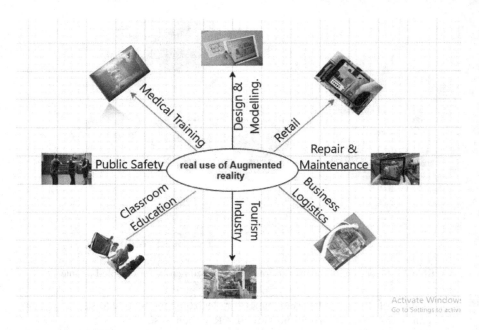

FIGURE 6.2 Real-time applications for augmented reality.

help the teacher to explain the lesson, provide visual cues, and help students test their knowledge

- **Public Safety:** AR can trick the brain into reusing or rerouting around neural pathways that had become disused due to disease or injury. By mapping the AR gear to display a disused right hand working in response to commands received, the brain will slowly process and correct the damage.

Figure 6.2 illustrates the real-time applications of AR in various domains. AR uses existing reality and physical objects to trigger computer-generated enhancements on top of reality in real time. Essentially, AR is a technology that renders computer-generated images at the user's perspective of the real world. These images are usually shaped as 3D models, videos, and information. The next section will review the recent advances in the area of AR.

6.2 RELATED WORK AND DISCUSSION

We have revived the potential work in the area of AR. The details and applications highlighted in the work have been tabulated in Table 6.1.

We have reviewed these papers to analyze the impact of AR in real time and to explain the technology advancement for empowering disabled people. The details related to the applications of AR for physically, visually, and mentally specially abled persons are discussed in the next section.

TABLE 6.1

Representation Work in the Domain of Augmented Reality

Authors	Applications	Summary
Caudell (1995) [4]	Headsets combined with head position sensing systems.	Describe the use of head-mounted display tools to increase the effectiveness and feature of human labours in their performance of industrial design, trade, and building, challenging, and repairing actions.
Saidin et al. (2015) [5]	Merging AR with education for interactive experience	Specifies the application of AR in various fields of subjects that includes medical, chemistry, arithmetic, astronomy, environmental science, and history.
Mirzaei et al. 2012 [6]	Specialized system to help deaf people	Integrated technologies to create a program which provide hearing support to deaf people.
Gopalakrishnan et al. (2020) [7]	Low vision care (LVC) clinic at a tertiary eye care center.	Examine the visual acuity enhancement in patients with low vision using AR device who presented to the LVC clinic at a tertiary eye care center.
Herskovitz et al. (2020) [8]	Mobile devices	Identify common constituent tasks in AR by analyzing existing mobile AR applications for iOS, and characterize the design space of tasks that require accessible alternatives.
Cakir and Korkmaz (2019) [9]	AR based teaching material	Interactive teaching material to enhance learning experience.
Bacca Acosta et al. (2014) [10]	Education	Highlighted the trends and vision towards the upcoming opportunities in AR for educational settings
Benda et al. (2015) [11]	Horticulture	Experimental analysis of the opportunities for consuming AR as a platform for display of educational resources in the field of horticulture in the real world for people with intellectual disabilities.
Akçayir and Akçayir (2017) [12]	Education	Review the challenges and advantages of deployment of AR in the educational field.
Maier et al. (2009) [13]	Education	Describe an approach for increasing the understanding and ease the learning of chemistry for students by providing visual virtual models of molecules.
Sumadio and Rambli (2010) [14]	Education	Introduce AR application in education for visual learning environment.
Ribeiro et al. (2012) [15]	3D sound system	Integrate AR technology with acoustic material to improve sound system.
Mallem (2010) [16]	Learning systems	Explain the issues and highlight the problems in developing AR learning systems.
Gybas et al. (2019) [17]	Education	Specify the use of AR for teaching students with mental disabilities.

6.3 TECHNOLOGY ADVANCEMENT USING AR FOR EMPOWERING DISABLED PEOPLE

Technology can reduce the barriers people with disabilities face in their daily lives, such as speaking, traveling, reading, and writing. This would enable them to participate in and enjoy the benefits of digital society, by gaining the same experience as everyone else. AR has provided many gadgets and apps to ease their day to day tasks [7].

With the help of investigators and some specialists, it is feasible to utilize AR technology for improving the life of a person with disabilities. In India, there are 2.69 crore people with some disability and there are more than 1 billion persons with disabilities globally. Therefore, the potential for a better lifestyle for people having disabilities is definitely a good message [6].

In this era, AR technology is one of the most important foundations of our modern society. This technique manifests in almost all humanitarian activities. It changes and translates into better programs every year and this involves extremely hard work with regard to technology.

Strategic Benefits of AR
- Creates unique customer experiences. The great advantage of AR is that it creates a unique digital experience that combines the best of the digital world with the body.
- Eliminates cognitive overload.
- Heightens user engagement.
- Competitive differentiation

Today, computer-assisted technology that uses AI and AR creates "intelligent" hearing aids that can detect the voice of a friend sitting in front of you in a noisy environment and filter out unwanted words. These hearing aids augment the voice with environmental friendly adjustment so that clear speech will be delivered to the intended person.

6.3.1 AR APPLICATIONS FOR THE PHYSICALLY DISABLED

Physical disability is limited to a person's physical activity, mobility, ability, or endurance. Other physical disabilities include disturbances that limit other aspects of daily life, such as respiratory distress, blindness, epilepsy, and sleep disturbances. AR technology presents countless opportunities to improve the lifestyle of people with disabilities [9]. Given below are some of the opportunities:

Improves Shopping Experience:
    Many people with disabilities cannot have much of a shopping experience. It is very difficult for people with disabilities to walk around the supermarket and pick up their products. With the help of AR technology, they can do shopping and enjoy their life. AR can be a great solution to provide your customers with a memorable experience. This will not only

allow your business to grow but will also provide your customers with the satisfaction of experiencing the product first-hand [9].

Improves Healthcare Quality:

AR is used in healthcare settings worldwide today, for applications including venous imaging, surgical imaging, and education. The latest hardware and software upgrades have reduced overhead costs while greatly improving user experience and assisting developers.

By using AR and VR technologies, people with disabilities have the potential to overcome their limitations, and to eventually improve their quality of life.

AR in Surgery:

The technology used by physicians to perform augmented and VR surgery has a headset with a clear display that projects images of the internal anatomy, such as bones and other tissues, based on computerized tomography scans, giving essentially X-ray vision to surgeons

Health Treatment Devices:

AR instruments and applications can be used for all kinds of medical remedies or therapy options. They are intelligent devices, which were originally evolved for gaming. Applications of AR are used in many areas. With the help of this technology, surgery has become very easy because the surgeon gets to see an overview of the internal organs on his screen. AR can also be helpful for the treatment of mentally specially abled persons and can improve their mental health [8].

Improving Education Skills:

A very important challenge facing people with disabilities is a lack of freedom, especially in dealing with everyday matters.

The technology of AR is very useful in supporting people with disabilities and teaching them very important lifestyle aspects. People can easily learn social, safety, and many more skills. We know that it is very difficult for a physically handicapped person to complete his or her education. But, by using AR, they can complete their education without leaving their homes [18].

6.3.2 AR Applications for the Visually Disabled

AR technology has provided many AR devices for visually impaired persons to raise their remaining perception of superior visual function. Worldwide, there are an estimated 285.8 million visually impaired people, and according to the report there are 39.5 million blind people and 246 million people are afflicted with low vision.

People who have lost their sight can express their feelings by reading and writing in a specialized language known as Braille. Now a days, a lot of accessories have specialized Braillian communication devices to communicate ideas online with the help of Internet. These accessories are easy and simple to use.

Smart AR glasses are described as AR wearable devices that resemble standard glasses and incorporate visual detail and physical information into the user's viewing field. To this end, AR is touching the lives of everyone including specially abled

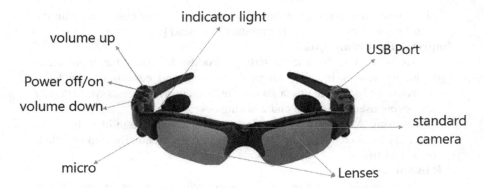

FIGURE 6.3 Component of augmented reality smart glasses for the visually impaired people.

persons by offering a world-class experience. People can participate in the virtual world with the help of AR and can better their lives.

Some components of AR smart glasses are shown in Figure 6.3. Here we can increase or decrease the volume, the power swtich is used to switch on or switch off the device, the indicator light indicates the on or off position of the device, Universal Serial Bus (USB) port is used for charging or connecting, and the camera is for capturing the images,

Smart AR glasses are portable devices that produce AR content for a user's benefit. Today, these types of smart glasses are great tools for the visually impaired or the blind, and have made life easier for those who use them. AR glasses have become their eyes and give them the requisite information to move around. And glasses with AR technology help patients with low vision conditions navigate better in their surroundings. Generally, people over the age of 40 years experience a condition known as low vision, which can be caused by retinitis pigmentosa, albinism, glaucoma, diabetes, and other conditions. These visual defects cannot be easily remedied with glasses, contact lenses, medications, or surgery [10]. Those who have loss of vision face many problems in their life. One of the main reasons of vision loss is myopia. It occurs when the pupil of the eye becomes too long or the curvature of the cornea (the outermost protective layer of the eye) is greatly increased. As a result, the light that enters the eye is not focused properly, due to which the images are focused slightly ahead of the retina. This makes the vision blurry. The devices created by AR have proved to be very useful in this area as well. With the help of these devices, a person gets a semblance of normalcy in his or her life [19].

Low Vision Aid:
Low Vision Aid is a device designed to help visually impaired people learn and see. Examples include standing and hand-held magnifiers, vertical and hand-held brackets, powerful magnifying glasses, glasses, and small telescopes with low-visibility devices designed to help the visually impaired to read and see. Nowadays, AR is making visual aids for handicapped persons, which are a boon for visually impaired persons [20].

AR Benefits the Visually Impaired:

Another augmented system helps those with almost complete vision loss by converting spatial information into high-contrast, color-coded visual patterns. The system measures, maintains, and changes the size and dimensions of the visible area around the wearer [21].

Medically Approved VR Low Vision Aid:

Vision Buddy helps the visually impaired read books, use household chores, and do daily chores independently. Vision Buddy helps visually impaired people to regain their sense of sight.

Listening Device:

In today's times, AR has become a very important technology. With the help of AR, listening devices have been created for the hearing impaired, which have proved to be very effective. These devices not only help them to hear but also bring back their lost confidence. Today, computer-assisted technology uses AI and AR to create "intelligent" hearing aids that can distinguish the voice of a friend sitting across you in a noisy environment and filter words other than that of your friend. They can adjust the expansion based on user locations and only make personalized speech audible [22].

Thanks to these AR technologies, people who have lost their vision can do many things like write texts, browse the internet, and send and receive emails. Screen reading software and special Braille speaking devices allow those of us who have no idea as to how to use computers, cell phones, and other electronic devices independently. Scientific studies have found that the use of hearing aids reduces dementia and the risk of dementia.

6.3.3   AR Applications for the Mentally Disabled

AR can help in treatment of mental illness that includes depression or suicidal tendencies [23]. AR-based devices can be used for meditation to rejuvenate the health of mentally disabled person.

Mental Illness:

Mental illnesses are health conditions that involve changes in feelings, thinking, or behavior, or a combination of all of these. Mental illnesses are associated with distress and/or problems with social, work, or family activities. Mental illness is common. Mental depression is caused by negative thoughts. This weakens one's confidence. People with depression have less sleep, panic, do not like to eat and drink, and like loneliness. Different facets of life should be shown to the person suffering from depression [12,24]. And, this is a new technology system that allows the presentation of visual content in the real world to work on the same representation and, in real time, improve the perception of the true user's senses.

AR can be defined as a set of strategies and tools that convert information into reality. These experiences may increase the natural suitability of AR in the treatment of psychiatric disorders. This works in treating a number of mental issues. It offers real-time environment and resources, which can communicate with the patients and help in their treatment [25]. Program planners can work as nurses to create real-life environments where people can experience very little exposure to problems that cause posttraumatic stress disorder, and slowly be exposed to more until their thought process gets them to realize that their fears are not the reality.

Mental illness is a dangerous disease in which a person loses his or her mind. It causes him or her a lot of trouble in doing his or her day-to-day activities. It is also called as psychological disorder. There are many types of mental disorders and some of them are described in Table 6.2.

AR Therapy Solutions for Good Health:

AR exposure therapy (ARET) is as an effective technology in the field of mental health. This study examines the ARET program used to treat cockroach phobia in a clinical setting. The results seem to indicate that the ARET system is working toward helping the therapist build a therapeutic relationship with the client. Users may perform like doctors to fabricate an illusive atmosphere in which they can execute little exposure to problems which are because of their mental illness, or gradually become more evidential unless their mindset makes them realize that they are not afraid of actuality.

Escapism:

Escape Temporary dementia is essential for maintaining good mental health. For some it is a sport, for others it is an art, for still others it is a prescription, and hallucinogens are easily tested as a treatment for depression and anxiety. This is a new evolution with real-time applications in AR. With this, patients can be made to believe that he has entered into a new world, which is secure and stress-free.

TABLE 6.2
Some Common Observed Disorders in Humans and Their Description

Psychological Disorder	Description
Anxiety disorders	Anxiety is born out of depression, despair, and sadness. When we ignore our feelings, they cause our unhappiness. Similarly, depression can take the form of anxiety if ignored. In this situation, the person is always afraid that something wrong is going to happen.
Depression, bipolar, or mood disorder	It is very common and normal to feel sad due to failure, struggle, and separation. But if feelings like unhappiness, sadness, helplessness, and hopelessness persist for a few days to a few months and make the person unable to carry on with his or her routine normally, then it can be a sign of a mental disease called depression.
Eating disorders	Your food or diet is a problem for you. You think you have anorexia or bulimia. Other people think you have lost too much weight.
Personality disorders	A personality disorder is a mental health condition that affects how a person thinks, understands, feels, or relates to others.

Fear Completion:

Fear is nothing but the reverse form of love. A bit like escape, this technology is suitable to bear down anything that causes psychological problems tested in the environment of illusive actuality and AR. The therapist creates a controlled environment in which he tested the patient to evacuate his/her fear of height. In this, the therapist gives an illusion of higher altitude to reduce the fear of height in the patients.

6.4 AR SOLUTIONS FOR TEACHING SPECIAL STUDENTS

With the help of this technology, classroom learning can become exceptional and more interactive, as AR teachers show concrete examples of concepts and add play materials to provide textbook content support. This will help students read faster and remember details. Human memory does not easily forget scenes [26]. During current seasons, VR and AR are combined for educators to teach, inspire, or enhance classroom interactions between all students having one or more type of disability by making teaching more reachable, unforgettable, actual, and interesting [13].

AR and VR technologies in learning create a synthetic world. And, this world is created by machines or computers. This will motive students to learn the tedious concepts quickly. Also, it simplifies the concepts and presents it in interactive way to improve the teaching and learning abilities [14].

6.4.1 ADVANTAGES OF AR IN EDUCATION

Sometimes people may simultaneously have more than one disability. Students with learning disabilities face many barriers with regard to awareness, infrastructure, teaching, project acquisition, project management, and mobility. It is important to take all these into account and devise a system that works on all of them to help students with learning difficulties. VR can also help students emotionally overcome situations of social awkwardness [15,16].

Probably one of the most popular AR applications in learning is to utilize AR applications directly in the classroom. In this case, they can help teachers explain the curriculum, give illusive characterization of the curriculum, and get relief from students testing their intelligence; it allows students and teachers to visualize 3D models in simulated, real-time, and large-scale environments. It helps to make learning focused and authentic, thus enjoyable and relevant to the students [17,27]. Learning disability in ordinary language refers to the lack or absence of learning ability. In order to understand learning difficulties, we must assess the factors influencing a child's learning. "Direct learning disability" means disruption of one or more of the basic cognitive processes involved in understanding or speaking a language, or in the use of the written form, which is impaired in hearing, thinking, speaking, reading, writing, spelling, or may manifest in the imperfect ability to perform mathematical calculations. There are mainly five learning disabilities, and a gist of them is given in Table 6.3. This table describes the different types of learning disabilities.

TABLE 6.3

Common Learning Disabilities Observed in Disabled People

Learning Disability	Definitions
Developmental dyslexia	Dyslexia is a learning disability that manifests primarily as difficulties with visual representation of speech or written language.
Developmental dyscalculia	Dyscalculia is a broad term used to describe a disability in mathematical skills.
Hyperactivity disorder	It is a disorder of attention deficit and hyperactivity disorder.
Autism spectrum disorder	Autism spectrum disorder is a brain disease. In this, the patient is neither able to speak properly, nor is he or she able to understand the point of others, nor is he or she able to establish communication with them.
Specific language impairment.	Children with this disorder talk much later than other children, and they struggle with many basic concepts in language.

6.5   AR ACCESSIBLE TECHNOLOGY TO PEOPLE

AR can improve access to buildings and community initiatives through mobile apps that allow the user to visualize architectural details accurately. It enables users to bypass natural boundaries and offer a new perspective and understanding of these spaces [8]. Building equipped with AR devices can make the indoor movement of the specialized people easy. With the help of illusive virtual subjects, AR contents create real-world scenarios to help the people in their work. In this research, we have found that there are many models, which makes it probabilistic to use AR for disabled users to offer several ideas for progression [10]. Assistive technology enables students with disabilities to compensate for certain disabilities. These specialized technologies promote independence and reduce the need for further support. Rehabilitative and assistive technology can enable individuals to care for themselves and their families. Untreated hearing loss increases the risk and the degree of distress, depression, somatization, loneliness, and becoming dependent on others [28].

AR technology generates a huge experimentation in recreational sports, education, marketing, and communication. The mix of physical and virtual contents creates visually appealing scenarios for the specially abled people. Some assistive technologies empowering the specially abled person are shown in Figure 6.4 and they are further described in the following paragraphs.

Mobility Devices:

Assistive devices such as wheelchairs have proved to be very useful for people with mobility problems. Incorporating technology will help advance the resource industry that helps businesses and individuals in need. One such example of a wise helper in improving the mobility of people with disabilities is a technology wheelchair. The standard electric wheelchair has low levels of control over the car with the help of a toy stick. Although these wheelchairs help with mobility, it depends on one's physical fitness [29].

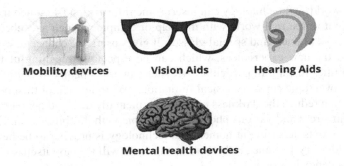

FIGURE 6.4   Devices for empowering the disabled with assistive technology.

Vision Aids:
   Smart visual aids are wearable devices for visually impaired people. They can guide users to their destination by helping them negotiate routes, roads, and corridors while avoiding obstacles. Smart visual aids can help both in indoor and outdoor environments. The user can be helped on his or her way and be warned of the dangers [25].

Hearing Aids:
   Smart hearing aids are growing in importance as a popular and effective treatment for people suffering from varying degrees of hearing loss. The functioning of intelligent hearing aids automatically filters background sounds to improve the desired sound in real time. Intelligent hearing aids make the process of restoring hearing as natural as possible as it is wireless [30].

Mental Health Devices:
   Mental health is one of the most neglected health issues. Assistive devices can not only help people with physical disabilities but also help people with mental illness. A common device such as a smartphone can help people with mental health problems [31]. Various apps are designed to provide a calm environment to reduce anger and frustration. In addition, an app can analyze person's behavior by monitoring its sleep cycle. They can also track inactive components such as breathing and heart rate to determine if a user needs professional medical attention [32–34]. In addition, IoT-based wearable devices were proposed for the diagnosis of chronic diseases [35].

6.6   CONCLUSION

We have reviewed the applications of AR and its operational principles. It has been well accepted that AR is a boon for physically challenged people. AR is touching lives in every domain and providing solutions to complicated tasks. AR has applications in various domains, namely, entertainment, medicines, education, and surgery. This technology has proved to be very effective for people with disabilities. Many AR devices have been developed to ease the lives of physically challenged people. AR allows users to look at two- or three-dimensional visual images that are depicted in the real world. AR technology can insert some information from the virtual world and display it in the real world with the help of equipment such as webcams, computers, android phones, and special glasses. It gives users the chance to explore new worlds and try new experiences, which can be especially meaningful for people with disabilities in cars. In particular, AR sites can allow people with disabilities in vehicles to overcome certain physical limitations. With the help of this, people with low vision can reduce the darkness of their life, mentally disabled people can reduce their mental stress and various phobias, and people with disabilities can enjoy various facilities outside sitting at home. This technology is proving to be beneficial in various fields very fast and in the coming times, it will develop itself so much that everyone is dependent on it.

REFERENCES

[1] Silva, R., Oliveira, J. C., & Giraldi, G. A. (2003). Introduction to augmented reality. *National Laboratory for Scientific Computation*, 11, 1–11.

[2] Hincapié, M., Caponio, A., Rios, H., & Mendívil, E. G. (2011). An introduction to augmented reality with applications in aeronautical maintenance. In *2011 13th International Conference on Transparent Optical Networks* (pp. 1–4). IEEE.

[3] McMahon, D. D., Smith, C. C., Cihak, D. F., Wright, R., & Gibbons, M. M. (2015). Effects of digital navigation aids on adults with intellectual disabilities: Comparison of paper map, Google maps, and augmented reality. *Journal of Special Education Technology*, 30(3), 157–165.

[4] Caudell, T. P. (1995) Introduction to augmented and virtual reality. *Proc. SPIE*, 2351, 272–281.

[5] Saidin, N. F., Halim, N. D. A., & Yahaya, N. (2015). A review of research on augmented reality in education: Advantages and applications. *International Education Studies*, 8(13), 1–8.

[6] Mirzaei, M. R., Ghorshi, S., & Mortazavi, M. (2012). Combining augmented reality and speech technologies to help deaf and hard of hearing people. In *2012 14th Symposium on Virtual and Augmented Reality* (pp. 174–181). IEEE.

[7] Gopalakrishnan, S., Suwalal, S. C., Bhaskaran, G., & Raman, R. (2020) Use of augmented reality technology for improving visual acuity of individuals with low vision. *Indian Journal of Ophthalmology*, 68(6), 1136–1142.

[8] Herskovitz, J., Wu, J., White, S., Pavel, A., Reyes, G., Guo, A., & Bigham, J. P. (2020) Making mobile augmented reality applications accessible. In *The 22nd International ACM SIGACCESS Conference on Computers and Accessibility*, Virtual Event, Greece (pp. 1–14). ACM, New York.

[9] Cakir, R., & Korkmaz, O (2019). The effectiveness of augmented reality environments on individuals with special education needs. *Education and Information Technologies*, 24(2), 1631–1659.

[10] Bacca Acosta, J. L., Baldiris Navarro, S. M., Fabregat Gesa, R., & Graf, S. (2014). Augmented reality trends in education: A systematic review of research and applications. *Educational Technology & Society*, 17(4), 133–149.

[11] Benda, P., Ulman, M., & Šmejkalová, M. (2015) Augmented reality as a working aid for intellectually disabled persons for work in horticulture. *AGRIS on-line Papers in Economics and Informatics*, 7(4), 31–37.

[12] Akçayir, M., and Akçayir, G. (2017). Advantages and challenges associated with AR for education: a systematic review of the literature. *Educational Research and Reviews*, 20, 1–11, doi: 10.1016/j.edurev.2016.11.002.

[13] Maier, P., Tönnis, M., & Klinker, G. (2009). Augmented Reality for teaching spatial relations. In *Conference of the International Journal of Arts & Sciences*, Toronto (pp. 1–8).

[14] Sumadio, D. D., & Rambli, D. R. A. (2010). Preliminary evaluation on user acceptance of the augmented reality use for education. In *2010 Second International Conference on Computer Engineering and Applications* (Vol. 2, pp. 461–465). IEEE.

[15] Ribeiro, F., Florêncio, D., Chou, P. A., & Zhang, Z. (2012) Auditory augmented reality: Object sonification for the visually impaired. In *14th International Workshop on Multimedia Signal Processing (MMSP)* (pp. 319–324), doi: 10.1109/MMSP.2012.6343462.

[16] Mallem, M. (2010) Augmented reality: Issues, trends and challenges. In *2nd International Conference on Image Processing Theory, Tools and Applications* (p. 8), doi: 10.1109/IPTA.2010.5586829.

[17] Gybas, V., Klubal, L., & Kostolányová, K. (2019) Using augmented reality for teaching students with mental disabilities. In *AIP Conference Proceedings* (Vol. 2116, No. 1, p. 060015). AIP Publishing LLC.

[18] McMahon, D. D. (2014) *Augmented Reality on Mobile Devices to Improve the Academic Achievement and Independence of Students with Disabilities*. University of Tennessee, Knoxville.

[19] Cascales-Martínez, A. (2017). Using an AR enhanced table top system to promote learning of mathematics: A case study with students with special educational needs. *EURASIA Journal of Mathematics, Science and Technology Education*, 13, 355–380.

[20] Quintero, J., Baldiris, S., Rubira, R., Cerón, J., & Velez, G. (2019). Augmented reality in educational inclusion. A systematic review on the last decade. *Frontiers in Psychology*, 10, 1835.

[21] Correa, A. G. D., De Assis, G. A., do Nascimento, M., Ficheman, I., & de Deus Lopes, R. (2007). Genvirtual: An augmented reality musical game for cognitive and motor rehabilitation. In *2007 Virtual Rehabilitation* (pp. 1–6). IEEE.

[22] Khan, T., Johnston, K., & Ophoff, J. (2019) The impact of an augmented reality application on learning motivation of students. *Advances in Human-Computer Interaction*, 2019, 7208494.

[23] Abas, H., & Badioze Zaman, H. (2011). Visual learning through augmented reality storybook for remedial student. In *International Visual Informatics Conference* (pp. 157–167). Springer, Berlin, Heidelberg.

[24] Lin, C. Y., & Chang, Y. M. (2015). Interactive augmented reality using Scratch 2.0 to improve physical activities for children with developmental disabilities. *Research in Developmental Disabilities*, 37, 1–8.

[25] Baragash, R. S., Al-Samarraie, H., Alzahrani, A. I., & Alfarraj, O. (2020). Augmented reality in special education: A meta-analysis of single-subject design studies. *European Journal of Special Needs Education*, 35(3), 382–397.

[26] Carmigniani, J., & Furht, B. (2011). Augmented reality: An overview. In *Handbook of Augmented Reality* (pp. 3–46), Springer.

[27] Torrado, J. C., Gomez, J., & Jaccheri, L. (2019) Supporting self-evaluation for children with mental disabilities through Augmented Reality In *IDC '19: Proceedings of the 18th ACM International Conference on Interaction Design and Children* (pp. 635–641).

[28] McMahon, D., Cihak, D. F., & Wright, R. (2015) Augmented reality as a navigation tool to employment opportunities for postsecondary education students with intellectual disabilities and autism. *Journal of Research on Technology in Education*, 47(3), 157–172.

[29] Bianco, M. L., Pedell, S., & Renda, G. (2016). Augmented reality and home modifications: a tool to empower older adults in fall prevention. In *Proceedings of the 28th Australian Conference on Computer-Human Interaction* (pp. 499–507).

[30] Rashid, Z., Melià-Seguí, J., Pous, R., & Peig, E. (2016). Using augmented reality and internet of things to improve accessibility of people with motor disabilities in the context of smart cities. *Future Generation Computer Systems*, 76, doi: 10.1016/j. future.2016.11.030.

[31] Richard, E., Billaudeau, V., Richard, P., & Gaudin, G. (2007). Augmented reality for rehabilitation of cognitive disabled children: A preliminary study. In *Virtual Rehabilitation, 2007* (pp. 102–108), doi: 10.1109/ICVR.2007.4362148.

[32] Alfian, G., Syafrudin, M., Ijaz, M. F., Syaekhoni, M. A., Fitriyani, N. L., & Rhee, J. (2018). A personalized healthcare monitoring system for diabetic patients by utilizing BLE-based sensors and real-time data processing. *Sensors*, 18(7), 2183.

[33] Ijaz, M. F., Alfian, G., Syafrudin, M., & Rhee, J. (2018). Hybrid prediction model for type 2 diabetes and hypertension using DBSCAN-based outlier detection, synthetic minority over sampling technique (SMOTE), and random forest. *Applied Sciences*, 8(8), 1325.

[34] Ijaz, M. F., Attique, M., & Son, Y. (2020). Data-driven cervical cancer prediction model with outlier detection and over-sampling methods. *Sensors*, 20(10), 2809.

[35] Awotunde, J. B., Folorunso, S. O., Bhoi, A. K., Adebayo, P. O., & Ijaz, M. F. (2021). Disease diagnosis system for IoT-based wearable body sensors with machine learning algorithm. In *Hybrid Artificial Intelligence and IoT in Healthcare* (pp. 201–222). Springer, Singapore.

7 Augmented Reality and Virtual Reality
Transforming the Future of Psychological and Medical Sciences

*Gurjinder Singh, Anjali Kataria, Shinnu Jangra,
Rubina Dutta, and Archana Mantri*
Chitkara University

Jasminder Kaur Sandhu
Chandigarh University

Thennarasan Sabapathy
Universiti Malaysia Perlis (UniMAP)

CONTENTS

DOI: 10.1201/9781003254119-7

7.1   INTRODUCTION

Disorders that affect the brain's ability to communicate, interact with others, learn, and perform tasks are known as neurodevelopmental disorders (Henderson et al., 2020). Attention Deficit Hyperactivity Disorder (ADHD), Autism Spectrum Disorder (ASD), communication disorders, global developmental delay, intellectual disability, motor disorders, and specific learning disorders are amongst the disorders that fall under neurodevelopmental disorders. A wide range of functional and social limitations are linked to a variety of neurodevelopmental disorders. The quality of life of individuals with neurodevelopmental disorders and their willpower can be enhanced with the help of effective communication (Chamak & Bonniau, 2016; Johnson et al., 2010). These interventions for various individuals with neurodevelopmental disorders are focused on improving their communication abilities (Ellis et al., 2013). Many of these programs emphasize the importance of delivering intensive treatment. A large number of families and individuals suffering from neurodevelopmental disorders cannot easily get treatment because of the geographic isolation and shortage of medical professionals in rural and remote areas (Bailey et al., 2021). Due to these issues, researchers focus on the viability of telemedical models for delivering services such as face-to-face communication that succeeds in using a telemedical model. Nowadays, researchers emphasize virtual reality (VR) and augmented reality (AR) technologies to revamp the effectiveness of communication interventions (Bryant et al., 2020).

AR and VR technologies are utilized in the education field to improve the teaching strategies for disabled students. It helps the students to acquire knowledge and skills in communication, behavior, and development (Cifuentes et al., 2016). For several decades, educational reform has been focused on disabled students. Individuals with cognitive and physical disabilities require assistance and special attention during their learning processes (Carberry & Mckenna, 2014). It is recommended that more effective teaching methods and practices must be provided to disabled people to accomplish this goal (Browder et al., 2006). Because of the proliferation of digital technologies, mobile devices, applications, and other innovative teaching–learning strategies could be beneficial for students who are suffering from neurodevelopmental disorders such as visual impairments, autism, cognitive disorder, and intellectual disabilities (Jdaitawi, 2019). VR technology becomes common and is utilized for academic, communication, and amusement purposes. New VR-based educational tools are being developed for disabled students (Rizzo et al., 2000). In the current scenario, some projects are created solely for the treatment of autistic individuals. Kids are more sensitive to the immersive VR experience than other people. Due to this, VR technology is sometimes denied by the people concerned. On the other hand, AR tools allow users to interact more safely and intuitively with 3D entities in the real world (Andreas & Billinghurst, 2011; Billinghurst et al., 2001). As a result, no mental barriers are erected when using AR to address specific problems or disabilities, such as natural speech or paralanguage. AR allows users to interact with digital information in the real world without having to look at a screen on a device. AR isn't just limited to the sense of sight. It can also be used for hearing, smell, and even touch, and help people to read and write even when they are suffering from disabilities (Akçayır & Akçayır, 2017).

7.1.1 AUGMENTED REALITY

AR technology can be described in various ways such as it augments the real world with virtually added information. AR technology is known to be a subset of VR technology. The individual interaction with the AR system is at all times immersed in their own reality, unlike the individual using VR technology. However, few VR systems mimic AR technology with the help of cameras by showing user surroundings included with supplementary information. This information is available as a synthetic feature of the virtual reality system. AR merges digital content with the real world by applying different techniques such as computer graphics, image processing, and computer vision (Yilmaz, 2018). Azuma defined AR as a system which contains the three important features such as a combination of the real and virtual worlds, interaction in real time, and 3D registration (Parker, 2018). Milgram defined AR as a subset of Mixed Reality (MR) that exists on a continuum of real to virtual environments shown in Figure 7.1. At one end is a reality, and at the other end is completely virtuality (Bhouri, 2009; Milgram, 2011).

The following steps should be considered during augmentation of data:

Step 1: A real-time view is captured with a device camera (smartphone, desktop, and head-mounted display).

Step 2: The captured scene is scanned with predefined algorithms to find the precise positions for overlaying the virtual content on top of the original image.

Step 3: To provide relevant virtual content for each location that has been identified, the system processor makes requests to predefined databases using the identifiers.

Step 4: Finally, the AR System creates a single view that incorporates both real and virtual information as demonstrated in Figure 7.2.

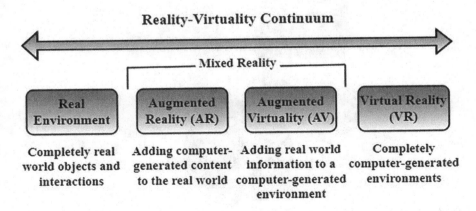

FIGURE 7.1 Adapted schema of virtuality continuum.

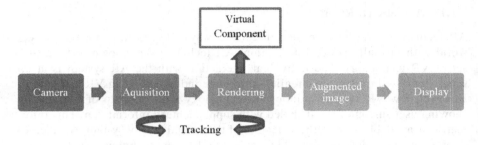

FIGURE 7.2   Marker-based AR system.

7.1.2 Types of Augmented Reality Systems

Figure 7.3 represents the distinct types of AR systems. The selection of each type is dependent on factors such as application, requirement, platform, and environment. The description of each type is as mentioned below:

  a. **Markers-Based AR:** AR utilizes a camera and visual markers to recognize a product only after it has been correctly identified by the reader. Using a camera, these applications can identify the difference between a real object and a marker in the environment. Like the QR code and fiducial markers, simple patterns are utilized. The QR codes and fiducial markers are used, allowing easy identification and less power consumption. In Figure 7.2, cameras scan the QR code and then place the augmented image on the screen.
  b. **Markerless/Location-Based AR:** It is a device comprising several components, namely, the compass (digital), accelerometer or velocity meter, and the Global Positioning System (GPS). The dynamic data are made available

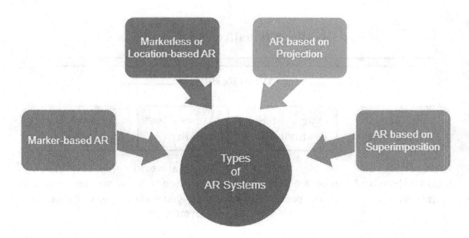

FIGURE 7.3   Types of AR.

depending on the user's location. The smartphone's location services feature plays a vital role in markerless AR technology. In the case of markerless, the camera of the mobile screen scans the specific space. Once it scans, important places nearby that area will be displayed on the screen. It works like Google Maps (Amin & Govilkar, 2015).

c. **Projection-Based AR:** It performs functions by projecting artificial light onto the surface of real-world objects. Its application allows for human-to-human interaction by first projecting light onto a surface and then sensing human interaction with the light projected. The distinction between known/expected projection and distorted projection allows for the detection of human interaction (Kugelmann et al., 2018).

d. **Superimposition-Based AR:** It is used to create an enlarged image of an object instead of looking directly at it. Thus, object recognition is critical to the superimposed technique of AR (Beglov et al., 2013).

7.1.3 COMPONENTS AND ASPECTS OF AR TECHNOLOGY

AR technology requires different components such as computational platforms, display devices, tracking and registration, interaction type, and access technology (Mekni & Lemieux, 2014). Table 7.1 summarizes the components of the AR system.

Following are the core technologies and aspects of AR:

i. **Tracking and Registration Technology**

One of the difficult techniques to master is tracking and registration, which calls for extremely precise and accurate orientation tracking. Using tracking and registration technology in a real-time scenario, rendered virtual objects would be placed in the correct location. Virtual objects should be placed in the new location to give the impression of a real scene when the camera's location and orientation change. The tracking and registration technology consists of two phases.

TABLE 7.1

AR System Components

Components	Descriptions
Computational Platform	Creates and controls virtual entities in real-world contexts.
Type of display	Mimicking virtual objects in real-world scenarios.
	Frequently used to deliver information by either comparing or fully substituting in case of a visual element.
Tracking and Registration	Accurately locating and annotating the physical entities related to virtual entities.
Interaction Technologies	Providing people with the ability to select, access, and visualize relevant information
Access Technology	Users can access real-world data using this application.

- **Registration Process**: To accomplish perfect superposition, the virtual item must entirely align itself to the correct position in the real environment.
- **Tracking Process**: The virtual object's position in the real scene must be recreated whenever the observer's position changes.

    It is further divided into three parts: hardware-based, vision-based, and software-based.

- **Hardware-Based Tracking and Registration Method**: Sensor data and signal sources are used to estimate the object's orientation and spatial position.
- **Vision-Based Tracking and Registration Method**: The data generated during the tracking phase are compared to previously stored data. The current direction and position are calculated. It is faster, simpler, and more scalable.
- **Hybrid Tracking and Registration Method**: Interior and exterior environmental issues can be addressed in this manner. Transplantation is both costly and complicated (Singh & Mantri, 2016).

ii. **Object Detection and Recognition Technology**

The primary goal is to find the object. There is a requirement to take initial steps for understanding object detection and classification. It can be performed using the enhanced supplemental data and information. For instance, the age and gender of a user in an AR application are displayed after the detection of the user's face. The next step is image matching, in which the picture features and their corresponding information are recorded in a database on the server (Guan & Wang, 2009). An AR system uses a mobile device's camera to record the current scene. The image is analyzed using recognition technology to find matches based on the value of the image's features. At last, the correct image appears in front of the camera's viewfinder.

iii. **Calibration**

The calibration uses pixels of the camera's image to put the objects back in their correct locations in three-dimensional space again. The main responsibility of this component is detecting and relaying information about the object's location and orientation. The following values for calibration are recorded during the testing process: vision range and camera parameters; sensor offset; deformation; and object location (Lee & Höllerer, 2007).

iv. **Model Rendering**

Two-dimensional images can be generated from 3D data using a process known as model rendering. A frame buffer is the most common location for storing the output image. Mobile devices use OpenGL ES rendering technology to display AR applications.

v. **Display Interaction Technology**

The main aim of AR technology is to use it on a mobile device. Due to the development of smartphones and tablets, there is an opportunity to reach a larger audience. Using a voice-activated interface, Google Glass lets users make and receive phone calls, send texts, and perform web searches without taking their hands off the device. Microsoft proposed the HoloLens in 2015, a device that allows users to visualize and communicate with holographic 3D virtual entities using audio, gaze, and hints in the form of gestures (Cen et al., 2020).

7.2   USE OF AR TECHNOLOGY IN MEDICAL SCIENCE

AR is applied in several fields of medical science such as in the training of medical students, neurological rehabilitation, medical study, telemedicine, and surgical techniques. The HoloLens device is used to perform surgeries on patients and to project an imaginary or realistic image on the screen digitally (Hsieh & Lee, 2018). Figure 7.4 shows that AR technology is used in various disabilities to improve the patient's health.

7.2.1   AR IN SURGICAL OPERATIONS

AR provides the best operational training to the students as well as doctors. This technology reduces operational errors and improves the surgical process (Yoon et al., 2018). Several industries have been developing AR surgical systems. AR technology is beneficial for surgeons and also provides a 3D environment, which is captured using the Stereoscopic Display Screen, as shown in Figure 7.5. There are several kinds of surgeries that already use AR technology.

7.2.1.1   Gastrointestinal Cancer Surgery

Gastrointestinal cancer is of various kinds such as pancreatic cancer, rectal cancer, large and small intestine cancer, anal cancer, colon cancer, esophageal cancer, bile duct cancer, gastrointestinal stromal tumor, and liver cancer. The treatment of all cancer surgeries was a little easy using AR Therapies.

AR therapies were used and applied in a Retero-scopic Camera for visualizing an internal organ of the body (Ahmed et al., 2022). There were two AR applications for gastrointestinal endoscopy.

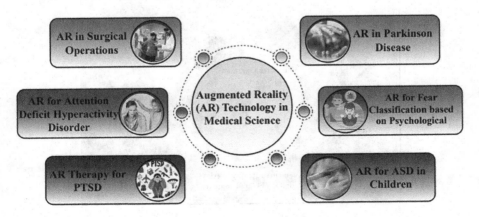

FIGURE 7.4   Augmented reality in medical science.

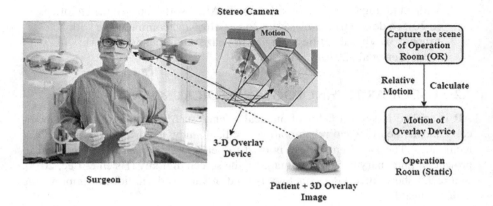

FIGURE 7.5   AR surgical navigation system using stereoscopy

Enhancement of Multi-Modality Image: There were various imaging approaches for gastrointestinal surgery endoscopy with the integration of AR technology, as shown in Figure 7.6. The first approach was endoscopic ultrasound, which could be used to describe the organs to trace the problem of the stomach. Secondly, Endoscopic Retrograde Cholangio-pancreatography (ERCP) with both endoscopy and fluoroscopy images was used for the evaluation of the pancreatico-biliary system (Mahmud et al., 2015). AR is applied for fluoroscopy in reference to the arena of cardiac interventions. It helps in analysis of the fluoroscopic structure or selection of optimal treatment for the patients.

Improvement of the Performance and Tracking: Due to the increasing pressure of endoscopists for the tracking of Polyp detection rates, AR is used to track and validate the performance of Polyp Detection. It also improves the testing aspects of endoscopy results of gastrointestinal problems.

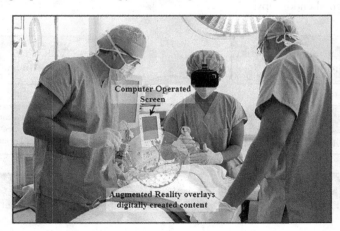

FIGURE 7.6   Use of augmented reality in gastrointestinal cancer surgery.

7.2.1.2 Knee Replacement Surgery

Digital surgery is utilized for the replacement of Knee like 3D visual perception, as shown in Figure 7.7. This kind of surgery has been done with the use of wearable headset devices because it shows a real-world 3D virtual perception to the doctors. There are several technologies for surgery and knee arthroplasty (Goh et al., 2021). Smart AR glasses are used nowadays for the surgery of knee replacement. But with the use of AR glasses, there were improvements in the process of knee surgery.

7.2.1.3 Brain Tumor Surgery

Neurology refers to the abnormal cells that have grown into the brain and these abnormal cells are malignant to the brain. It is a very serious health issue because these abnormal tissues damage normal tissues of the brain. So, in this condition, brain surgery is inevitable. However, when a human suffers from this stage, the surgeon faces several issues in proceeding with the patient's surgery. That is why, to improve this problem of surgery for the surgeon as well as the patient, AR devices like HoloLens can be utilized. (Lee & Wong, 2019). The first surgery was performed with the use of an Augmented Stereo Microscope in 1995. Nowadays, AR technology has been enhanced because it shows the digital image on the screen when the surgeon is doing surgery on any human and improves the procedure of the surgery, as shown in Figure 7.8.

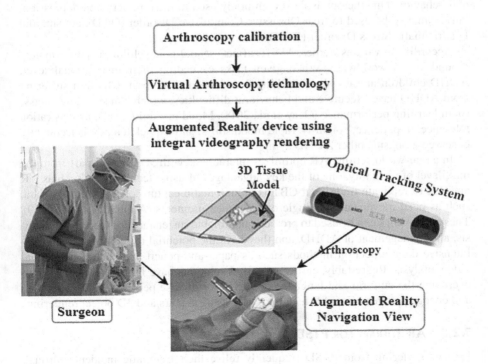

FIGURE 7.7 Use of augmented reality in knee replacement surgery.

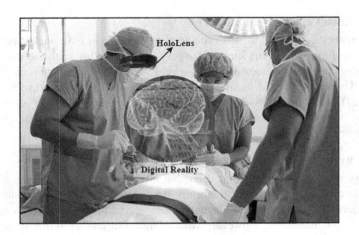

FIGURE 7.8   Augmented reality in brain tumor surgery.

7.2.2   AR THERAPY FOR ADHD

Distraction, hyperactivity, and aggressiveness are all symptoms of ADHD, which is the most common type of neurodevelopmental disorder. Persons who require psychological treatment use Cognitive Behavioral Therapy (CBT) to improve their thinking and behavior. This therapy is most commonly used to treat anxiety and depression, but it can also be used to treat Obsessive Compulsive Disorder (OCD), autism, and Posttraumatic Stress Disorder (PTSD).

According to various studies, ADHD affects school-going children approximately around age 5 worldwide. When given tasks exceeding their instructional level, ADHD children are at risk of walking out or becoming upset. Children suffering from ADHD have executive and behavioral difficulties, which can slowdown classroom learning performance (Ocay et al., 2018). Mood instability, such as frustration tolerance, impatience, volatility, rapid mood shifts, and a quick temper, is frequently observed alongside other ADHD symptoms.

In a real-world setting, AR optimizes interactions with 3D items. Apart from the multilevel of virtuality, one of the key advantages of using technologies such as VR and AR to replicate traditional CBT is an automatic capture of multisensory data, such as head movement and angle of view measurements (Alqithami et al., 2019). These recordings can be used to provide quantifiable sustenance for the care, diagnosis, and management of ADHD, and they have the potential to replace recent labor-intensive data collection methods such as paper-and-pencil approaches or manual video analysis. Regrettably, earlier promised solutions have failed to deliver: (a) To overcome the cultural and language obstacles for diverse persons. (b) To speed up and engage patients using AR technology by using avatars and 3D object rendering.

7.2.3   AR THERAPY FOR PTSD

Patients suffering from PTSD frequently relive their traumatic incidents through flashbacks and nightmares. People who have PTSD may also be very afraid when they see things that are similar to what happened in their past (Eshuis et al., 2021). They may also avoid situations that are responsible for trauma. People who have PTSD have a lot of mental and physical alertness, as well as insomnia, irritability, hypervigilance, low focus, and reckless and self-destructive activities. In PTSD, trauma-related incidents are usually followed by uncomfortable physiological responses, which lead to cognitive and behavioral avoidance, a coping mechanism for reducing psychological distress and physiological hyperarousal. This avoidance serves to strengthen the fear of adaptive processing of traumatic memories, thus maintaining PTSD symptoms.

7.2.4 AR IN PARKINSON'S DISEASE (PD)

PD occurs in about 1% of the people over the age group of 60 years. A person suffering from this disease often has symptoms of slow movement and tremors. AR acts as an assistive technology for PD.

PD is a brain disorder that begins slowly but worsens over time. It tends to affect the motor and nonmotor symptoms. As the disease progresses, an individual may face challenges in walking and talking, loss of posture reflexes, tremors, and rigidity (Massano & Bhatia, 2012). There is no well-defined clinical diagnostic procedure for this disease. Figure 7.9 shows the symptoms of PD and contributes to the identification of the disease. The targeted detection of this disease can provide new avenues in the identification of PD patients and hence help in development of novel neuroprotective therapies.

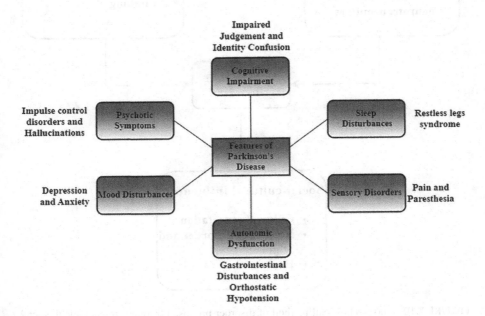

FIGURE 7.9 Symptoms affecting Parkinson's disease.

7.2.5 AR FOR FEAR CLASSIFICATION BASED ON PSYCHOLOGICAL DISORDER

A psychological disorder is dangerous for society due to the distressed behavior of the person. This disorder is a medical disorder in which the patient's behavior is not under his or her control. It can be treated by using expensive drugs, which can be covered by health insurance. Psychological disorders have both real-time environment and biotic influences, which reflect the biopsychosocial method of an ailment (Chicchi Giglioli et al., 2015).

Biopsychosocial method of an ailment is the system of determining the ailment through certain psychological, social, and biological factors, as shown in Figure 7.10.

1. The basic element of the biopsychosocial method is the biological factor. This factor determines the functioning of the human body. The genetically inherited features play a vital role and make some patients more in danger of disorder as compared to the rest of the people and affect neurotransmitters.
2. The psychological component is the second factor of the biopsychosocial method. These parameters come from individual human beings from their

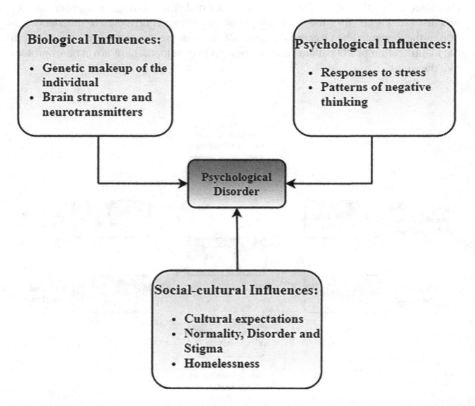

FIGURE 7.10 Biopsychosocial method of disorder proposed through psychological, social cultural, and biological factors.

level of thinking. This includes negative thinking patterns and the response to variable levels of stress.

3. The social cultural influence of biopsychosocial relates to an ailment because of the social or cultural conditions of an individual. These include conditions such as socioeconomic status, abuse, discrimination, and homelessness.

7.2.6 AR FOR ASD KIDS

ASD is a neurodevelopmental disorder that affects the behavior, interests, and communication of children's lives. AR is used to show digitally everything like the real world by using glasses and head-mounted displays. This technology attracts children who are suffering from ASD disorder. AR is used to provide social interaction, positive emotions, and attention to the kids (Berenguer et al., 2020). In this article, researchers talked about the AR-based application "MOSOCO," which helps children to enhance their social skills and learning power (Almurashi et al., 2022). Figure 7.11 represents AR technique that improves social skills of Autism kids.

1. AR application is used to check the brainpower of the children and 3D videos are used for enjoyment purposes so as to increase the engagement level.
2. AR technology enhances the awareness of facial expression and increases the focus of the children in this kind of 3D video and games. It provides scores to the kids so that they are engaged more and learn more.
3. Three-dimensional stories using AR glasses and headsets attract attention, increases the learning power of the children and their strength.

7.3 CHALLENGES AND OPPORTUNITIES

There is high demand to study the merits and demerits of AR technology in the domain of medical and health science. The analysis of AR-based applications in medical science is still in the developing stages. The goal of this study is to determine and comprehend the effect of an AR mobile application for learning encouragement in the fields of surgical operations, mental disorders, physical handicaps, PD, stress disorder, and spectrum disorder kids. As compared to other technologies, AR doesn't require special hardware because it can be simply accessed by PCs or mobile devices. The main problem of the AR system is usability faced by doctors and patients. These are some of the main challenges faced by users in the medical field.

1. Users of AR immersive technology encounter issues related to usability and technical concerns. Sometimes, many users are confused by the technology. There is also no evidence that usability issues are created by AR technology. They can be caused by a need for technological experience, interface design faults, technical challenges, and negative points of view.
2. The content provided by using AR applications is usually inflexible, restricting the doctor's authority over the content and preventing patient-specific customization to fulfill the needs of patients.

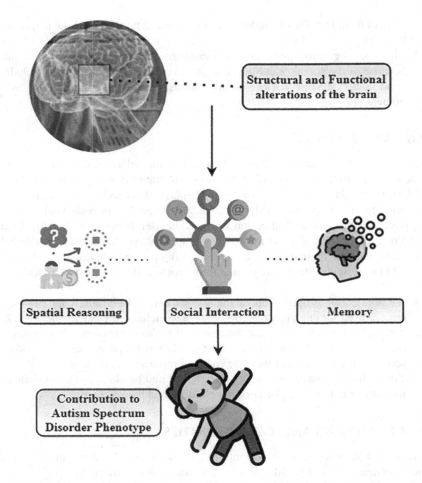

FIGURE 7.11   Augmented reality technology improves social skills of autism kids.

3. Another problem faced by the users is the stability of smartphones. AR-based applications cannot be positive. If the AR devices lack well-designed communications and guidance, then difficulties may occur. Due to this, the technology may become useless and excessively complicated.

4. The staff are not familiar with the technology and require training regarding how to use the equipment.

5. If the immersive techniques for sensitivity and compassion training are not performed correctly, then these techniques can have drawbacks. These interventions might actually reinforce preconceptions.

6. Researchers assume that AR techniques will be incorporated as standard equipment in orthopedic treatment. It will provide a great technological advance in the field of medicine. There is a growing number of research studies and researchers working on the adoption of AR technology in ordinary clinical operations (Casari et al., 2021).

TABLE 7.2

Comparison of Existing Studies

S. No.	Authors	Title	Name of Journal, Publisher	Year	Disease	Tools/ Technologies	Description
1	Min-Chai Hsieh and Jia-Jin Lee	Preliminary Study of VR and AR Applications in Medical and Healthcare Education	*Journal of Nursing and Health Studies*, iMedPub	2018	Autism, Phantom Limb Pain	AR technology, Google glasses	• Virtual reality, augmented reality, and mixed reality provide more attention in the field of healthcare. • Google glasses help the children who suffer from autism spectrum disorders. • To improve from autism spectrum disorder use google glasses.
2	Jang W. Yoon, Robert E. Chen, Esther J. Kim, Oluwaseun O. Akinduro, Panagiotis Kerezoudis, Phillip K. Han, Phong Si, William D. Freeman, Roberto J. Diaz, Ricardo J. Komotar, Stephen M. Pirris, Benjamin L. Brown, Mohamad Bydon, Michael Y. Wang, Robert E. Wharen Jr, Alfredo Quinones-Hinojosa	Augmented reality for the surgeon: Systematic review	*The International Journal of Medical Robotics and Computer-Assisted Surgery*, WILEY	2018	Neurosurgery, ophthalmology, surgical oncology. plastic surgery, urology, vascular surgery, maxillofacial surgery, and interventional radiology	Google glasses, Oculus Rift, HoloLens	• The use of google glasses for capturing the medical images and electronic medical records. • Then visualizing the signals of physiologic concepts involved peripheral vascular resistance, dynamic operating blood level, cardiac index, hematocrit, and venous saturation.

(Continued)

TABLE 7.2 (*Continued*)
Comparison of Existing Studies

S. No.	Authors	Title	Name of Journal, Publisher	Year	Disease	Tools/ Technologies	Description
3	Graham S. Goh, Ryan Lohre, Javad Parvizi, Danny P. Goel	Virtual and augmented reality for surgical training and simulation in knee arthroplasty	*Archives of Orthopedic and Trauma Surgery, Knee Arthroplasty*	2021	Knee replacement surgery	Oculus Rift and Quest, HTC Vive	• With the use of augmented reality, painless knee surgery has been implemented. • So to decrease the cutting error in surgery and to reduce the chronic pain during knee replacement use augmented reality.
4	Chester Lee, George Kwok Chu Wong	Virtual Reality and Augmented Reality in the management of intracranial tumors: A review	*Journal of Clinical Neuroscience,* Elsevier	2018	Brain and intracranial tumor	AR system–based 3D slicer	• To improve an issue of the surgery for surgeons as well as patients, apply augmented reality devices, namely, HoloLens. • The first surgery has been done with the use of an augmented stereo microscope and nowadays augmented reality technology has been enhanced.

(*Continued*)

TABLE 7.2 (*Continued*)
Comparison of Existing Studies

S. No.	Authors	Title	Name of Journal, Publisher	Year	Disease	Tools/ Technologies	Description
5	Patricia Perez-Fuster, Gerardo Herrera, Lila Kossyyaki, and Antonio Ferrer	Enhancing Joint Attention Skills in Children on the Autism Spectrum through an Augmented Reality Technology-Mediated Intervention	*Children*, MDPI	2022	Joint attention skills and mediated intervention	AR smart glasses	• AR technology has emerged in the area of autism spectrum disorders, and it is very effective in different health care treatments such as for mental health treatment and diagnosis.
6	Haneen Almurashi, Rahma Bouaziz, Wallaa Alharthi, Mohammed Al-Sarem, Mohammed Hadwan, and Slim Kammoun	Augmented Reality, Serious Games and Picture Exchange Communication System for People with ASD: Systematic Literature Review and Future Directions	*Sensors*, MDPI	2022	Communication system for people with autism spectrum disorder	Develop serious games through augmented reality	• Augmented reality technology enhances the awareness of facial expression and increases the focus of children in this kind of 3D video and games. They provide scores to the kids so that they are engaged more and learn more.

(*Continued*)

TABLE 7.2 (Continued)

Comparison of Existing Studies

S. No.	Authors	Title	Name of Journal, Publisher	Year	Disease	Tools/ Technologies	Description
7	Carmen Berenguer, Inmaculada Baixauli, Soledad Gomez, Maria de El Puig Andres, and Simona De Stasio	Exploring the Impact of Augmented Reality in Children and Adolescents with Autism Spectrum Disorder: A Systematic Review	*International Journal of Environment Research and Public Health*, MDPI	2020	Autism spectrum disorder in adolescents and children	Design attractive learning games applications with the use of augmented reality	• To enhance the treatment process in the field of medicare and to teach nursing medical students to use augmented reality. • To help children suffering with autism disorder and apply AR treatment.
8	Chien-Hsu Chen, I-Jui Lee, and Ling-Yi Lin	Augmented reality-based video-modeling storybook of nonverbal facial cues for children with autism spectrum disorder to improve their perceptions and judgments of facial expressions and emotions.	*Computers in Human Behavior*, Elsevier	2016	Autism spectrum disorder	Unity 3D and Vuforia Platform	• Video modeling story books were designed through augmented reality. • AR technology enhances the social communication in autism spectrum defect (ASD) disorder.

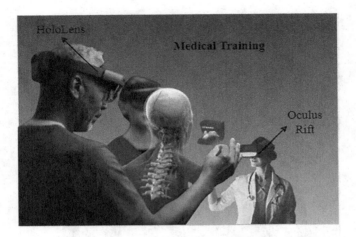

FIGURE 7.12 Augmented reality in medical training in the operation room.

Immersive technology is rapidly altering our perceptions of the world. Due to these technologies, several games come to mind. Immersive technology, on the other hand, has found new applications. There are now numerous AR and VR applications for disabled people (Tang et al., 2019). Figure 7.12 shows the use of AR technology in the operation room. The several examples based on modern technologies that improve the lives of persons with disabilities are:

1. Not everyone has complete hearing or vision loss. Some people suffer partial hearing or vision loss. The majority of them have only partial vision loss and can benefit from AR or VR applications that improve their senses. Color blindness can be corrected with AR glasses (Mehra et al., 2020).
2. Social skill development using AR/VR technology. People with ASD have a hard time engaging with others. It's embarrassing and overwhelming for them. This obstacle can be overcome by practice. The Brain Power Scheme is the world's first AR smart glasses–based autism system (Zhao et al., 2022).
3. AR applications improve the speech and hearing disabilities of people. Communication is one of the most difficult tasks for those who are facing the issue of speech and hearing impairments. A lot of assistive and wearable technology has been developed for disabled people to communicate in a more efficient manner. Now, VR and AR are seeking to take it to the next level (Barua & Das, 2021).
4. Travelling is difficult for people who have mobility issues. They must focus on the areas that are easily accessible. Ramps and wheelchair-accessible bathrooms may go unnoticed by nondisabled persons, yet they are critical for people with disabilities. VR and AR tour of a site allows them to explore the area and check for accessibility difficulties.
5. Handicapped people comprehend the reality of never being able to walk again. This prompted a group of Duke University scientists to develop the

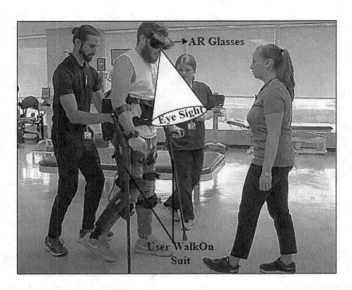

FIGURE 7.13 The WalkON Suit in the hands of a completely paraplegic patient: (a) walking and (b) changing the mode.

Walk Again Project, which combines brain–machine interfaces with a VR system to assist patients with paraplegia, as shown in Figure 7.13. These brain–machine systems with VR can assist paralyzed people in regaining muscle control. According to the researchers, VR allows patients to visualize when their legs hit the ground or are extended (Manns et al., 2019; Talaty et al., 2013).

6. The first AR surgery in living patients was done by Johns Hopkins neurosurgeons. On June 8, 2020, the doctors implanted six screws into a patient's spine for major surgery to fuse three vertebrae and alleviate the patient's chronic, painful back pain. On June 10, surgeons removed a malignant growth known as a neurological illness from a patient's spine in the second surgery. Both patients are doing well, according to the doctors. Approximately eight out of ten people will suffer from debilitating back pain at some point in their lives (Choi et al., 2018). Surgery may be a possibility if medication and lifestyle changes aren't enough to ease discomfort. Each year, around 1.6 million people in the United States undergo spinal fusions, with 60%–70% of patients reporting decreased pain as a result of the procedure. The most well-known therapies are surgery and radiation using this technology. The surgeons use AR surgery technology that includes a headset with a watch eye display that projects images of the patient's interior anatomy, such as skeletons and other tissues, based on computed tomography (CT) scans, giving them X-ray visibility (Navab, 2012). It's like having a GPS navigator in front of your eyes in a natural way while using AR in the surgery room, so that you don't have to

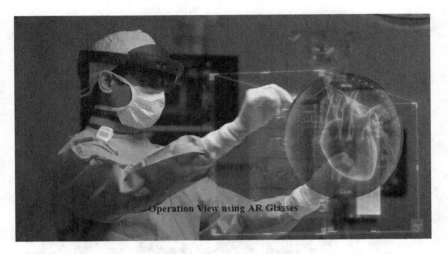

Operation View using AR Glasses

FIGURE 7.14 Surgeon's operation view using augmented reality.

glance at a separate screen to see a patient's CT scan. Moving from training to routine use in surgery, on the other hand, is taking a little longer. Google Glass was used to pilot orthopedic shoulder replacement at the University of Alabama and Emory University, and Stanford University is creating its gadget. Figure 7.14 shows the use of AR technology in surgeon operations.

7. Digital technologies have made a significant contribution to closing opportunity gaps, particularly among underserved and disadvantaged people. These technologies have encouraged innovative solutions to inequity, from assistive technologies that allow people with disabilities to live more independently to social networks that help isolated users discover new systems of support to telehealth and e-learning platforms that provide access to healthcare services and educational opportunities to underserved populations (Rodríguez et al., 2016). Immersive empathy therapies should not just result in a shift in emotions or viewpoint but also in action or behavioral changes that could lead to larger social change.

8. Games create an unsatisfactory playing experience when player ability levels are not matched. To overcome this issue, player balance is utilized in a variety of digital game genres, but it hasn't been employed in video games (Rogers et al., 2018). Co-located AR table games were investigated where boosts and handicaps can be used to accommodate for different situations and skill levels of the players. In the AR table football game, we used projected icons to prominently display game balancing mechanics. Researchers investigated numerous triggers for this type of game balance, as well as their implications on player experience, with this game table shown in Figure 7.15.

FIGURE 7.15   Augmented reality table football for handicap.

7.4   CONCLUSION

AR and VR in medical science, clinical research, and psychology are increasing day by day. Immersive technologies have encouraged innovative solutions to inequity, from assistive technologies that allow people with disabilities to live more independently to social networks. Immersive technologies help doctors, psychologists, and patients suffering from different neurological disorders such as ADHD, ASD, language disorders, general developmental gap, and mental disability. The development of AR interactive games, applications, and AR-based interactive books could aid in treating these disorders as AR can provide a simulated environment similar to real-life situations, which can help the patients improve their behavior and mental state. This present work focuses on how AR and VR can help doctors, surgeons, psychologists, and people with disabilities.

AR is becoming widely popular and attractive in providing a learning environment to perform surgeries and operations in medical science. AR provides immersive operational training to doctors, surgeons, and practitioners, as it reduces operational errors and improves the surgical process. The surgeon has employed AR surgery technology that included a headset with a watch eye display that projected images of the patient's interior anatomies, such as skeletons and other tissue, based on CT scans, giving them X-ray visibility. Also, digital surgery for a knee replacement was performed with the help of 3D visual perception techniques. This kind of surgery was done with the help of wearable headset devices as it presents virtual information augmented in a real-world scene that helps the doctors to understand the process and body parts easily. However, with the use of AR glasses, there were improvements in the process of knee surgery.

The present work discussed the use of immersive technologies in medical science and clinical research with real-world applications. AR and VR technologies can ease down the complex processes and provide training to professionals. AR can help in giving e-instructions through digital learning platforms of any process, whereas VR can take the person to a simulated situation with the help of virtual environments. Immersive technologies allow users to interact with virtual things, enhancing their experience and improving their understanding and confidence to work on real scenarios. The deliberations and case studies discussed in this paper provide pathways to future research and opportunities to implement immersive technologies in other fields in an effective way.

REFERENCES

Ahmed, S., Bosma, N., Moser, M., Ahmed, S., Brunet, B., Davies, J., Doll, C., Dueck, D., Kim, C. A., Ji, S., Le, D., Lee-ying, R., Lim, H., Mcghie, J. P., Mulder, K., Park, J., Ravi, D., Renouf, D. J., Schellenberg, D., ... Zaidi, A. (2022). Systemic therapy and its surgical implications in patients with resectable liver colorectal cancer metastases. A report from the Western Canadian Gastrointestinal Cancer Consensus Conference. *Current Oncology, 29*(3), 1796–1807.

Akçayır, M., & Akçayır, G. (2017). Advantages and challenges associated with augmented reality for education: A systematic review of the literature. *Educational Research Review, 20*, 1–11. https://doi.org/10.1016/j.edurev.2016.11.002

Almurashi, H., Bouaziz, R., Alharthi, W., Al-Sarem, M., Hadwan, M., & Kammoun, S. (2022). Augmented reality, serious games and picture exchange communication system for people with ASD: Systematic literature review and future directions. *Sensors, 22*(3), 1–47. https://doi.org/10.3390/s22031250

Alqithami, S., Alzahrani, M., Alzahrani, A., & Mustafa, A. (2019). AR-therapist: Design and simulation of an AR-game environment as a CBT for patients with ADHD. *Healthcare, 7*(4). https://doi.org/10.3390/healthcare7040146

Amin, D., & Govilkar, S. (2015). Comparative study of augmented reality SDK's. *International Journal on Computational Science & Applications, 5*(1), 11–26. https://doi.org/10.5121/ijcsa.2015.5102

Andreas, D., & Billinghurst, M. (2011). Handbook of augmented reality. In *Handbook of Augmented Reality*, 289–307. https://doi.org/10.1007/978-1-4614-0064-6

Bailey, B., Bryant, L., & Hemsley, B. (2021). Virtual reality and augmented reality for children, adolescents, and adults with communication disability and neurodevelopmental disorders: A systematic review. *Review Journal of Autism and Developmental Disorders*. https://doi.org/10.1007/s40489-020-00230-x

Barua, R., & Das, S. (2021). Improvements of virtual and augmented reality for advanced treatments in urology. In *Emerging Advancements for Virtual and Augmented Reality in Healthcare* (pp. 117–131). IGI Global. https://doi.org/10.4018/978-1-7998-8371-5.ch008

Beglov, V., Hauta-Kasari, M., & Bochko, V. (2013). *Object information based on marker recognition* (Master's thesis, Itä-Suomen yliopisto).

Berenguer, C., Baixauli, I., Gómez, S., Andrés, M. D E. P., & De Stasio, S. (2020). Exploring the impact of augmented reality in children and adolescents with autism spectrum disorder: A systematic review. *International Journal of Environmental Research and Public Health, 17*(17), 1–15. https://doi.org/10.3390/ijerph17176143

Bhouri, I. (2009). On the projections of generalized upper Lq-spectrum. *Chaos, Solitons and Fractals, 42*(3), 1451–1462. https://doi.org/10.1016/j.chaos.2009.03.056

Billinghurst, M., Kato, H., & Poupyrev, I. (2001). The MagicBook: A transitional AR interface. *Computers and Graphics, 25*(5), 745–753. https://doi.org/10.1016/S0097-8493(01)00117-0

Browder, D. M., Wakeman, S. Y., Spooner, F., Ahlgrim-Delzell, L., & Algozzine, B. (2006). Research on reading instruction for individuals with significant cognitive disabilities. *Exceptional Children, 72*(4), 392–408. https://doi.org/10.1177/001440290607200401

Bryant, L., Brunner, M., & Hemsley, B. (2020). A review of virtual reality technologies in the field of communication disability: Implications for practice and research. *Disability and Rehabilitation. Assistive Technology, 15*(4), 365–372. https://doi.org/10.1080/1748 3107.2018.1549276

Carberry, A. R., & Mckenna, A. F. (2014). Exploring student conceptions of modeling and modeling uses in engineering design. *Journal of Engineering Education, 103*(1), 77–91. https://doi.org/10.1002/jee.20033

Casari, F. A., Navab, N., Hruby, L. A., Kriechling, P., Nakamura, R., Tori, R., de Lourdes dos Santos Nunes, F., Queiroz, M. C., Fürnstahl, P., & Farshad, M. (2021). Augmented reality in orthopedic surgery is emerging from proof of concept towards clinical studies: a literature review explaining the technology and current state of the art. *Current Reviews in Musculoskeletal Medicine, 14*(2), 192–203.

Cen, L., Ruta, D., Al Qassem, L. M. M. S., & Ng, J. (2020). Augmented immersive reality (AIR) for improved learning performance: A quantitative evaluation. *IEEE Transactions on Learning Technologies, 13*(2), 283–296. https://doi.org/10.1109/TLT.2019.2937525

Chamak, B., & Bonniau, B. (2016). Trajectories, long-term outcomes and family experiences of 76 adults with autism spectrum disorder. *Journal of Autism and Developmental Disorders, 46*(3), 1084–1095. https://doi.org/10.1007/s10803-015-2656-6

Chicchi Giglioli, I. A., Pallavicini, F., Pedroli, E., Serino, S., & Riva, G. (2015). Augmented reality: A brand new challenge for the assessment and treatment of psychological disorders. *Computational and Mathematical Methods in Medicine, 2015*, 862942. https://doi.org/10.1155/2015/862942

Choi, H., Na, B., Lee, J., & Kong, K. (2018). A user interface system with see-through display for WalkON suit : A powered exoskeleton for complete paraplegics. *Applied Sciences, 8*(11), 2287. https://doi.org/10.3390/app8112287

Cifuentes, S. C., García, S. G., Andrés-Sebastiá, M. P., Camba, J. D., & Contero, M. (2016). Augmented Reality experiences in therapeutic pedagogy: A study with special needs students. In *Proceedings - IEEE 16th International Conference on Advanced Learning Technologies, ICALT 2016* (pp. 431–435). https://doi.org/10.1109/ICALT.2016.23

Ellis, R. S., McLure, R. J., Dunlop, J. S., Robertson, B. E., Ono, Y., Schenker, M. A., Koekemoer, A., Bowler, R. A. A., Ouchi, M., Rogers, A. B., Curtis-Lake, E., Schneider, E., Charlot, S., Stark, D. P., Furlanetto, S. R., & Cirasuolo, M. (2013). The abundance of star-forming galaxies in the redshift range 8.5–12: New results from the 2012 Hubble ultra deep field campaign. *Astrophysical Journal Letters, 763*(1), 8–13. https://doi.org/10.1088/2041-8205/763/1/L7

Eshuis, L. V., van Gelderen, M. J., van Zuiden, M., Nijdam, M. J., Vermetten, E., Olff, M., & Bakker, A. (2021). Efficacy of immersive PTSD treatments: A systematic review of virtual and augmented reality exposure therapy and a meta-analysis of virtual reality exposure therapy. *Journal of Psychiatric Research, 143*(May), 516–527. https://doi.org/10.1016/j.jpsychires.2020.11.030

Goh, G. S., Lohre, R., Parvizi, J., & Goel, D. P. (2021). Virtual and augmented reality for surgical training and simulation in knee arthroplasty. *Archives of Orthopaedic and Trauma Surgery, 141*(12), 2303–2312. https://doi.org/10.1007/s00402-021-04037-1

Guan, T., & Wang, C. (2009). Registration based on scene recognition and natural features tracking techniques for wide-area augmented reality systems. *IEEE Transactions on Multimedia*, *11*(8), 1393–1406. https://doi.org/10.1109/TMM.2009.2032684

Henderson, T. A., van Lierop, M. J., McLean, M., Uszler, J. M., Thornton, J. F., Siow, Y. H., Pavel, D. G., Cardaci, J., & Cohen, P. (2020). Functional neuroimaging in psychiatry—aiding in diagnosis and guiding treatment. What the American Psychiatric Association does not know. *Frontiers in Psychiatry*, *11*(April), 1–19. https://doi.org/10.3389/fpsyt.2020.00276

Hsieh, M. C., & Lee, J. J. (2018). Preliminary study of VR and AR applications in medical and healthcare education. *Journal of Nursing and Health Studies*, *3*(1), 1–5. https://doi.org/10.21767/2574-2825.100030

Jdaitawi, M. (2019). The effect of flipped classroom strategy on students learning outcomes. *International Journal of Instruction*, *12*(3), 665–680. https://doi.org/10.29333/iji.2019.12340a

Johnson, J., Gooding, P. A., Wood, A. M., Taylor, P. J., Pratt, D., & Tarrier, N. (2010). Resilience to suicidal ideation in psychosis: Positive self-appraisals buffer the impact of hopelessness. *Behaviour Research and Therapy*, *48*(9), 883–889. https://doi.org/10.1016/j.brat.2010.05.013

Kugelmann, D., Stratmann, L., Nühlen, N., Bork, F., Hoffmann, S., Samarbarksh, G., Pferschy, A., von der Heide, A. M., Eimannsberger, A., Fallavollita, P., Navab, N., & Waschke, J. (2018). An augmented reality magic mirror as additive teaching device for gross anatomy. *Annals of Anatomy*, *215*, 71–77. https://doi.org/10.1016/j.aanat.2017.09.011

Lee, C., & Wong, G. K. C. (2019). Virtual reality and augmented reality in the management of intracranial tumors: A review. *Journal of Clinical Neuroscience*, *62*, 14–20. https://doi.org/10.1016/j.jocn.2018.12.036

Lee, T., & Höllerer, T. (2007). Handy AR: Markerless inspection of augmented reality objects using fingertip tracking. In *Proceedings - International Symposium on Wearable Computers, ISWC* (pp. 83–90). https://doi.org/10.1109/ISWC.2007.4373785

Mahmud, N., Cohen, J., Tsourides, K., & Berzin, T. M. (2015). Computer vision and augmented reality in gastrointestinal endoscopy. *Gastroenterology Report*, *3*(3), 179–184. https://doi.org/10.1093/gastro/gov027

Manns, P. J., Hurd, C., & Yang, J. F. (2019). Perspectives of people with spinal cord injury learning to walk using a powered exoskeleton. *Journal of Neuroengineering and Rehabilitation*, *16*, 1–10.

Massano, J., & Bhatia, K. P. (2012). Clinical approach to Parkinson's disease: features, diagnosis, and principles of management. *Cold Spring Harbor Laboratory Press*, *2*(6), a008870.

Mehra, R., Brimijoin, O., Robinson, P., & Lunner, T. (2020). Potential of augmented reality platforms to improve individual hearing aids and to support more ecologically valid research. *Ear and Hearing*, *41*(Suppl 1), 140S.

Mekni, M., & Lemieux, A. (2014). Augmented reality: Applications, challenges and future trends. *Applied Computational Science*, *20*, 205–214.

Milgram, P. (2011). A taxonomy of mixed reality visual displays. *Industrial Engineering*, *12*, 1–14.

Navab, N., Blum, T., Wang, L., Okur, A. and Wendler, T. (2012). First deployments of augmented reality in operating rooms. *Computer*, *45*(7), 48–55.

Ocay, A. B., Rustia, R. A., & Palaoag, T. D. (2018). Utilizing augmented reality in improving the frustration tolerance of ADHD learners: An experimental study. In *Proceedings of the 2nd International Conference on Digital Technology in Education* (pp. 58–63). https://doi.org/10.1145/3284497.3284499

Parker, O. (2018). Innovations in smart packaging. *Graphic Arts Monthly*, *21*(6), 13–18. https://doi.org/10.1007/978-981-10-2419-1

Rizzo, A. A., Buckwalter, J. G., Bowerly, T., Van Der Zaag, C., Humphrey, L., Neumann, U., Chua, C., Kyriakakis, C., Van Rooyen, A., & Sisemore, D. (2000). The virtual classroom: A virtual reality environment for the assessment and rehabilitation of attention deficits. *Cyberpsychology and Behavior, 3*(3), 483–499. https://doi.org/10.1089/10949310050078940

Rodríguez, H. B. M., Salem, S. J., & Gomez, I. T. J. (2016). Feasibility and safety of augmented reality - assisted urological surgery using smartglass. *World Journal of Urology, 35*(6), 967–972. https://doi.org/10.1007/s00345-016-1956-6

Rogers, K., Colley, M., Lehr, D., Frommel, J., Walch, M., Nacke, L. E., & Weber, M. (2018). KickAR : Exploring game balancing through boosts and handicaps in augmented reality table football. In *Proceedings of the 2018 CHI Conference on Human Factors in Computing Systems* (pp. 1–12).

Singh, G., & Mantri, A. (2016). Ubiquitous hybrid tracking techniques for augmented reality applications. In *2015 2nd International Conference on Recent Advances in Engineering and Computational Sciences, RAECS 2015, December*. https://doi.org/10.1109/RAECS.2015.7453420

Talaty, M., Esquenazi, A., & Briceño, J. E. (2013). Differentiating ability in users of the ReWalk™ powered exoskeleton an analysis of walking kinematics. In *2013 IEEE 13th international conference on rehabilitation robotics (ICORR)* (pp. 1–5). IEEE.

Tang, K. S., Cheng, D. L., Mi, E., & Greenberg, P. B. (2019). Augmented reality in medical education: A systematic review. *Canadian Medical Education Journal, 11*(1), 81–96. https://doi.org/10.36834/cmej.61705

Yilmaz, R. M. (2018). Augmented reality trends in education between 2016 and 2017 years. In *State of the Art Virtual Reality and Augmented Reality Knowhow*. https://doi.org/10.5772/intechopen.74943

Yoon, J. W., Chen, R. E., Kim, E. J., Akinduro, O. O., Kerezoudis, P., Han, P. K., Si, P., Freeman, W. D., Diaz, R. J., Komotar, R. J., Pirris, S. M., Brown, B. L., Bydon, M., Wang, M. Y., Wharen, R. E., & Quinones-Hinojosa, A. (2018). Augmented reality for the surgeon: Systematic review. *International Journal of Medical Robotics and Computer Assisted Surgery, 14*(4), 1–13. https://doi.org/10.1002/rcs.1914

Zhao, R., Li, D., Wei, M., & Li, X. (2022). The contents and methods of knowledge network from the perspective of bibliometrics. *Technology Analysis & Strategic Management, 34*(3), 245–257. https://doi.org/10.1080/09537325.2021.1894329

8 Artificial Intelligence in Healthcare
Perspectives from Post-Pandemic Times

Tapash Rudra
Amity University

Shyam Bihari Goyal
City University

CONTENTS

8.1 ORGANIZATION OF THE CHAPTER

The onslaught of the devastating pandemic has been rampaging since the last two and half years. It has been a global massacre without doubt. However, the healthcare sector has been majorly affected, among others. Therefore, alongside conventional ways, we must think about advanced technology-based aids to revamp the medical set-up in the days to come. In this chapter, we highlighted implications of artificial intelligence (AI)-guided algorithms and relevant attributes to be inculcated in the existing medical set-up. At the onset, we gave an account of the pre-pandemic scenario of AI in clinical practice in brief. Moving forward, we addressed the major issues of medical practice where artificial algorithms would be instrumental; ethics, clinical trials, therapeutics, vaccine development, etc. to name a few. On top of that, we also mentioned about strategic planning involving various aspects of AI from a clinical point of view during post-pandemic times. Last but not the least, we concluded the chapter with a relevant discussion considering AI as the major force to be reckoned with to have an additional cushion in the medical sectors.

8.2   INTRODUCTION

Any catastrophic event marks significant indentations even after it disappears. The ongoing global pandemic is not an exception either. Taking into account the First World War and Plague, we can say that history does always encompass considerable amount of compassion and empathy across the global community. It is beyond doubt that the healthcare sector is the worst hit since the onset of the running global catastrophe. Therefore, it is imperative to look out for alternative options to revitalize the healthcare aspects.

The primary question to be asked during the post-pandemic times is: *"what are the expertise and skills that we need to restore the medical health sectors"?* The frontline workers including doctors and paramedics have been relentlessly serving the global community since the very beginning of the ongoing disaster. In fact, their herculean efforts have made it possible to minimize the damage to a fair extent. Collective strategies and the subsequent implementation undertaken by the medical personnel stabilized the healthcare organizations as well as the occupational safety during this deadly event [1].

Furthermore, continuous support and overwhelming dedication of the healthcare workers even during the vaccine rollouts have been the major breakthroughs for rapid inoculation of vaccines among the masses. Moreover, proper monitoring, provision of adequate service to the community, and necessary follow-up are the other useful aids [2]. Along with medical and health personnel, nurses also have been pivotal in providing emergency services and separation of suspected individuals from the rest to curtail the spread of Covid-19 infection [2,3].

In the above context, the advanced and innovative concept of AI aids is of real importance to release the burden from the shoulders of frontline workers. Indeed, machine learning (ML) and various computational algorithms might be the roadmap towards the post-pandemic healthcare organizing sectors [4,5] (Figure 8.1).

8.3   APPLICATIONS OF ARTIFICIAL INTELLIGENCE IN HEALTHCARE BEFORE THE COVID-19 PANDEMIC

Even though the influence of AI has been distinctly evident during the ongoing Covid-19 pandemic, the impact of AI algorithms was also prominent even before that. Substantial impact has been found in the literature, especially in the various domains of healthcare and medical sectors even before the ongoing pandemic.

Among the different attributes, one of them is the enhancement of radiological imaging of patients by tagging AI algorithms to fetch an additional database [6,7], as shown in Table 8.1. Other clinical studies have been reported where anomalous

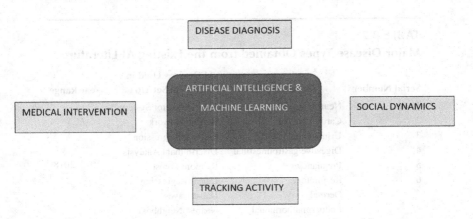

FIGURE 8.1 Implication of artificial intelligence and machine learning techniques in healthcare sectors.

TABLE 8.1

Major Database Obtained from the Existing AI Literature

Serial Number	Data Types	Sub Types	Year Range
1.	Radio imaging	Magnetic resonance imaging (MRI), CT scan, Ultrasound, Arthrogram	
2.	Electrodiagnosis	Nerve conduction studies (NCS), Electromyography (EMG)	
3.	Genetics	Disease genomics, Proteomics, Transcriptomics, and Metabolomics	2013–2018
4.	Disability assessment	Rubrics, Focus Groups, Surveys	
5.	Physiological evaluation	Norm-referenced psychological tests, Informal tests and surveys, Interview information, School or medical records, medical evaluation, and observational data	
6.	Mass screening	Pap smear or liquid-based cytology, Mammography, Colonoscopy	
7.	Miscellaneous	Bioinformatic tools	

Source: Retrieved from PubMed, as of 2018.

TABLE 8.2

Major Disease Types Obtained from the Existing AI Literature

Serial Number	Disease Types	AI Devices Used in Clinical Set-Up	Year Range
1.	Neurological	Support Vector System	
2.	Cardiovascular	Neural Network	
3.	Urinogenital	Logistic Regression	
4.	Digestive/gastrointestinal	Discriminant Analysis	
5.	Pregnancy	Random Forest	2013–2018
6.	Respiratory	Linear Regression	
7.	Dermal	Naïve Bayes	
8.	Endocrinal/hormonal	Nearest Neighbour	
9.	Nutritional	Hidden Markov	
10.	Neoplasms	Decision Tree	

Source: Retrieved from PubMed, as of 2018.

gene expression was used in the long non-coding ribonucleic acid (RNA) segments to depict gastric cancer [8]. On a similar note, another study has been published that developed electrodiagnostic modelling to interpret neural injuries [9], as shown in Table 8.2. AI techniques have also been utilized to find phenotypes from case studies to retrieve congenital abnormalities [10].

8.4 AN ACCOUNT OF ARTIFICIAL INTELLIGENCE–GUIDED AIDS IN HEALTHCARE: SCENARIO FROM POST-PANDEMIC TIMES

Considerable evidence has been reported about the sustenance of natural ecosystems including the floral and faunal restoration during the Covid-19 pandemic. Sporadic lockdowns and restricted human activities have been the principal reasons behind. However, collective combatting of the civilians against the ongoing viral outbreak has also been the hallmark of the crisis [11,12]. In the post-pandemic times, following AI-aided applications will be profound in the healthcare sectors.

8.4.1 ETHICAL CONSIDERATIONS

Ethical issues have always been a matter of concern in medical as well as healthcare setups. However, keeping in mind the nature and trajectory of the ongoing health crisis, the ethical aspects would be much more pronounced during the post-pandemic scenario. With the advent of innovative AI aids, post-pandemic healthcare research including strategic development and policy-making should be more sustainable and vigorous to say the least. Moreover, with the introduction of numerous contact tracing applications, AI-guided sensors would surely add to the "Overall Quality of Life" to a fair degree [8,9]. To add to it, serving the needs of patients, identifying specific healthcare issues, and avoiding discrimination among the sufferers are the other attributes that should be of significant interest in line with AI-mediated practice in post-pandemic times [10]. The end of the ongoing global outbreak will bring about a paradigm shift as far as reshaping of ethical considerations in healthcare practice is concerned and invariably AI tools should be the potential forces to be reckoned with [13,14].

8.4.2 IN RAPID AND EFFECTIVE COVID-19 VACCINE DEVELOPMENT

It seems there is a constant tussle between the SARS-CoV-2 virus and the leading Biotech companies across the world regarding vaccine development. Over the years, AI-enabled tools have been used successfully in several areas of modern healthcare. Since the outbreak of Covid-19 in China, the scientific fraternity has been using a handful of AI-guided machineries alongside other advanced improvisations. It has been evidenced that AI systems not only hastened the identification of the disease pathogen but also provided comprehensive coverage of recovering from the same. Furthermore, improvised AI systems, namely, distributed computational algorithms and open data projects, have given a new dimension to the vaccine research. These have improved a lot of aspects ranging from fast and accurate recognition of the pathogen, generation of adequate response against the pathogen, and providing appropriate preventive measures leading to the holistic vaccine research [5,15].

One of the arguable areas around the vaccine development for Covid-19 has been the scarcity of clinical trials. Significant amount of dilemma exists whether the data are sufficient before the mass roll out of the vaccines. Not only civilians, even the scientific community has not been entirely convinced regarding the formulation, sampling, and duration of the patient trials. With relevance to the clinical trials, AI-enabled technologies have already been implied in tandem with molecular biology and biotechnology. One of the fascinating innovations in the context of vaccine development is the Blue Dot. This recognizes pathogenic variants as well as the spot patterns with sizable accuracy. Several trials have been carried out so far utilizing the Blue Dot. In the same regard, Deep Learning–based therapeutic screening has been deployed to depict the specific protein–ligand interaction. It facilitates the assessment of the right combination of drugs combating Covid-19 infections. Similarly, precise ML modelling has been constructed to identify the intensity of infection among the patients involving age and gender as variables [16]. Scientists also developed search algorithm for ligand (SAL), which is an AI programme specifically designed to select the right candidate for the clinical trials. This categorically shortens the duration for vaccine development. Therefore, this kind of AI-guided aids should be the perfect choice for anti-viral development during the post-pandemic times [5]. Last but not the least, "Human Immunomics Initiative," which itself is a part of the human vaccine project, has been added to AI algorithms to accelerate the proceedings of vaccine and therapeutics development primarily targeting the elderly section of the community [17].

8.4.3 STRATEGIC IMPLICATIONS IN HEALTHCARE SECTORS USING AI-ENABLED AIDS

Modern era is all about innovations. It will be even more significant during the post-pandemic period. Therefore, meaningful AI techniques should be of vital importance to figure out complex matters into relatively simpler ones regarding medical research, healthcare, and society [18]. This immensely benefits the societal decorum for overall reshaping of future [19]. ML modelling could be applied in the form of Gaussian processes, generative adversarial networks, and deep neural networks respectively. These in turn would interpret the individualistic data from the set of observational ones without sorting the randomized trials. Again, omics data could be also coordinated with the same [20–22]. These new innovations have made the treatment accurate in relevance to the choice of drugs is concerned [23]. Health practitioners have more options for the patient groups whether to go for Remdesivir, Lopinavir/Ritonavir or Ivermectin. Implementation of longitudinal observational databases together with AI modelling is another improvisation in this context. By virtue of the dynamic approach, clinicians would be able to assess and intervene in patients' past medical profile more effectively. They would go for sequential intervention leading to precise prognosis [24]. This innovative modelling would be able to determine the specific duration of usage of life support devices for individual patients. Moreover, it would also depict the timeframe during which a patient could live without mechanical ventilator in intensive care unit (ICU)/intensive therapy unit (ITU), especially during the times of scarcity of the required life support device.

8.4.4 FORMULATION OF AI ALGORITHM–BASED BIOMARKERS

AI, ML, support vector machine (SVM) algorithm, and random forest (RF) networking systems have also been employed to manifest the severity of Covid-19 infections among the various groups of patients. It has already proven to be a potent tool for predicting the patient data being used with statistical regression. The sophisticated RF algorithm is a combination of as many as 11 biomarkers interlinked with Covid-19 severity scores. The system not only gives an idea of the clinical parameters of the patients but also evaluates the mortality rate using the statistics-based algorithm [25]. In fact, this newly developed algorithm has become an accurate technique since the time of its formulation.

8.4.5 AI-ENABLED TREATMENTS/THERAPEUTICS AGAINST COVID-19

Another significant influence of ML techniques is to accurately screen the useful therapeutics against SARS-CoV-2 virus by selecting the exact drugs. This allows the broadening of the circumference of available drugs with advanced options. This approach helps in identifying the 3D structure of the chosen drug, thereby depicting the drug–viral interaction to fix the viral inhibition. Together, these ML approaches facilitate the widening of the drug repositories for choosing the appropriate drugs against SARS-CoV-2 virus [26].

8.5 DISCUSSION

- As discussed above, AI-mediated aids would be the future roadmap during the post-pandemic scenario—AI-aided therapeutic innovations, virtual communication, and telehealth; telemedicine should be practiced with more vigour to curtail the possibilities of resurgence of potential waves of Covid-19 infection [27].

- It is well known that newly emerging variants (including rapidly transmitting Delta, Lambda, and recently emerging omicron variants of concern) of the SARS-CoV-2 virus are the major reasons behind the massive severity of the second/third waves across the globe. However, consistent hard work and dedication of the frontline workers have successfully evaded the second wave of the infection considerably. Therefore, robust monitoring should be instrumental for averting any possibilities of hostility among civilians. AI and associated computational attributes should be prioritized along with the existing medical set-up [28–30].

- AI-based technologies should have a holistic approach if they are utilized with the correct intent. It has already been evidenced that AI algorithms and ML techniques are extremely useful in the diagnosis, recognition of infections, accurate monitoring, precise prediction, and even tracing of the prognosis. So, they are not only a handful against Covid-19 infections but also could be equally viable in tackling other existing diseases [18].

- To say the least, advanced AI modelling has all the potential to be the future force in medical and healthcare sectors and would provide a sustainable society in the days to come [31–33].

8.6 CONCLUSION

In the context of the above factorials, it is understandable that the ongoing global pandemic has influenced us in both adversely as well as positive ways. The ongoing pandemic has been instrumental in demolishing billions of lives across the globe so far. Both civilians and healthcare workers have been the sufferers across the world due to this deadly disaster. Therefore, it is imperative to resurrect the healthcare sector with effective means to be combat Covid-19. On the contrary, the ongoing global crisis has presented with a window of opportunity to use AI algorithms in the best possible ways in healthcare and medical sectors. The dynamics of the AI industry could collectively improve the quality of life (QOL) of the global community in the post-pandemic era.

Every problem creates solutions; creativity is the outcome of every crisis. Undoubtedly, the ongoing Covid-19 pandemic is the classical example of the same. This global disaster has shown the significance of a stable healthcare sector in the society including the role of doctors, nurses, and other caregivers, respectively. Over the years, a multidimensional approach has been accepted in all the fields of science, and healthcare sector is not an exception. So, these new innovations should be practiced on a regular basis for combatting similar epidemics in the future. We must remember that most of the children population have not been vaccinated, and we never know what the consequences of further waves of Covid-19 will be if it ever comes back. Under such circumstances, AI technologies should be the perfect choice along with the existing medical set-up to tackle pandemics in the future.

8.7 DISCLOSURE

The author confirms that there is no conflict of interest for the concerned chapter.

REFERENCES

1. World Health Organization (WHO). 2021. *Coronavirus Disease (Covid-19) Outbreak: Rights, Roles and Responsibilities of Health Workers, Including Key Considerations for Occupational Safety and Health, 19 March 2020* (No. WHO/2019-nCov/HCW_advice/2020.2). World Health Organization.
2. World Health Organization and the United Nations Children's Fund (UNICEF). 2021. *The Role of Community Health Workers in COVID-19 Vaccination: Implementation Support guide, 26 April 2021* (No. WHO/2019-nCoV/NDVP/CHWs_role/2021.1). World Health Organization.
3. Al Thobaitya, A. and Alshammari, F. 2020. Nurses on the frontline against the COVID-19 pandemic: an integrative review. *Dubai Med J* 3:87–92.
4. Lahner, E., Dilaghi, E., Prestigiacomo, C., et al. 2020. Prevalence of Sars-CoV-2 infection in health workers (HWs) and diagnostic test performance: the experience of a teaching hospital in central Italy. *Int J Environ Res Public Health* 17(12):1–12.
5. Laudanski, K., Shea, G., DiMeglio, M, Rastrepo, M. and Solomon, C. 2020. What can covid-19 teach us about using AI in pandemics? *Healthcare* 8:1–14.
6. Administration UFaD. 2017. Guidance for industry: electronic source data in clinical investigations. Accessed 1 Jun. https://www.fda.gov/downloads/drugs/guidance/ucm328691.pdf
7. Gillies, R. J., Kinahan, P. E. and Hricak, H. 2016. Radiomics: images are more than pictures, they are data. *Radiology* 278:563–77.
8. Li, C. Y., Liang, G. Y. and Yao, W. Z., et al. 2016. Integrated analysis of long noncoding RNA competing interactions reveals the potential role in progression of human gastric cancer. *Int J Oncol* 48:1965–76.
9. Shin, H., Kim, K. H. and Song, C., et al. 2010. Electrodiagnosis support system for localizing neural injury in an upper limb. *J Am Med Inform Assoc* 17: 345–7.
10. Karakülah, G. Dicle, O. and Koşaner, O., et al. 2014. Computer based extraction of phenotypic features of human congenital anomalies from the digital literature with natural language processing techniques. *Stud Health Technol Inform* 205: 570–4.
11. Gulseven, O., Al Harmoodi, F., Al Falasi, M. and ALshomali, I. 2020. How will the COVID-19 pandemic affect the UN sustainable development goals (SDGs)? *SSRN Elec J* 1–28. doi:10.2139/ssrn.3592933.
12. Srivastava, A. Sharma, R. K. and Suresh A. 2020. Impact of Covid-19 on sustainable development goals. *Int J Advan Sci Technol* 29(9 Special Issue):4968–72.
13. WHO. Ethics and covid-19; 2021. Available from: https://www.who.int/teams/health-ethics-governance/diseases/covid-19. Accessed April 30, 2020.
14. Robert, R., Kentish-Barnes, N., Boyer, A., Laurent, A., Azoulay, E. and Reignier, J. 2020. Ethical dilemmas due to the Covid-19 pandemic. *Ann Intensive Care* 10(1):1–9. doi:10.1186/s13613-020-00702-7.
15. McGuire, A.L., Aulisio, M.P., Davis, F.D., et al. 2020. Ethical challenges arising in the COVID-19 pandemic: an overview from the Association of Bioethics Program Directors (ABPD) task force. *Am J Bioethics* 20(7):15–27. doi:10.1080/15265161.2020.1 76413854.
16. Baines, P., Draper, H., Chiumento, A., Fovargue, S. and Frith, L. 2020. COVID-19 and beyond: the ethical challenges of resetting health services during and after public health emergencies. *J Med Ethics* 46(11):715–16. doi:10.1136/medethics-2020-106965.

17. Organization for Economic Co-operation and Development. 2020a. Using artificial intelligence to help combat COVID-19. https://www.oecd.org/coronavirus/policy-responses/using-artificial-intelligence-to-help-combat-covid-19-ae4c5c21/

18. Arora, N., Banerjee, A. K. and Narasu, M. L. 2020. The role of artificial intelligence in tackling COVID-19. *Future Virol* 1–8. doi:10.2217/fvl-2020-0130.

19. Kannan, S., Subbaram, K., Ali, S. and Kannan, H. 2020. The role of artificial intelligence and machine learning techniques: race for covid-19 vaccine. *Arch Clin Infect Dis* 15(2):2–9. doi:10.5812/ archcid.103232.

20. Ahuja, A. S., Reddy, V. P. and Marques, O. 2020. Artificial intelligence and COVID-19: a multidisciplinary approach. *Integr Med Res* 9(3):100434.

21. Kaushik, A. C., Raj, U. 2020. AI-driven drug discovery: a boon against COVID-19? *AI Open* 1:1–4. doi:10.1016/j.aiopen.2020.07.001.

22. Piccialli, F., di Cola, V. S., Giampaolo, F. and Cuomo, S. 2021. The role of artificial intelligence in fighting the covid-19 pandemic. *Inf Syst Front* 1–31. doi:10.1007/s10796-021-10131-x.

23. Noya, A., Bulakovskiy, M. and Rijpens, J. 2020b. Social economy and the COVID-19 crisis: current and future roles. https://www.oecd.org/coronavirus/policy-responses/social-economy-and-the-covid-19-crisis-current-and-future-roles-f904b89f

24. Ahmed, M. A., Van der Schaar, M. (2017). Bayesian inference of individualized treatment effects using multi-task Gaussian processes. In *31st Conference on Neural Information Processing Systems (NIPS 2017)*, Long Beach, CA, USA.

25. Yoon, J., James, J. and van der Schaar, M. 2018. GANITE: estimation of individualized treatment effects using generative adversarial nets. In *International Conference on Learning Representations (ICLR)*.

26. Zhang, Y., Jarrett, D. and van der Schaar, M. 2020. Stepwise model selection for sequence prediction via deep kernel learning. In *International Conference on Artificial Intelligence and Statistics (AISTATS)*.

27. Gao, J., Zhenxue, T. and Xu, Y. 2020. Breakthrough: chloroquine phosphate has shown apparent efficacy in treatment of COVID-19 associated pneumonia in clinical studies. *BioScience Trends* 14(1):72–3.

28. Ferguson, N. M., Daniel, L., Gemma, N. -G., et al. 2020. *Impact of non-Pharmaceutical Interventions (NPIs) to Reduce COVID-19 Mortality and Healthcare Demand.* London: Imperial College COVID-19 Response Team.

29. McRae, M. P., Simmons, G. W., Christodoulides, N. J., et al. 2020. Clinical decision support tool and rapid point-of-care platform for determining disease severity in patients with COVID-19. *medRxiv*. doi:10.1101/2020.04.16.20068411

30. Caruso, F. P., Scala, G., Cerulo, L. and Ceccarelli, M. 2021. A review of COVID-19 biomarkers and drug targets: resources and tools. *Briefings Bioinf* 22(2):701–13.

31. Salyer, S. J., Maeda, J., Sembuche, S. et al. 2021. The first and second waves of the COVID-19 pandemic in Africa: a cross-sectional study. *Lancet* 397(10281):1265–75.

32. Stiles-Shields, C., Plevinsky, J. M., Psihogios, A. M. and Holmbeck, G. N. 2020. Considerations and future directions for conducting clinical research with pediatric populations during the COVID-19 pandemic. *J Pediatr Psychol* 45(7):720–24. doi:10.1093/jpepsy/jsaa055

33. AL-Hashimi, M. and Hamdan, A. 2021. Artificial intelligence and coronavirus COVID-19: Applications, impact and future implications. In: Alareeni, B., Hamdan, A., and Elgedawy, I., editors. *The Importance of New Technologies and Entrepreneurship in Business Development: In the Context of Economic Diversity in Developing Countries*, vol. 194. Cham: Springer International Publishing.

9 Bioweapons versus Computer-Based Counter Measure Techniques and Mathematical Modelling for the Prediction of COVID-19

Joginder Singh and Gurinderjit Kaur
Chandigarh Group of Colleges

*Rinkesh Mittal, Sukhdeep Kaur,
and Kuldeep Sharma*
Chandigarh Engineering College

CONTENTS

DOI: 10.1201/9781003254119-9

9.1 INTRODUCTION AND HISTORY

In today's society, we confront risks of bioweapons and bioterrorism using genetically altered agents, in addition to natural calamities. Genetic engineering [1] is the technique of transferring biological organisms to functioning genes (DNA) by human intervention. Bioweapons are created by manipulating genes to create new types of genes with pathogenic features (infectivity, higher survival, virulence, drug resistance and infectivity, for example) [2]. One of the most serious threats we face is the exploitation of "black biology" to manufacture bioweapons. Production of bioweapons began in 1991 during the Gulf War, and over 20 nations are now involved in the dissemination of such weapons [3]. Genetic engineering came into focus in the 1970s, and by the 1980s, it had grown into a multibillion-dollar worldwide business. In the later decades of the twentieth century, knowledge of molecular biology grew at an exponential rate. Many hostile bioweapons can be manufactured using genetically modified diseases. In 1918, influenza, often known as Spanish flu, infected 500 million people (about a quarter of the world's population) and killed 50 million people worldwide. Coughing and sneezing spread it. During World War I, enormous troop deployments and tight quarters intensified the epidemic [4,5].

In 1979, there was an outbreak of anthrax infection. A military facility breakout anthrax pores which victimized 105 people and lead to the death of 64 people. In 2001, anthrax spores were mailed in letters through the US Postal service. Eighteen people got sick with some sort of disease and five people died of inhalation of anthrax. In the 2014 outbreak, seven people died and the Indian government quarantined 30 houses. In 2016 anthrax outbreak, 100 people were infected and 2,300 reindeer died in Russia [6]. In 1965, a common cold named B814 came into existence when Tyrrell and Bynoe were studying samples of human embryonic trachea taken from the respiratory tract of an adult. At the same time period, Hamre and Procknow obtained samples from medical students with cold and cultured a virus in tissue culture showing unusual properties. They named it Hamre's virus. Later on, it came to be known as 229E. The relation between B814 and 229E viruses with myxoviruses or paramyxoviruses known at that time was not found to be close enough. In the late 1960s, morphological constraints were found to be having similarity between certain animal viruses such as mouse hepatitis virus, swine flu, gastroenteritis virus and infectious bronchitis virus with some human strains as studied by Tyrrell along with a group of virologists working together. Crown-like appearance of this new group of virus was officially named as coronavirus [7].

H1N1 is the subtype of influenza A virus, which was caused in 2009, and has an association with the outbreak of Spanish flu in 1918. During the flu pandemic of 2009, in the United States, patients were isolated from the virus and it was found out that H1N1 virus was constituted by the genetic elements of four different viruses [8]. The outbreak of this pandemic started in Mexico in 2009 and then in the United States. H1N1 was declared a pandemic on 11th June 2009 by World Health Organization

(WHO) and was declared a national emergency by the US President on 25th October 2009. At least 213 countries were affected by the H1N1 pandemic by 21st March 2011 and 16,931 deaths were reported. The preparedness alert of H1N1 pandemic was issued by WHO in 2011 [9].

SARS virus was an animal virus identified in 2003. It was thought to be spread from bats and other animals, which perhaps transferred to humans in China in 2002. Twenty-six countries were affected by the SARS epidemic and 8,000 cases were reported in 2003. The SARS virus transmission is from person to person. The symptoms of this disease include malaria, headache, shivering, diarrhoea, shortness of breath and cough. The countries that were affected by the SARS epidemic in 2002–2003 were China, Canada, Singapore, Hong Kong and Vietnam. The vaccines for SARS-CoV are still under development [10,11].

MERS is an abbreviation for Middle East Respiratory Syndrome. This viral respiratory illness was originally detected in Saudi Arabia in 2012. MERS symptoms include pneumonia, shortness of breath, coughing and fever. The MERS virus has killed 35% of the victims. Since 2012, the World Health Organization has documented 2494 cases, including 858 fatalities. It is a zoonotic virus, which means it spreads between humans and animals. According to research, infected camels transmit the virus to people [12]. The MERS virus does not spread from person to person. Since 2012, 27 nations have been afflicted by the MERS virus, including China, France, Bahrain, Egypt, Malaysia, Germany and Saudi Arabia, among others. Human cases were recorded in 80% of the instances. Most of the outbreaks of MERS virus have occurred in the Middle East. The vaccines for MERS virus are not currently available and are still under development [13].

The evolution of bioweapons can be categorized in four phases. The first phase was experienced in World War 1 in which gaseous chemicals like phosgene and chlorine were used. The World War 2 experienced the second phase in which a cholinesterase inhibitor, nerve agents, e.g., tabun, and plague bombs and anthrax were used. The third phase constituted in 1970 was used in the Vietnam War; a mixture of herbicides-stimulated hormonal function was used for defoliation and destruction of crops. Also, a new group of "Novichok" and mid-spectrum agents like bioregulators, auxins and physiologically active compounds were used. In the fourth phase, genetic engineering and biotechnical evolution are used to generate gene-designed organisms and can be used for a wide variety of bioweapons [14]. Gene-engineered organisms can be used to produce microorganisms with enhanced environmental stability and aerosol; microscopic factor producing a venom, toxin or bioregulator; microorganism that resists antibiotics, therapeutics and routine vaccines; microorganisms with altered immunological profile; and microorganisms that can escape detection by antibody sensor system.

The biological weapon is a device with a delivery system that expedites dispersion and appropriate dissemination of the designed biological agent in such a way that it targets the object of choice (human, crop, etc.) with its effect. It can be used to inject the virus/bacteria, spray from airplane on the area of denial, or as a handheld spray weapon [4].

Also, bioweapons can release pathogenic and harmful microorganisms that can kill crops and destroy reserves of enemies [15]. Anticrop warfare with the use of

bioweapons results in malnutrition, debilitating famines, food insecurity and deci-
mation of agriculture-based economies. In the Vietnam war, defoliants have been
widely used as anticrop warfare agents. Wheat smut caused by fungus *T. foetida* or
Tilettia caries was used as a bioweapon. In 1984, deliberate contamination of salad
bars with *Salmonella typhimrium* was done in the USA to incapacitate voters. In
1995, Aum shinrikyo released nerve agent (sarin) in Japan in the Tokyo subway [16].

9.2   GENETICALLY ENGINEERED PATHOGENS

There are six types of genetically engineered pathogens, which can be used as
bioweapons.

9.2.1   DESIGNER GENES

A human molecular blueprint was provided by the human genome project, which
decoded alphabets of life, which has the complete genome sequence and is known
for 205 naturally occurring plasmids, 599 viruses, 1 fungus, 31 bacteria, 1 plant, and
2 animals. These blueprints enable a manufacturer of bioweapons to make microorganisms that are more harmful and critically affect the targets. From the designer
genes, the microbiologist can develop synthetic virus, synthetic genes, or also a new
microorganism. Some of bacteria develop resistance to antiviral agents or antibiotics,
leads to identifying antibiotic resistance genes in an organism, which can be developed to render its resistance to antibody. Gene with beta-lactamase codes defeats the
action of penicillin [17].

Analogous to natural mutation, entire viruses may be created. By swapping out
variant or synthetic genes or by inducing hybridization of viral strains, a new strain
of influenza can be created. Altering common virus influenza slightly can make it
more deadly. It is possible to choose the most lethal characteristics as the database
of microbial genomes with its part list is available. The entire gene could be stitched
together with some animal viruses [18].

9.2.2   BINARY BIOWEAPON

To use the form of pathogen, two component systems containing innocuous parts are
mixed. Multiple plasmids that code for virulence or any special characteristics are
contained by many pathogenic bacteria. The virulence of plague, anthrax and other
diseases are enhanced by these plasmids and they can be transferred often across
species barrier to different kinds of bacteria [19]. A virulent plasmid and host bacteria can be produced in the required quantity for bioweapons.

9.2.3   GENE THERAPY AS BIOWEAPON

Gene therapy is permanent replacement in the genetic composition of any person
by replacing a faulty gene or repairing it. The two classes of gene therapy involve
somatic cell line (therapeutic) and germ cell line (reproductive). Changes in DNA of
the somatic cell could not be passed onto next generations but only affects individuals.

However, changes in DNA of the germ cell would be followed by next generations. The first genetically altered primate was produced by virus of jellyfish gene into rhesus monkey egg [20].

9.2.4 STEALTH VIRUS

A cryptic viral infection, which enters the human genome and remains dormant for extended time, is the stealth virus. The triggering of this virus is done by external stimulants later on. Through this external stimulus, the virus gets activated and causes disease. Herpes virus is carried by many humans, which can be activated to cause genital lesions or oral lesions. Some people who had chicken pox earlier in life carry the varicella virus. Segments of DNA (Oncogenes) when triggered can initiate misbehaviour and wild cellular growth. Some genes can cause cancer [21].

A stealth virus can infect the genome of population through a bioweapon and can be triggered anytime at the targeted population or the government can be blackmailed by threat of triggering [22].

9.2.5 HOT SWAPPING DISEASE

A zoonotic disease is transmissible to humans by a virus in the animal species. These viruses have a natural animal reservoir in which they reside and cause no damage or very little damage to that animal. However when transferred to humans they cause significant disease. Examples of natural animal reservoir are water fowl for eastern equine encephalitis, birds for west line virus, bat for Ebola virus and corona virus, and rodents for hantavirus. HIV virus, which is the natural reservoir for chimpanzee, becomes AIDS in humans [22]. A bioweapon can contain these viruses taken from animals as hot swapping disease.

9.2.6 DESIGNER DISEASE

Molecular biology has reached a point where symptoms of hypothetical disease can be proposed, designed and created. These pathogens are known as designer disease. These designer diseases in bioweapons can cause disease by inducing specific cells to multiply or divide rapidly, turning of the immune system and programmed cell death [23].

9.3 COUNTER MEASURE BY COMPUTER-BASED TECHNIQUES

Biodetection has accelerated as a result of the development of biorobots. Robotic insects that employ computerized artificial systems to replicate some biological processes can aid in virus identification. Computerized procedures can be used to do single-operation tasks such as blood sample screening, DNA processing, gene identification, virus/bacteria detection and monitoring of genetic cell activity. For detecting microbes in food, military applications and clinical procedures, biosensors employing electrochemical devices or fibre optics are utilized. An immune sensor is used to detect *Candida albicans*. *Bacillus anthracis* is detected using an optical sensor. In USA, several systems have been developed to detect bioweapons. To detect biological agents that cause metabolic damage, polyvalent immune-sensor has been developed. Combination of neural informational network, electronic nose and laser eyes to detect particle densities with alarm has been developed.

9.3.1 COMPUTER AND ARTIFICIAL INTELLIGENCE– BASED COUNTER MEASURE TECHNIQUES

The implementation of computer-based technology and artificial intelligence in health sector means that the patients who require care are diagnosed and treated using sensors embedded in smartphones and computers. Although it seems like the diagnosis and treatment are quite simple steps, there are so many unseen background factors to be taken care of to properly treat the patient. The unseen factors include data collection through various modes such as calls and interviews, results are processed and analyzed, and accurate and proper diagnosis is done using multiple sources of the data. The treatment method to be chosen is prepared and administered, which includes continuous monitoring of the patient and the aftercare which includes follow-up appointments [24]. Figure 9.1 shows the stages in which the computer technology can be implemented in the health sector and provides a solution to combat various diseases spread by bioweapons.

There are four solution stages for computer-based technology, which are dependent on each other. There is an interconnection between all the four stages of the architecture such that the data from the first stage is processed to the next stage. In the first step, the interconnected devices, such as sensors from computer-connected devices, collect the data. These devices include sensors, monitors, actuators, camera, detectors, etc. embedded or connected with computers. The second step includes the preprocessing and standardization of the data, which are moved to the cloud network in the third step. At the fourth and final stage, the analysis and management of data are done [25].

Using holographic telescope, the intensity of light scattered off an object can be captured. The researcher took 400 individual spores of five different species of

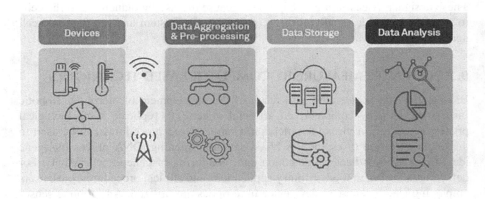

FIGURE 9.1   Solution stages for computer-based technology.

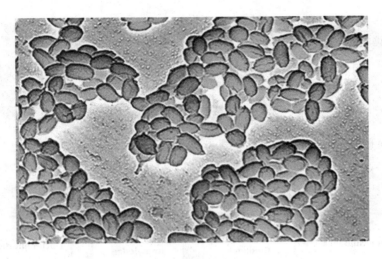

FIGURE 9.2   Anthrax spores at 12,000× microscope.

bacteria out of which one is *Bacillus anthracis* (anthrax) and trained the neural network algorithm to detect the spores; the AI detected the spores [26] (Figure 9.2).

9.3.2 COMPUTER-ASSISTED SURGERY AS A COUNTER MEASURE

During the spread of any virus/bacteria during a bio-war, the systems have been updated to provide computer-assisted surgery (CAS). When computer technology is used for planning and guiding surgical intervention, it is called CAS. The surgical process is improved through CAS by integrating the computer technology. CAS aims to increase the accuracy and reduce invasiveness and costs related to the procedures of surgery [27]. Figure 9.3 shows the pipeline of the CAS.

Acquiring the data of the patient is the first step in the pipeline. This data acquisition is based on imaging such as X-ray, computed tomography (CT) scan, magnetic resonance imaging (MRI) and any other type of measurement taken from the optical tracking system. The processing of the data takes place so that the information of a higher level can be extracted, which is usually done through segmentation. The data are then prepared for the stage of visualization. Surgical planning is done in the visualization stage. The anatomy of the patient is studied by the surgeon. The surgical procedure is virtually performed by studying the pathology of the patient-specific data acquired in the first step [28]. The surgical outcomes which are predicted are examined in some cases. All these three steps of image acquisition, image processing and visualization comprise preoperative planning. Next is the transfer of the whole surgical plan to the operating room so that it can be applied to the process of surgery. The plan is implemented in the surgical process through image guidance, mechanical guidance, or with the surgeon's mental model that he or she had prepared in the planning stage. Image guidance and mechanical guidance are explicit in nature while the documentation is implicit guidance. In CAS, visualization has a very significant role. It comes under the planning phase where the acquired data, predicted outcomes of the surgery and the derived measurements of the patient are displayed [29]. The

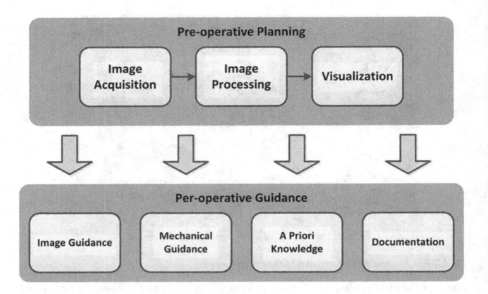

FIGURE 9.3 Pipeline of computer-assisted surgery.

efficient interaction of the surgeon with various components is also enabled through visualization. Many general tasks are facilitated in CAS for planning and guiding the surgery. These tasks include spatially understanding of the anatomy and pathology, access planning, resection planning, reconstruction planning and implant planning. The patient data visualization is explored by the surgeon, which comes under spatially understanding the patient data anatomy in the specific region. This task is very important and basic in complex anatomy [30].

The hand motions of the surgeons are facilitated with the help of CAS. Also known as robotic surgery, it limits the operation space of the surgeons. The various advantages of the devices used in CAS are magnified vision, improved access and stabilization in implementing the instruments. The operative dexterity is reduced significantly in the instruments of standard endoscopy whose degree of freedom is four. The reversed hand motions are required by the operator where the motion of the trocar is dependent on fulcrum. Moreover, the manipulation of operating tips in the shaft shear instrument leads to fatigue in the hand muscle as high forces are induced. Also, in endoscopic surgery, there is incompatibility between the skills of human motor and visual motor. All these limitations are overcome by enhancing the computer-assisted or robot-assisted surgery. The robotic arms are mounted with microwrist instruments that reproduce the motion in scaled proportions with the help of the computer interface. The activity of the wrist is emulated to all the axes of the wrist through the instrument. In confined spaces of operation, the enhancement of dexterity is being transformed from motion scaling and tremor filtering. Figure 9.4 shows a console from where the surgeon operates in the 3-D field of operation. It is a robot-assisted tele-manipulation system with a camera and two instrument arms [31].

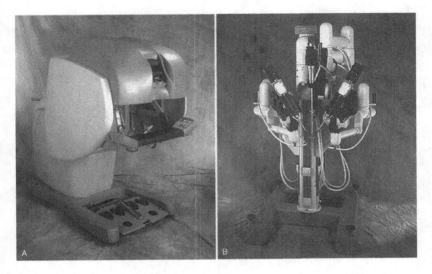

FIGURE 9.4   Computer-assisted tele-manipulation system.

9.3.3   BIG DATA AS HEALTHCARE

The prevention, diagnosis and treatment of human health are the main aims of any healthcare system. Health professionals, facilities and funding companies fall under the domain of healthcare. The health professionals include doctors and nurses, healthcare facilities include clinics and hospitals, whereas funding companies are those that run the healthcare facilities. The various health sectors include medicine, psychology, nursing, dentistry and so on [32]. The healthcare professionals include doctors, scientists, surgeons, dermatologists, neurologists and so on. The patients' medical history is required by the doctors at such levels, which include the personal history and medical data required for the treatment of the patients. EHR (Electronic Health Records) are in practice nowadays and they store all the necessary information of the patient required for treatment. Figure 9.5 shows big data in healthcare applications

The transmission, reception, storage and manipulation of data are all possible with computer-aided technology. All these data are required by the healthcare sectors and departments to work efficiently [33].

There are many data care components related to healthcare that gather the patient information, which results in quality improvement and makes the service efficient by reducing the costs and errors in healthcare and medical sectors. Some healthcare-related data components include medical practice management (MPM) and personal health record (PHR). Cost control and health improvement are the factors to be taken care of in the healthcare field, which is possible through big data. Various healthcare centres receive the data for further investigation making it confidential. A large amount of information related to diseases makes their treatment possible through computer-aided technology. Vast amount of data is stored in the data warehouses from different sources through Big Data Analytics [34]. Analytic pipelines are used to process these stored data so that affordable and smarter options are obtained.

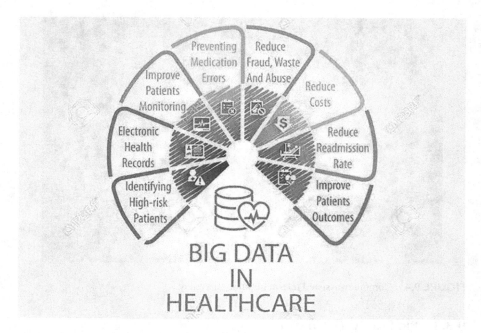

FIGURE 9.5   Big data in healthcare.

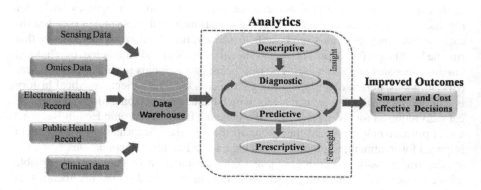

FIGURE 9.6   Analysis using big data.

Figure 9.6 shows analysis of big data. The healthcare sector has been digitalized with the help of big data, which further enables to deal with healthcare problems and provide improvement in preventive care and discovery of new medicines in the healthcare field.

9.3.4 Computer-Assisted Decision-Making

With every passing day, computers have become a very significant entity in the daily lives of a broad section of people. As microcomputers were invented in the late seventies and due to the enhancement in their performance in the eighties, computers have got a very significant role in our lives. The whole lifestyle is being revolutionalized with computers. Computer-based techniques have a great social impact due to their medical field applications. Large hospitals are being run depending on computer-based measures and techniques. The facilities provided by the computers have been integral in the equipment of diagnosis. In the medical field, the computers are majorly used in information systems for hospitals, medical imaging, analysis of data in medicine, monitoring of the patients, computer-assisted surgery, decision-making and therapy, treatment of critical patients, telemedicine, electronic health records, medical databases, and research and application of computers in offices and hospital administration [35]. Computers can accept, store and access the data automatically to produce the output results. Data in very large amounts can be stored and processed in computers to provide the user with required information as well as rapid and accurate calculations are being performed. The informatics in the medical field is growing very rapidly. The organization and management of the information for patient care seems to be very significant. The medical informatics seeks education and research in the biomedical field through the use of information networks and computers. If the information system of the hospital is computerized, then the data can be continuously transmitted, stored and monitored at all transactions. Valuable information regarding patient care is easily accessible through this. All information can be accessed by the physicians directly through the application of computer-based techniques [36]. The information system in the hospital covers registration, billing, diet, pharmacy, accounts and biomedical maintenance. There are various software available, which are customized according to the needs and requirements of the hospital information system. The data are collected in large numbers in medical research. Then, there is compilation, analysis and interpretation of the data. For this, the application of various statistical methods becomes necessary. They calculate the standard deviation, error, t test, Z test and chi square test. All these statistical methods consume a huge amount of time. But with the aid of computer-based techniques, all these calculations can be done in a very short time. The various statistical packages of good quality include biomedical computer package, statistical package for social sciences (SPSS), Genstat, and Epi-Info. The first package to be developed was BMD and statistical programmes of advanced level were provided. SPSS provides various statistical options for the analysis of multivariant and simple statistics. The most powerful package is the Genstat, which is used for variance analysis. WHO developed a package called Epi-Info for the study of epidemics. This package can process the word and analyze the data for graphical abilities. WHO and Centre for Disease Control (CDC) made this non-copyrighted package available for statistical programming [37].

Laboratory computing is one of the applications of computer-based techniques in the medical field. The analysis of laboratory includes photometry, blood chemistry, microbiology and so on. Proper validation of the results with patient identification is done. This contributes to the efficiency of the care system of patients. The monitoring machines based on the computers can automatically collect the heart rate, blood pressure and respiratory activity of the patient in digital form. The chart of the patient is updated automatically and the hospital staff are notified of vital changes [38]. The

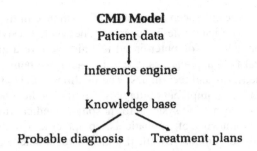

FIGURE 9.7   Decision-making model assisted by computers.

decision-making based on the computers is CMD, which is an interactive system as the doctors can be assisted in the task of clinical decision-making. The natural abilities of the doctors to make judgments are complemented with the vast memory of the computer through this system. Figure 9.7 shows the model of decision-making assisted by computers.

Large interventions of therapy are required to predict the survival of critically ill patients. For this, there is frequent collection of variables and the derived data are provided to the doctors. The recorded data to be significant should be clear as the information can be in a very large quantity. The intensive care unit (ICU) computerizes all the necessary and required information so that there is perfect management of the patient's data. There has been the development of closed loop system for vasodilator infusions [38]. The computer techniques–based therapy includes various methods to plan, monitor and adjust the dosage of toxic drugs such as in antibiotics. The regimens of dosage can be planned by the physicians through the target peak selection. Various surgical procedures can be planned, taught and performed with the aid of computer-based technologies. Robotically assisted surgery (RAS) is one of the major and recent developments in the medical field. The use of computer software and robotic devices allows the surgeons to implement minimal-invasive techniques. The images of high resolution can be generated with computer-assisted techniques. The human body images are created with the technology of medical imaging. The hardware and software are dedicated for this purpose so that high resolution images are obtained in CT scans, gamma cameras, ultrasound and MRI. The information system of the hospitals can be integrated with these workstations. There are various technologies in the field of medicine, which have helped transforming it completely. These technologies include 3-D printing, artificial intelligence, BCI and BBI's, robotics, electronic diagnosis, technologies related with the interaction between patient and physician. Three-dimensional printing can be used in future to test the toxicity of a specific drug on the human body. The use of artificial intelligence in the field of medicine includes the evaluation and analysis of patient's personal and biometric data including all the levels of diet and activities. A whole new understanding level can be achieved through artificial intelligence. The complex connections of human and computers are incorporated with the advancement of the interface between human brain and computer. With the advancement in technology, the healthcare has become efficient, better, more accurate and easier for patients, physicians and hospital staff [39].

9.3.5 COMPUTER VISION–BASED TECHNIQUES AS A COUNTER MEASURE

While using the computer-based technology to diagnose disease, the data are stored through the sensors present in the computer chip. For example, the CT scan of lungs is stored in the camera sensor. The other symptoms are also identified through the sensors embedded in the computer. All of these data are then aggregated and configured. The configuration is done by running the algorithm in the applications of smartphones and computers. All the symptoms of disease are recorded and configured separately through the computer-based technology. These data are then stored and analyzed. To identify the presence of virus in the lungs through CT scan images, many reports of radiology are trained in order to get a better diagnosis. Since the computational techniques have become very advanced, CPUs and GPUs are required, which are provided by the cloud in the form of virtual machines. The progressive CT scan images of the lungs are shown in Figure 9.8. The key technique for detecting the COVID-19 disease is the CT scan. The increase in the volume and density of CT scan images is the evidence for confirmed COVID-19 case. The proposed framework allows the radiologists to efficiently decide the suspected cases, which would otherwise take longer time if done manually by the radiologists [40].

Using deep learning, COVID-19 can be predicted using X-ray images. The epithelial cells of respiratory systems are affected by the presence of COVID-19. So, X-ray can be used to analyze the presence of COVID-19. The dataset of X-ray of normal

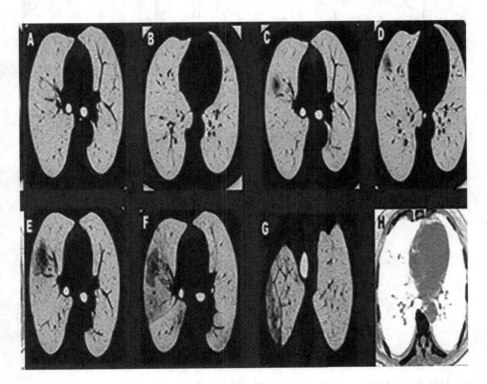

FIGURE 9.8 CT scan images of a suspected COVID-19 case.

people and X-ray of COVID-19 people can be used to train the model and with the use of CNN and deep learning, the model will be able to detect the presence of COVID-19 virus in X-ray [41]. Figure 9.9 shows the X-ray dataset of normal and COVID-19 positive people and Figure 9.10 shows detection of COVID-19 using algorithm.

Medical imaging and the analysis of medical image data are growing very rapidly in the medical field. Due to advancement in the imaging technologies, large amount of data is available due to which medical applications have risen and the need for better methods of data analysis and algorithms has increased in demand. The operation of minimal intervention is one such example. Due to the advancement of methods in

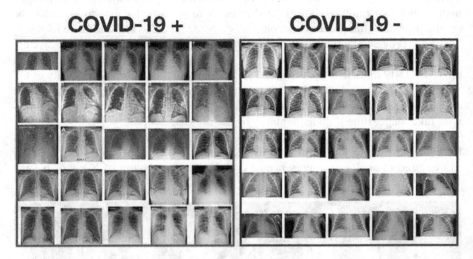

FIGURE 9.9   Dataset of normal and COVID 19 people.

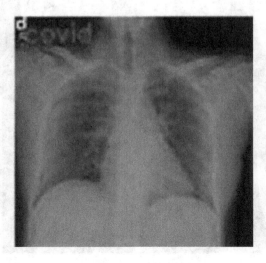

FIGURE 9.10   Detection of the presence of COVID-19.

real-time imaging, major surgeries are being possible, which also require the surgical tools having precise and automatic tracking. The methodologies in Deep Learning help in the analysis of medical image data by significant frameworks in the medical field [42]. Brain Tumour Segmentation is one of the applications of computer vision–based Deep Learning. In the United States, more than 20,000 people are diagnosed with tumour of spinal cord and brain of primary stage every year. The image processing of the brain tumour can be used to detect the tumour fall extensions where the anatomical structure is being segmented. The anatomical structures having unexpected shapes such as tumours in soft tissues can be challenging for automatic segmentation and the supervision of humans is required for complete segmentation [43]. Figure 9.11 shows the segmentation of the tumour in the brain. Active contours can be employed for tumour delineating with the aid of probabilistic maps. The successful segmentation of the brain tumour comes from the convergence of active contours at the level set.

Another application of the computer-based vision in deep learning is the measuring the density of damaged cartilage. The shock impulses are damped and absorbed between the between the thigh and shin bones with the help of knee cartilage. The tissue of the cartilage layer is very flexible due to which the pressure on the knee joint is eased, which is caused by walking or body weight. The damage to cartilage layer needs a clinical intervention such as encouraging new cartilage by drilling small holes or by totally replacing the knee cartilage. The ultrasonic imaging can be used to observe the state of erosion [44]. Figure 9.12 shows the ultrasound image of damaged cartilage tissue. The level of intervention is evaluated by trained orthopaedics and the physicians access the knee cartilage thickness. The computational tools measure and analyze the output images.

Segmentation of skeletons and bones is another application of computer vision–based deep learning. The image of the bone can be easily obtained by CT scan. Figure 9.13 shows the CT scan of the bones and skeleton. This is because the bone tissue can be easily identified through simple thresholding. The fractured bones can be observed by 3-D modelling, which has become necessary and significant in medical applications. The bone density can be assessed as a measurement in the CT scan,

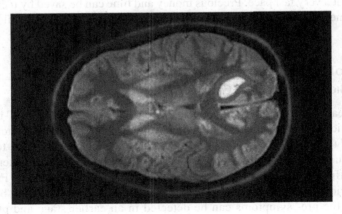

FIGURE 9.11   Segmentation of the brain tumour.

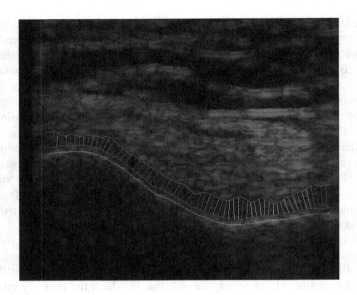

FIGURE 9.12   Ultrasound image of damaged cartilage tissue.

which is the actual rate of intensity. Manual segmenting used for bone geometry segmentation is a very long process and full of errors. Deep learning models combined with the computer vision technology are able to provide the algorithm that segments the bones accurately in CT scans with robustness and high speed [45].

The tumour cells can be automatically segmented through machine learning methods. Examining the tumour cells manually and visually is highly time-consuming and in the case of rapid intervention, this method is not readily available. This makes the manual segmentation very unpractical task by the experts. Therefore, the algorithms based on computer vision and machine learning are proposed in which the tumour cells could be automatically segmented. The quantification tasks can be autonomously performed by these algorithms, which scan and analyze the histological tissue at a very fast pace. Precious money and time can be saved by incorporating learning methods based on computer vision in the system of tumour cell segmentation [46].

9.3.6 IoT-Based System as Counter Measure for Bioweapon against Crop-War

In the threats described in the previous section, smart farming and IoT-based sensors (humidity, soil moisture, light, temperature, pesticide detection, etc.) are used to combat the attack of bioweapons. Furthermore, these are also used to increase crop production and weather forecast–based automatic irrigation system is used, which optimizes water usage and eliminates wastage of water [47]. Figure 9.14 shows various applications of IoT in the agriculture industry. During bio-attacks on crops, the pre- symptoms can be detected in an earlier stage and proper precautions and fertilizers can be provided to plants. Several applications have been

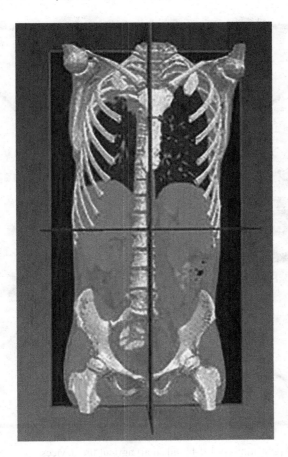

FIGURE 9.13 CT scan of bones and skeleton.

developed through computer vision and deep learning, which can detect the type of disease in plants and also provide suggestions to cure. Figure 9.15 shows the data set for deep learning. The algorithm using deep learning and image processing is able to recognise the infected leaf and stem, measure the affected area, find the shape of the infected region, determine the colour of the infected region, and also influence the shape and size of the crop [48]. The farmer can click the photograph of the crop and upload via desktop application or mobile app. Using artificial intelligence and deep learning, through the uploaded image, the disease can be detected.

9.4 MATHEMATICAL MODEL FOR COVID-19 PREDICTION

The SIR model is commonly used to study the count of individuals in a population suffering from an infectious disease. It categorizes the population under three parameters.

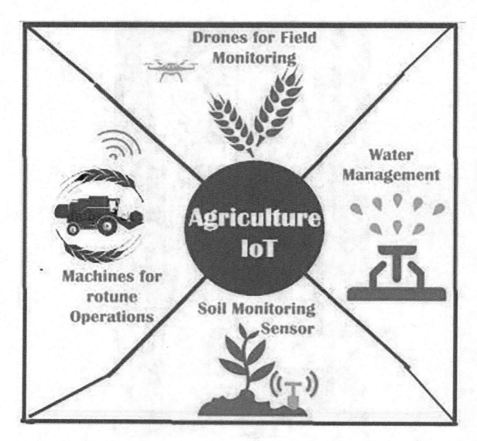

FIGURE 9.14   Applications of IoT-based smart agriculture devices.

Susceptible (S): Individuals not yet infected but are potentially vulnerable to get infected.

Infectious (I): Individuals infected at present (active cases) and could potentially infect people who come in contact with them.

Recovered (R): Recovered individuals from the disease and are therefore immune to any further infections.

The three categories or compartments have a certain number of persons each day. However, that number varies from day to day, as individuals shift from one category to another. Those persons of compartment S, who get infected, will move to the compartment I. Similarly, infected people in compartment I, who recover or die from the disease, will shift to the recovered R compartment.

It is expected that the cumulative populations in the three compartments (S + I + R) would always remain constant. It refers to the overall population of the territory under question. This model ignores the reality that continual births and deaths occur in the region. However, for short-term epidemics lasting a few months, this is a realistic assumption to make.

FIGURE 9.15 Image set for deep learning.

Natural population birth and death rates must also be included when modelling other diseases such as recurrent childhood infectious diseases like measles. For disorders such as COVID-19, another category known as "Exposed" (E) must be considered. Asymptomatic individuals are those who may have the virus but may not exhibit any symptoms. They are located between the vulnerable and diseased compartments. Despite the fact that they are asymptomatic, these people can still transmit the disease to others. As a result, we acquire a novel model known as the "SEIR model." More compartments, such as "Quarantined" or "Isolated," can be added to the model to allow for a more in-depth examination of disease management techniques. The Susceptible-Exposed-Infectious-Removed (SEIR) Model is a popular and straightforward model for predicting human-to-human transmission during an epidemic [49–51]. During any epidemic, the model divides the population into four different partitions with different variables. In the SEIR model, by adding the exposed/latent person population (E-exposed) and letting infected persons move from S (susceptible) to E (exposed) and from E (exposed) to I (infected), the delay between the acquisition of infection and the state of infection can be incorporated. Figure 9.16 shows the SEIR model.

In the model, persons can flow from S to E partition with the β rate, from E towards I with the ε rate, and from I towards R with the γ rate. However, a person can move from I to D (dead) with the α rate. R does not return to S as they are assumed to be immune.

If a person had some sort of contact with any infected person, he/she comes into the susceptible compartment (S). The probability is product of number of susceptible

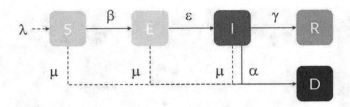

FIGURE 9.16   S-E-I-R Model for prediction.

people in the population and the fraction of infected people. Considering β as the transmission rate, the exposure rate can be given as:

$$r_{nE} = \frac{\beta}{N} SI \tag{9.1}$$

β can be given as

$$\beta = \frac{R_0}{n_{id}} \tag{9.2}$$

where R_0 is the basic reproduction number and n_{id} is the average number of days when an individual is infectious. For simulation purposes, balance in population of birth and natural deaths is assumed. With the increase in new exposed cases, the number of susceptible persons decreases and is given as:

$$\frac{dS}{dt} = -\frac{\beta}{N} SI \tag{9.3}$$

where N denotes the population size.

For the number of exposed (E),

$$\frac{dS}{dt} = \frac{\beta}{N} SI - \varepsilon E \tag{9.4}$$

where ε is the rate of progression towards infectious (per day) and if the length of incubation increases, this will decrease. The rate at which a person is isolated, dead or recovered, the εE decreases otherwise it increases. The rate is inversely proportional to the average number of days that a person is infectious and is shown as:

$$\gamma = \frac{1}{n_{id}} \tag{9.5}$$

The rate at which infectious persons die due to disease is given as αI and I is given as:

$$\frac{dI}{dt} = \varepsilon E - \gamma I - \alpha I \tag{9.6}$$

R variable shows those who have built immunity and are no longer susceptible; the equation of R can be given as:

$$\frac{dR}{dt} = \gamma I \tag{9.7}$$

However, for the D which dies due to disease, the equation can be written as:

$$\frac{dD}{dt} = \alpha I \tag{9.8}$$

For case prediction of COVID-19 using the preceding mathematics, a model is created in COMSOL software. The model is being used to forecast cases for India. The population is assumed to be 1,391,790,362, new cases are assumed to be 1012 on May 16, 2020, and active cases are assumed to be 3,618,423 [52], while the basic reproduction number for India is assumed to be 1.379 [53]. Erlang mean rate (r) is assumed to be 2.414, and reduction in transmission rate (β) is assumed to be 0.3 in weekend lockdown state. Figure 9.17 depicts the input parameters.

Figure 9.18 depicts the model's output after 100 days of computing. The graph depicts the number of instances that have been exposed, infected, recovered and died. According to the forecast, the death rate will continue to climb on an exponential scale until flattening out after 50+ days.

Population:	0.13917903262E10	
Mortality at entry to infectious state:	0.065	
End of simulation time:	100	day

Fitted Parameters
☐ Use from the latest Parameter Estimation

Basic reproduction number:	0.006932
Erlang mean rate ϵ:	2.414
Peak rate of import cases:	2174

▼ Reductions

Reduction of the transmission rate β:	0.3

FIGURE 9.17 Input parameter for model.

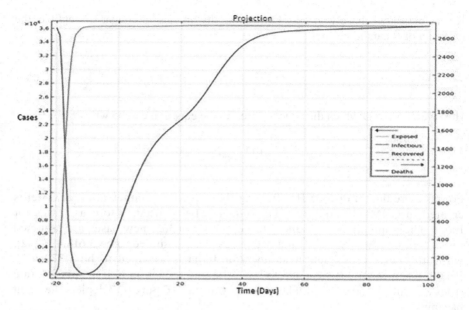

FIGURE 9.18   Projection by model.

9.5 CONCLUSION

Aside from natural disasters, genetically engineered agents constitute a bioweapon and bioterrorism threat. The number of bioweapons that may infect individuals and crops by injecting, spraying or shooting projectiles containing genetically altered DNA is increasing by the day. This work examines several genetically engineered illnesses as well as the impact of biological agents. To fight the effects propagated by these bio-agents, several computer-based solutions are used. Algorithms that combine computer vision and deep learning to provide faster, more accurate results assist the medical industry. In the event of a pandemic, artificial intelligence, big data, computer vision, computer-aided systems and IoT-based systems are offering solutions. Computer-assisted surgery is extremely beneficial to doctors. Even physicians can do surgery in faraway locales. Smart agricultural devices based on IoT are not only used to boost crop yield but also to monitor crop damage caused by any biological agent during crop war and to recommend a remedy to farmers. Countermeasures employing computer-assisted procedures are becoming more common as biowarfare technology advances. The mathematical model may also be used to forecast communicable diseases, as well as provide a full explanation of the prediction of COVID-19 coronavirus cases.

REFERENCES

[1] Hassani, Morad, Mahesh C. Patel, and Liise-anne Pirofski. "Vaccines for the prevention of diseases caused by potential bioweapons." *Clinical Immunology* 111, no. 1 (2004): 1–15.

[2] Murch, Randall S. "Forensic perspective on bioterrorism and the proliferation of bioweapons." In *Firepower in the Lab: Automation in the Fight Against Infectious Diseases and Bioterrorism*, Joseph Henry Press, p. 211. 2001.

[3] Ainscough, Michael. "Next generation bioweapons: genetic engineering and BW." In *The Gathering Biological Warfare Storm*, US Air Force Counterproliferation Center Future Warfare Series No. 14, pp. 269–270, 2004.

[4] Rumyantsev, Sergey N. "The best defence against bioweapons has already been invented by evolution." *Infection, Genetics and Evolution* 4, no. 2 (2004): 159–166.

[5] Boddie, Crystal, Matthew Watson, Gary Ackerman, and Gigi Kwik Gronvall. "Assessing the bioweapons threat." *Science* 349, no. 6250 (2015): 792–793.

[6] Tucker, Jonathan B. "The current bioweapons threat." In *Biopreparedness and Public Health*, pp. 7–16. Springer, Dordrecht, 2013. https://link.springer.com/chapter/10.1007/978-94-007-5273-3_2

[7] Sharma, Manvinder and Harjinder Singh (2022) "Contactless methods for respiration monitoring and design of SIW-LWA for real-time respiratory rate monitoring." *IETE Journal of Research*. DOI: 10.1080/03772063.2022.2069167

[8] Novel Swine-Origin Influenza A (H1N1) Virus Investigation Team. "Emergence of a novel swine-origin influenza A (H1N1) virus in humans." *New England Journal of Medicine* 360, no. 25 (2009): 2605–2615.

[9] Writing Committee of the WHO Consultation on Clinical Aspects of Pandemic (H1N1) 2009 Influenza. "Clinical aspects of pandemic 2009 influenza A (H1N1) virus infection." *New England Journal of Medicine* 362, no. 18 (2010): 1708–1719.

[10] Martina, Byron E. E., Bart L. Haagmans, Thijs Kuiken, Ron A. M. Fouchier, Guus F. Rimmelzwaan, Geert Van Amerongen, J. S. Malik Peiris, Wilina Lim, and Albert D. M. E. Osterhaus. "SARS virus infection of cats and ferrets." *Nature* 425, no. 6961 (2003): 915–915.

[11] Stadler, Konrad, Vega Masignani, Markus Eickmann, Stephan Becker, Sergio Abrignani, Hans-Dieter Klenk, and Rino Rappuoli. "SARS—beginning to understand a new virus." *Nature Reviews Microbiology* 1, no. 3 (2003): 209–218.

[12] Haagmans, Bart L., Judith M. A. van den Brand, V. Stalin Raj, Asisa Volz, Peter Wohlsein, Saskia L. Smits, Debby Schipper et al. "An orthopoxvirus-based vaccine reduces virus excretion after MERS-CoV infection in dromedary camels." *Science* 351, no. 6268 (2016): 77–81.

[13] Tang, Xian-Chun, Sudhakar S. Agnihothram, Yongjun Jiao, Jeremy Stanhope, Rachel L. Graham, Eric C. Peterson, Yuval Avnir et al. "Identification of human neutralizing antibodies against MERS-CoV and their role in virus adaptive evolution." *Proceedings of the National Academy of Sciences* 111, no. 19 (2014): E2018–E2026.

[14] Marimuthu, S., Melvin Joy, B. Malavika, Ambily Nadaraj, Edwin Sam Asirvatham, and L. Jeyaseelan. "Modelling of reproduction number for COVID-19 in India and high incidence states." *Clinical Epidemiology and Global Health* 9 (2021): 57–61.

[15] Alper, Joseph (1999). "From the bioweapons trenches, new tools for battling microbes." *Science* 284:1754–1755.

[16] Atlas, Ronald M. (1998). "Biological weapons pose challenge for microbiological community." *ASM News* 64: 383–388.

[17] Cole, Leonard A. (1996). "The spectre of biological weapons." *Scientific American* 275: 60–65.

[18] Steidler, Lothar. "Genetically engineered probiotics." *Best Practice & Research Clinical Gastroenterology* 17, no. 5 (2003): 861–876.

[19] MacIntyre, Raina C. "Biopreparedness in the age of genetically engineered pathogens and open access science: an urgent need for a paradigm shift." *Military Medicine* 180, no. 9 (2015): 943–949.

[20] Sharma, Manvinder, Harjinder Singh, and Digvijay Pandey. "Parametric considerations and dielectric materials impacts on the performance of 10 GHzSIW-LWA for respiration monitoring." *Journal of Electronic Materials* 51, no. 5 (2022): 2131–2141.

[21] Aldhous, Peter. "Biologists urged to address risk of data aiding bioweapon design." *Nature* 414, no. 6861 (2001): 237–239.

[22] Martin, John. "Severe stealth virus encephalopathy following chronic-fatigue-syndrome-like illness: clinical and histopathological features." *Pathobiology* 64, no. 1 (1996): 1–8.

[23] Sackstein, Robert. "A revision of Billingham's tenets: the central role of lymphocyte migration in acute graft-versus-host disease." *Biology of Blood and Marrow Transplantation* 12, no. 1 (2006): 2–8.

[24] Zhao, Xiaojun, and Shuguang Zhang. "Molecular designer self-assembling peptides." Chemical Society Reviews 35, no. 11 (2006): 1105–1110.

[25] Sikchi, Smita Sushil, Sushil Sikchi, and M. S. Ali. "Artificial intelligence in medical diagnosis." *International Journal of Applied Engineering Research* 7, no. 11 (2012): 2012.

[26] Hosny, Ahmed, Chintan Parmar, John Quackenbush, Lawrence H. Schwartz, and Hugo J. W. L. Aerts. "Artificial intelligence in radiology." *Nature Reviews Cancer* 18, no. 8 (2018): 500–510.

[27] Sharma, Manvinder, and Harjinder Singh. "Substrate integrated waveguide based leaky wave antenna for high frequency applications and IoT." *International Journal of Sensors Wireless Communications and Control* 11, no. 1 (2021): 5–13.

[28] Adams, Ludwig, Werner Krybus, Dietrich Meyer-Ebrecht, Rainer Rueger, Joachim M. Gilsbach, Ralph Moesges, and Georg Schloendorff. "Computer-assisted surgery." *IEEE Computer Graphics and Applications* 10, no. 3 (1990): 43–51.

[29] Wang, Yulun, Modjtaba Ghodoussi, Darrin Uecker, James Wright, and Amante Mangaser. "Modularity system for computer assisted surgery." U.S. Patent 6,728,599, issued April 27, 2004.

[30] DiGioia III, Anthony M., David A. Simon, Branislav Jaramaz, Michael K. Blackwell, Frederick M. Morgan, Robert V. O'toole, and Takeo Kanade. "Computer-assisted surgery planner and intra-operative guidance system." U.S. Patent 6,205,411, issued March 20, 2001.

[31] Kienzle III, Thomas C. "Enhanced graphic features for computer assisted surgery system." U.S. Patent 6,917,827, issued July 12, 2005.

[32] Wang, Yulun, Modjtaba Ghodoussi, Darrin Uecker, James Wright, and Amante Mangaser. "Modularity system for computer assisted surgery." U.S. Patent 6,892,112, issued May 10, 2005.

[33] Bates, David W., Suchi Saria, Lucila Ohno-Machado, Anand Shah, and Gabriel Escobar. "Big data in health care: using analytics to identify and manage high-risk and high-cost patients." *Health Affairs* 33, no. 7 (2014): 1123–1131.

[34] Dimitrov, Dimiter V. "Medical internet of things and big data in healthcare." *Healthcare Informatics Research* 22, no. 3 (2016): 156–163.

[35] Andreu-Perez, Javier, Carmen C. Y. Poon, Robert D. Merrifield, Stephen T. C. Wong, and Guang-Zhong Yang. "Big data for health." *IEEE Journal of Biomedical and Health Informatics* 19, no. 4 (2015): 1193–1208.

[36] Schurink, C. A. M., P. J. F. Lucas, I. M. Hoepelman, and M. J. M. Bonten. "Computer-assisted decision support for the diagnosis and treatment of infectious diseases in intensive care units." *The Lancet Infectious Diseases* 5, no. 5 (2005): 305–312.

[37] Ji, Soo-Yeon, Rebecca Smith, Toan Huynh, and Kayvan Najarian. "A comparative analysis of multi-level computer-assisted decision making systems for traumatic injuries." *BMC Medical Informatics and Decision Making* 9, no. 1 (2009): 2.

[38] Nachtigall, I., S. Tafelski, M. Deja, E. Halle, M. C. Grebe, A. Tamarkin, A. Rothbart et al. "Long-term effect of computer-assisted decision support for antibiotic treatment in critically ill patients: a prospective 'before/after'cohort study." *BMJ Open* 4, no. 12 (2014): e005370.

[39] Gil, Miguel, Pedro Pinto, Alexandra S. Simões, Pedro Póvoa, MM da Silva, and L. Lapão. "Co-design of a computer-assisted medical decision support system to manage antibiotic prescription in an ICU ward." *Studies in Health Technology and Informatics* 228 (2016).

[40] Wahabi, Hayfaa Abdelmageed, Samia Ahmed Esmaeil, Khawater Hassan Bahkali, Maher Abdelraheim Titi, Yasser Sami Amer, Amel Ahmed Fayed, Amr Jamal et al. "Medical doctors' offline computer-assisted digital education: systematic review by the digital health education collaboration." *Journal of Medical Internet Research* 21, no. 3 (2019): e12998.

[41] Sharma, Manvinder, Bikramjit Sharma, Anuj Kumar Gupta, Dishant Khosla, Sumeet Goyal, and Digvijay Pandey. "A study and novel AI/ML-based framework to detect COVID-19 virus using smartphone embedded sensors." In Agrawal, R., Mittal, M., Goyal, L.M. *Sustainability Measures for COVID-19 Pandemic*, pp. 59–74. Springer, Singapore, 2021.

[42] Gupta, Anuj Kumar, Manvinder Sharma, Ankit Sharma, and Vikas Menon. "A study on SARS-CoV-2 (COVID-19) and machine learning based approach to detect COVID-19 through X-ray images." *International Journal of Image and Graphics* 22, no. 03 (2020): 2140010.

[43] Lee, June-Goo, Sanghoon Jun, Young-Won Cho, Hyunna Lee, Guk Bae Kim, Joon Beom Seo, and Namkug Kim. "Deep learning in medical imaging: general overview." *Korean Journal of Radiology* 18, no. 4 (2017): 570–584.

[44] Zhao, Xiaomei, Yihong Wu, Guidong Song, Zhenye Li, Yazhuo Zhang, and Yong Fan. "A deep learning model integrating FCNNs and CRFs for brain tumor segmentation." *Medical Image Analysis* 43 (2018): 98–111.

[45] Zhang, Minjie, Sriniwasan B. Mani, Yao He, Amber M. Hall, Lin Xu, Yefu Li, David Zurakowski, Gregory D. Jay, and Matthew L. Warman. "Induced superficial chondrocyte death reduces catabolic cartilage damage in murine posttraumatic osteoarthritis." *The Journal of Clinical Investigation* 126, no. 8 (2016): 2893–2902.

[46] Gjertsson, Konrad, Kerstin Johnsson, Jens Richter, Karl Sjöstrand, Lars Edenbrandt, and Aseem Anand. "A novel automated deep learning algorithm for segmentation of the skeleton in low-dose CT for [(18) F] DCFPyL PET/CT hybrid imaging in patients with metastatic prostate cancer." (2019).

[47] Işın, Ali, Cem Direkoğlu, and Melike Şah. "Review of MRI-based brain tumor image segmentation using deep learning methods." *Procedia Computer Science* 102 (2016): 317–324.

[48] Balakrishna Reddy, G., and K. Ratna Kumar. "Quality improvement in organic food supply chain using blockchain technology." In Deepak, B.B.V.L., Parhi, D.R.K., Jena, P.C. *Innovative Product Design and Intelligent Manufacturing Systems*, pp. 887–896. Springer, Singapore, 2020.

[49] Elgabry, Mariam, Darren Nesbeth, and Shane D. Johnson. "A systematic review protocol for crime trends facilitated by synthetic biology." *Systematic Reviews* 9, no. 1 (2020): 22.

[50] Li, Michael Y., and James S. Muldowney. "Global stability for the SEIR model in epidemiology." *Mathematical Biosciences* 125, no. 2 (1995): 155–164.

[51] Sharma, Manvinder, Digvijay Pandey, Dishant Khosla, Sumeet Goyal, Binay Kumar Pandey, and Anuj Kumar Gupta. "Design of a GaN-based flip chip light emitting diode (FC-LED) with au bumps & thermal analysis with different sizes and adhesive materials for performance considerations." *Silicon* 14, no. 12 (2021): 7109–7120.

[52] Zivkovic, Miodrag, Nebojsa Bacanin, K. Venkatachalam, Anand Nayyar, Aleksandar Djordjevic, Ivana Strumberger, and Fadi Al-Turjman. "COVID-19 cases prediction by using hybrid machine learning and beetle antennae search approach." *Sustainable Cities and Society* 66 (2021): 102669. https://doi.org/10.1016/j.scs.2020.102669

[53] https://www.worldometers.info/coronavirus/

10 Evolution of Healthcare Sector and Evolving Cyberattacks—A Summary

Jai Ganesh Sekar, Arun Chokkalingam, and Dhivya Kesavan
RMK College of Engineering and Technology

CONTENTS

10.1 HEALTHCARE INDUSTRY AND ITS REVOLUTION

In the past 25 years, the healthcare industry has developed in alignment with technology and with a focus on sufficing the patient's requirements. This development has been rapid in the 21st century due to the Covid-19 pandemic with the support of 3D technology (printing) and artificial intelligence (AI) [1]. We have seen that the interest in engineering approaches in the healthcare industry has developed rapidly with the introduction of information technology tools for analysing the medical data along with the advanced medical infrastructure. Today's healthcare industry (4.0) has evolved, and technologies like electronic health records (EHR), health monitoring systems, wearable devices, etc. have created a breakthrough in the modern healthcare sector. These advancements had a significant impact on the lives of people as well as on the global economy by contributing 20% of the gross domestic product. This economic breakthrough provided the space for people from different industries to invest, research, and develop the healthcare sector. In the contemporary Industry 4.0 era, there is a shift towards the new paradigm by being innovative, connected, and employing cost-efficient manufacturing processes that yield quality products, which improve the satisfaction level of customers in healthcare services. Not only the

DOI: 10.1201/9781003254119-10

hospitals and clinics, even the homes are now equipped with various diagnostic and therapeutic options that are presented progressively and transparently, with extensive data and reporting that is composed of many wireless sensors and equipment. In this cognitive scenario, human intelligence is mimicked by AI techniques providing solutions to more complex problems that are emerging. This is supported by computers with high computational power. It is exciting to look at the transition of the healthcare sector from industry 1.0 to industry 4.0. Understanding this technological shift will also help us contrast the significance of the distributed system in the healthcare sector.

The first healthcare revolution was referred to as *healthcare 1.0*, which originated in the 18th century and was prolonged all the way up to the mid-19th century. Healthcare 1.0 was more aligned towards the doctors. It refers to the traditional patient–doctor scenario. In this era, the patient goes to the clinic and consults with a doctor and healthcare professionals. After a detailed check-up, the doctor prescribes medications. This was practiced for more than a century. In this generation, the doctor maintains the health records of every patient, and it is more doctor-centric. This generation of the healthcare sector was more focused on providing solutions for major public health problems. The approaches were evidence-based. Both preventing diseases with vaccination and purifying the drinking water were aspects concerning this generation of the healthcare sector.

The second healthcare revolution was referred to as *healthcare 2.0*, which started after a decade from the previous generation. With the invention of new and modern medical equipment, such as computed tomography (CT) scan, ultrasound scan, and magnetic resonance imaging (MRI) for imaging; Pulse Oximeter for monitoring; chest tubes and da Vinci Robots as life supporting equipment, their usage in the healthcare industry has increased. This development is called as Healthcare 2.0. This generation of healthcare systems was more connected, and all the health monitoring devices were networked. All health records were digitized and stored as EHRs. These EHRs were very helpful to the doctors as they could better understand the patient's health condition over time. Clinical imaging systems were also a part of the EHR, and this facilitated the doctors to get a better insight into the patient. Moreover, industry 2.0 was more focused on enhancing the performance of the systems in 1.0.

The third healthcare revolution was referred to as *healthcare 3.0*, which was in existence for a decade from 2005. The health industry experts witnessed the development of genomic information and the advancements in electronics, communication, and computing; the size of the computing devices dramatically reduced, giving birth to wearable devices and implants. This revolution integrated all patient-related data along with interconnected EHR systems, paved the way for real-time tracking of patients' health, and allowed these data to be stored electronically for later retrieval or analysis to get deeper and better insights into a patient's health. This generation has also faced several challenges in maintaining the patient data securely and in preserving the integrity of the stored data. Most of the activities are recorded in the EHR along with the pertinent timestamps, and most of the manual processes are digitized. In addition, technologies such as computer networks and remote care enabled telehealth, and electronic visits were made possible to replace face-to-face meetings between doctors and patients. Computers were also becoming more advanced in this era; it has improved the possibilities of detecting diseases earlier and more accurately. The Internet helped to keep the devices connected round the clock and provided continuous access to the stored electronic records, irrespective of the geographic location.

What we witness now is *healthcare 4.0*. The aforementioned technologies and features were bundled together and coupled with data collection. This revolution made it possible to keep the health records in a centralized system to monitor the patient's real-time health status and to offer uninterrupted services either physically or remotely. This is referred to as tele healthcare. Wearable devices and implantable equipped with lots of sensors were used to measure different health parameters of a patient, such as blood pressure, glucose and oxygen levels, heart rate, and body temperature. All the collected data will be stored in a centralized server to help the doctors to monitor the patients even more insightfully. The Internet of Things (IoT) along with tele healthcare facilitated improved disease monitoring and management. Healthcare IoT is a system interconnected with communication protocols such as WIFI, Bluetooth, and Zigbee.

The revolution in healthcare industry transformed the healthcare sector into a cyber-physical system [2]. To establish an intelligent and networked healthcare industry, programming technologies, such as cloud computing with the help of IoT, data analyzing techniques, machine learning (ML) platforms, are clubbed together with physical tools, such as wearable sensors and surgical robots. Healthcare 4.0 links the hospitals and patient care facilities to the patient's home. This enables the healthcare professionals to monitor and access the patient's health condition, medical records, and financial statements remotely. Furthermore, we can anticipate proactive therapy, early disease prediction and prevention, tailored medication, and improved patient-centric care using AI techniques. As a result, the paradigm of Health Care 4.0 emerges from a smart, widespread, and networked healthcare community [3–5].

Looking at the evolution of the manufacturing industry from Industry 1.0 to Industry 4.0, as shown in Figure 10.1, we can see that we started with simple manufacturing devices and technologies and evolved to more advanced and intelligent processes and procedures. With this new state-of-the-art healthcare industry, doctors can diagnose many deadly diseases very early. They can be treated with high precision and accuracy, saving many patients' lives.

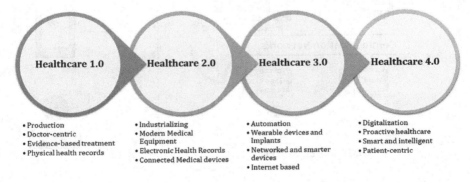

FIGURE 10.1 Industry revolution.

10.2 ROLE OF DISTRIBUTED SYSTEM IN HEALTHCARE

Before we understand the role of the distributed system in healthcare, we should first understand what a distributed system is. This basic knowledge on the distributed system will have its significance in understanding the role of distributed system specific to healthcare systems while highlighting the significant advantages of distributed system for the same.

We come across many distributed systems in our day-to-day activities like Amazon platforms, Netflix, search engines, online banking, shopping, and gaming, and the list goes on and on. The simplest example that we consider for our discussion is a simple client-server communication or a model. To answer the simple question, what is a distributed system? Independent nodes either hardware or software are connected together by a network to perform a wide range of operations, which is represented as the distributed system. These nodes will work together simultaneously to fulfil one goal or task. In most cases, the links between the nodes are highly structured, and in some instances, the links may be unstructured as well. The node links being structured or unstructured depends on the system requirements. In general, the complexity of the node link is hidden from the end-user, whoever is accessing it for a particular task. The end-user may be a human or a mobile device connected to the Internet. The entire nodes that are linked together appear as a single computer to its end-users. So basically, distributed systems are a bunch of independent computers that cooperate to solve a problem together. The above discussion can be visualized from Figure 10.2, which shows the schematic representation of distributed systems.

A distributed system may contain physically separable nodes that are connected together by a network, which enables the path for communication among the nodes, and works in tandem. Distributed system software has to be installed in all of these nodes. The operation of a distributed system can be understood using a simple example like rendering a long video, which would take a long day when rendered using a single computer. A distributed system begins with a task to render a video, like a

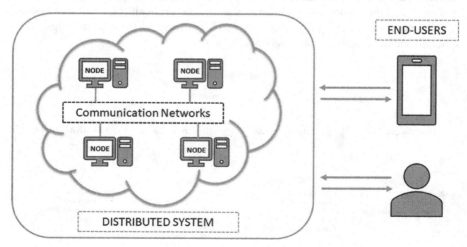

FIGURE 10.2 Distributed system.

video editor on a client computer (nodes), by splitting the job into many pieces. In this example, the algorithm assigns each frame of the video to different nodes to complete the process of rendering. Once the frame is complete, the application that manages the process assigns the node with a new frame to process. This process continues until all the frames of the video are finished, and all the pieces are put back together.

At the same time, the readers should understand that two applications running and communicating with each other within the same computer are necessarily not a distributed system even though they are trying to achieve the same goal. In order to designate the group of nodes working in coordination as a distributed system, they need to satisfy the below-mentioned characteristics [6–8].

- The nodes should not have a shared clock (Timers).
- The nodes must be independent.
- The nodes should not have shared memory.
- Multiple nodes should have the ability to process the same function independently at the same time, with the tasks being executed concurrently.
- Heterogeneity among the nodes is another crucial characteristic of a distributed system, as different nodes use different and independent operating systems and are built on different architectures.

Distributed systems carry several advantages such as greater flexibility, reliability, speed of computing, geo-distribution, etc. Rendering a video is one simple example to demonstrate the working of a distributed system. But, that's not the end of the list; distributed system also has its applications in telecommunication networks, scientific computing, genetic research, reservation systems, multiuser video conferencing, cryptocurrency, peer-to-peer file sharing systems, online video games with multiplayer facility, global supply chain management, etc. Its long list of advantages makes the distributed system suitable for enormous applications, including the healthcare sector [9].

Now it's time to dive in and understand the role of the distributed system with respect to healthcare industries. When a person is affected by any disease, getting proper treatment and getting recovered is a tedious process. Earlier, healthcare services were primarily introduced at home. At first, doctors and nurses visited the patient's home. Later, hospitals replaced this system with tremendous advancement in modern medicines and specialized clinics. Hospitals can be equipped with high-end facilities to treat patients. But, at the same time, there were two drawbacks. First, having high-end facilities and state-of-the-art infrastructure raises the cost of treatment. Second, with time, there are more and more patients approaching the hospitals, and the hospitals struggle to manage the overflow of patients every week. The only solution for this problem is to keep the patients out of hospitals, but at the same time, they should get proper treatment at the right time. This embraces the distributed system into healthcare.

The concept of providing decentralized patient care, including services like patient monitoring system and tests for diagnosing illness to people in need, is termed as distributed healthcare. This enables patients to access these services from their homes and get guidance and support. This home-based healthcare system aims at providing hospital-level care at patients' premises with continuous monitoring of serious illness. This approach reduces the cost of treatment and also improves the quality of treatment, and enhances the overall healthcare experience. This approach is well suited for aged patients and patients with less mobility. These systems monitor the significant vitals of the patient, and if any critical situation is identified, then all sorts of proactive arrangements are made to prevent the patient from further hospitalization. Distributed care, if it is to become the next model for healthcare, will require technology that allows healthcare professionals and other teams to collaborate. A data platform that can combine information from many systems and create a holistic, electronic medical record for a patient is a basic prerequisite for distributed care. These medical records of the patient are made available for a variety of healthcare professionals for diagnosing the patient's health. Since these are personal records, an individual can decide to whom the data must be visible and will have complete control over who can access his or her health records (Electronic Health Records).

These electronic health records of a patient are distributed and facilitate a wide range of applications. It is challenging for doctors to make any clinical decisions without knowing the medical history of the patient or without having sufficient data. Distributed healthcare systems allow doctors to access medical information from a shared platform so as to make effective decisions on time. These data can also be used by researchers to explore the genetic architecture of any new or unknown disease-causing cells. Patients in intensive care units need continuous monitoring of their vitals for proper medical examinations. Sensors enabled with Internet connectivity can be placed on the patient's body, and these devices will upload the real-time signals of electrocardiogram (ECG), heartbeat, body temperature, etc. These data can be accessed by health professionals at any point in the world so as to give personalized and accurate prescriptions to the patients on time without visiting the patient's home or hospitals. Furthermore, technologies like big data, data analytics, and data Science will facilitate the researchers, doctors, and even the patients to get more valuable insights based on the previous health records. There are countless possibilities in the healthcare industry to evolve, such as remote patient monitoring systems, health-related mobile applications, telemedicine in real-time, etc.

Healthcare 4.0 aims at delivering smart and interlinked healthcare in the near future. This can be achieved by promoting research activities in health and bioinformatics with the introduction of information technology into the healthcare industry for modelling, maximizing, and to maintain the collected healthcare data securely. In this complex organizational work design, it is equally significant to device a communication protocol that connects healthcare professionals, patients, and the monitoring devices by considering the entire system as patient-centric.

While discussing the advantages and possibilities of modern smart healthcare systems, it is worth to throw some light on the critical challenges and drawbacks as well.

- **Data Compatibility**: It is clearly evident that the patient's records are to be stored, maintained, and accessed in a database. In this case, there are several database management systems from various vendors that use different formats to store the data. Hence, data compatibility becomes a critical issue in order to make the health records distributed among many systems.

- **Data Availability and Security**: The entire smartness of the distributed systems depends on the data that are collected from the patients. Diagnosis, treatment, and medications will be prescribed purely based on these available data. In the Internet world, nothing is secure. Keeping the private data confidential and securing the information from any unauthorized access is a significant issue to be addressed.

- **Prediction Models and Their Accuracy**: Most of the features of healthcare 4.0, such as telemedicine, auto diagnostics, etc. rely on AI and ML models. Unfortunately, these technologies rely on predefined models to predict certain outcomes and the accuracy of the prediction depends on the number of datasets available for training the model and choosing the correct parameters. In the medical field, there are enormous amounts of uncertainties for treating a disease, as it depends on several factors, such as individual nature, previous medical history, etc. Thus, it becomes more challenging for the healthcare professionals to decide on which vitals/samples to collect from the patients.

To make a closing statement, the latest healthcare evolution 4.0 might sound promising with all the latest technologies. However, managing, securing, and monitoring the device fleets with reliable and efficient technology in healthcare is an upcoming challenge.

10.3 WHY HEALTHCARE IS THE BIGGEST TARGET FOR CYBERATTACKERS?

The rise of healthcare 4.0 is what we are experiencing now. All of these technologies are coming together, along with real-time data collecting, more AI use, and an overlay of invisible user interfaces. Healthcare will become more predictive and individualized as a result of an emphasis on teamwork, coherence, and convergence. Simultaneously, these technological improvements allow attackers to launch a variety of security assaults, including data privacy, confidentiality, and integrity attacks, all of which are quite concerning. Healthcare organizations become increasingly susceptible to online attacks compromising confidential patient data [10]. At the same time, healthcare officials do not have sufficient awareness or avenues to educate themselves about online risks. Sadly, the risk for an organization is just too big even to consider. Many healthcare organizations are ready to spend a huge amount of money on cybersecurity. On the other side, new threats are uncovered day by day, making it difficult for healthcare organizations to secure patient information. In this session, we will discuss the various reasons for why the healthcare sector is becoming a popular target for cyberattackers.

Patients' Private Information Is Worth Huge Money to Attackers: Several healthcare organizations store an incredible amount of data of their patients. Cybercriminals try to access this private information as they can sell this information on the black market for huge money. Now you may be wondering what they would do with a health record? Here is a glimpse of activities that an attacker or cybercriminals would do with your health record. Cybercriminals are very much interested in health records because they have hell a lot of information about an individual, such as a patient's full name, residential address, financial information, credit/debit card details, and other personal identification numbers. This information is enough to take out a loan or to initiate a purchase against a patient's credit cards. This information can also be used to fake an identity to purchase drugs, claim false insurance, etc. Most hackers steal health records and sell them in the darknet for profit, but the impact of this data theft depends on who buys this information and how it is used. The attackers can even infect the hospital or healthcare organization with ransomware, preventing the healthcare officials from accessing the medical records, and they will demand a ransom to unlock the system.

Medical Devices are Vulnerable to Cyberattacks: With technological advancements, many medical devices were reduced in size so that they can be injected or implanted on the patient's body itself. One such well-known medical device is the pacemaker. In addition to pacemakers, insulin pumps, and cardioverter defibrillators are a few other examples of medical devices that can be implanted in a patient's body. Not only these devices but most of the medical devices are designed for a specific purpose, such as monitoring or automated dispensing of drugs. These devices are not designed like many other devices that connect to the Internet such as laptops and mobile phones, keeping security in mind. Due to this reason, medical devices become an easy target for hackers to gain access. An attacker needs a backdoor to gain access to the internal circuitry of a medical device. Generally, these backdoors are installed or designed by the product manufacturers for testing and calibration purposes. The software company can also install a backdoor for debugging or installing any future updates. All the hackers know that the medical devices do not hold or store any medical records of the patient, but still, they can gain control over the devices and upload malicious ransomware or bots into the healthcare organization servers. In turn, the attacker would get complete access to the server or to the organization's network. Other intentions of the hacker also include gaining knowledge of how the device works, to reverse engineer it, to damage the device and harm the patient, etc.

Remote Access and Collaborative Working Open Up Doors for Cyberattacks: In the distributed healthcare system, the patient's records will be accessed by many health professionals to provide the best healthcare to the patient. Also, a distributed healthcare system allows healthcare professionals and individuals to access the information remotely from any device. Though these are key features of distributed healthcare, connecting to a network from new devices and untrusted networks is risky, as the devices are not secured (sometimes). In addition to this, most healthcare professionals lack awareness about best practices in cybersecurity. It is very difficult to manage the devices that the stakeholders use to connect to the healthcare network and access private information. Even one compromised device can leave a whole organization wide open for critical cyberattacks.

Healthcare Professionals Have the Least Awareness about Cybersecurity: Most of the healthcare professionals are very busy and work with tight deadlines. This work culture cuts off the opportunity for a healthcare worker to learn about the online security process. Due to tight work schedules, healthcare professionals often avoid the security layer of authentication, such as logging into a web service with a password to access information as they tend to access a lot of information several times a day. This negligence often attracts cybercriminals to gain access to healthcare organizations.

Healthcare Industries Have Tight Budgets for Security and Outdated Technologies: The majority of the clinics have outdated systems and infrastructure that are not completely equipped for modern cyber threats. Among all the industries, healthcare industries are the slowest to adopt the best practices on cybersecurity and related technologies. Most of the hospitals and healthcare organizations are failing to upgrade due to fear that their services may get disrupted. Outdated technologies and infrastructures will not detect the modern and recent threats on the Internet. The attackers can make the healthcare professionals download malware-infected attachments, which paves the way for a data breach into the network.

The list of reasons for the healthcare sector being an easy target for cyberattacks is exhaustive, and they are susceptible to cyberattacks for various other reasons as well.

10.4   CYBERATTACKS IN HEALTHCARE INDUSTRIES—AN INFOGRAPHIC

According to HIPAA (The Health Insurance Portability and Accountability Act 1996) Journal, data breaches in the healthcare sector are rampant than ever before [11]. Very few and important cyberattacks that occurred in the healthcare sectors are listed here, and these figures give us a greater insight into how big the threat would be.

- In the year 2021, it has been reported that around 686 healthcare data breaches have occurred. It is predicted that this may increase in future. It is worthy to note that 642 data breaches were reported in 2020.
- Over 4,49,93,618 healthcare records were exposed or stolen in 2021 alone.

These huge figures show that the healthcare industry has always been a prime target for cybercriminals, and 2021 is the worst year as the healthcare sector has been a victim of many cyberattacks. Table 10.1 summarizes the largest data breaches in the healthcare sector during the year 2021 alone. Each of the data breaches mentioned below involves exposure of protected personal health records of more than 1 million individuals [12].

TABLE 10.1

Largest Data Breaches in the Healthcare Sector During the Year 2021

Name of the Entity/ Victim	Origin of Entity/ Victim	Records Breached/ Stolen/Exposed	Cause of Breach
Accellion FTA Hack	An US-based firewall vendor	3.51 million records were stolen. More than 100 companies were affected	Hacked due to four vulnerabilities in file transfer appliance
Florida Healthy Kids Corporation	Florida health plan	3.5 million individual records were exposed	Hacked due to the vulnerabilities in the website have not been fixed for the period of 7 years.
20/20 Eye Care Network, Inc	A Florida-based eye and ear care service provider	3,253,822 personal and protected health information was exposed	Hacked due to webservices from Amazon were misconfigured
NEC Networks, LLC dba CaptureRx	Texas-based NEC networks	2.42 million individuals were affected	Victim of the largest healthcare ransomware attack
Forefront Dermatology, S.C.	Wisconsin-based healthcare provider	2,413,553 secured health records of individuals may be exposed	Unauthorized intruders had gained access to its network
Eskenazi Health	Indiana-based healthcare provider	1,515,918 records including socially identifiable information and financial reports were breached	Ransomware attack by the Vice ransomware gang
The Kroger Co	Ohio-based grocery chain and pharmacy operator	1,474,284 records including socially identifiable information and financial reports were breached	Hacked due to vulnerabilities in file transfer appliance
St. Joseph's/Candler Health System, Inc.	Georgia-based health system	1,400,000 records including socially identifiable information and financial reports were breached	Ransomware attack
University Medical Center	Nevada-based healthcare provider	1,300,000 patient's records were stolen and $12 million was demanded as ransom	Ransomware attack

(Continued)

TABLE 10.1 (*Continued*)
Largest Data Breaches in the Healthcare Sector During the Year 2021

Name of the Entity/ Victim	Origin of Entity/ Victim	Records Breached/ Stolen/Exposed	Cause of Breach
American Anesthesiology, Inc	New York–based American Anaesthesiology	1,269,074 patient records were compromised. Attacker intended to divert the payrolls of employees	Affected by a phishing attack. Employees' credentials were exposed as they responded to phishing emails
Practicefirst Medical Management Solutions and PBS Medcode Corp	New York practice management company	1,210,688 protected health records of individuals were exposed	Ransomware attack
Personal Touch Holding Corp.	New York– based business associate	7,53,107 protected health records were stolen and exposed	Ransomware attack
Oregon Anesthesiology Group, P.C.	Oregon-based healthcare provider	7,50,500 protected health records were stolen and exposed	Victim of an attempted ransomware attack
UF Health Central Florida	Florida-based healthcare provider	7,00,981 protected health records were stolen and exposed	Victim of an attempted ransomware attack
Sea Mar Community Health Centers	Washington-based healthcare provider	6,88,000 protected health records were stolen and exposed	An unspecified attack resulted in theft of data
Health Net Community Solutions	California-based health plan	6,86,556 protected health records were stolen and exposed	Theft of data due to vulnerability in file transfer appliance and extortion attack
Community Medical Centers, Inc.	California-based healthcare provider	6,56,047 protected health records were stolen and exposed	An unspecified attack
DuPage Medical Group, Ltd.	Illinois-based healthcare provider	6,55,384 protected health records were stolen and exposed	Victim of an attempted ransomware attack
Hendrick Health	Texas-based healthcare provider	6,40,436 protected health records were stolen and exposed	Victim of an attempted ransomware attack
UNM Health	New Mexico– based healthcare provider	6,37,252 protected health records were stolen and exposed	An unspecified attack resulted in theft of data
Trinity Health	Michigan-based business associate	5,86,869 protected health records were stolen and exposed	Theft of data due to vulnerability in file transfer appliance and extortion attack

(Continued)

TABLE 10.1 (*Continued*)
Largest Data Breaches in the Healthcare Sector During the Year 2021

Name of the Entity/ Victim	Origin of Entity/ Victim	Records Breached/ Stolen/Exposed	Cause of Breach
Utah Imaging Associates, Inc.	Utah-based healthcare provider	5,82,170 protected health records were stolen and exposed	An unspecified attack
Texas ENT Specialists	Texas-based healthcare provider	5,35,489 protected health records were stolen and exposed	Victim of an attempted ransomware attack
Wolfe Clinic, P.C.	Iowa-based healthcare provider	5,27,378 protected health records were stolen and exposed	Victim of an attempted ransomware attack
State of Alaska Department of Health and Social Services	Alaska-based health plan	5,00,000 protected health records were stolen and exposed	Unspecified hacking incident by nation-state espionage group

10.5   MOST FREQUENT ATTACKS IN HEALTH INDUSTRIES AND REMEDIAL MEASURES

A cyberattack on the healthcare sector is more than an attack imposed on computers as the attack is on vulnerable people and the people who need medical care/attention. The attacks on the healthcare sector are not only limited to the organizations providing the healthcare facilities but also include hospitals, mental health facilities, pharmaceutical companies, and diagnostic centres. Healthcare sectors are becoming easy and popular targets for cybercriminals due to one or many reasons [13], as we previously discussed. According to the infographic figures shown in the previous section, it is evident that healthcare cyberattacks are rising every year. A study also says that the cyber threat for the healthcare industry in over 30 countries is rising rapidly. There are several types of cyberattacks being executed for several reasons but, with respect to the healthcare sector, 10 of 15 attacks are ransomware attacks. Likewise, there are only a few types of attacks that are majorly executed on the healthcare system organizations. We will discuss each type of attack briefly in this section.

> **Ransomware Attacks**: In recent times, an increasing number of hospitals have been subjected to ransomware attacks. Ransomware is a kind of malicious software, also called malware, which blocks access to data stored on a computer by encrypting all the files until the victim pays the ransom demanded by the attacker. In most cases, the ransomware attack comes with a deadline, and if the ransom is not paid within the deadline, the data are lost forever. Ransomware attacks have become more common in the healthcare sector, and most healthcare organizations have fallen victim to them. There are two types of approaches in which the ransomware attack can be executed, Encryptors and Screen Lockers. In Encryptors, the malicious

software injected into the system or network will encrypt all the files on the system, making the files unusable without the decryption key. In the case of Screen Lockers, the malicious software simply blocks access to the system by imposing a screen lock.

In both cases, the victims are notified on the lock screen that their system/network is hacked, and the attacker demands the victim to pay a ransom. Usually, the victims are asked to pay the ransom in the form of cryptocurrencies like Bitcoin to keep the transaction anonymous. In most cases, even if the ransom is paid, the victim may not get the proper decryption key to recover the data, and sometimes the victim never receives the decryption key. Typically, the ransomware attack infects the system or network in one of the three ways:

- Through phishing emails that contain malicious attachments.
- Making the victim click on the malicious link.
- Viewing an advertisement containing malware is generally called malvertising.

Through any one of these methods, the attacker injects the ransomware agent into the system. This agent then starts encrypting the files on the infected machine. Once the agent completes encrypting all the data in the machine, it then displays a programmed message on the victim's screen on what has happened and the ways to pay the attacker. Generally, these types of attacks are targeted at medium to large-sized organizations as they can pay more ransom than an individual as it becomes critical for organizations to resume their daily operations.

Data Breaches: On the illicit market, personal health information (PHI) is more valuable. As a result, fraudsters benefit more when they target health records. They frequently sell or use the PHI for their own personal advantage. The health industry, according to the Ponemon Institute and Verizon Data Breach Investigations Report, has more data breaches than any other industry. Breaches are mostly observed in the healthcare sector. A data breach is when confidential, sensitive, or protected information is disclosed to an unapproved person or community. Without the authorization of the data's true owner, the files in the cyberattack are viewed or shared. Data breaches pose a huge risk for individuals as well as organizations of various sizes. Credential-stealing malware, an insider who purposely or accidentally releases patient data, or stolen laptops or other devices are all examples of incidents that might lead to this. These are the several ways in which the data breach takes place:

- **Accidental Insider**: When an employee examines the files on a co-worker's device without authorization, the employee is breaking the law. Here, though the employee does not have any malicious intention, the data are considered to be breached as they are exposed to an unauthorized person without the proper permission of the owner.
- **Malicious Insider**: When a person accesses or shares the data with the intention of causing harm to an individual or entity then, it is referred to as an insider threat.

- **Stolen Devices**: Data breaches may happen if the device is lost and it contains any sensitive information on the hard disk that is not protected or encrypted.
- **Malicious Outsiders**: They are the actors outside an organization who practice several attack vectors and collect information from an individual or a network.

  In most of the general cases, an attacker (especially malicious outsiders) researches the victim's vulnerabilities in the network or servers such as outdated software, weak credentials, already breached credentials but not updated yet, compromised assets, third-party access points, compromised mobile device, etc. These vulnerabilities act as the entry points for the attacker to enter into the network and search for the required data.

Distributed Denial of Service (DDoS) Attacks: Here, the attacker floods the network with fake Internet traffic and overwhelms a network to the point of in-operability. This type of attack takes advantage of limitations in the network's maximum capacity to handle Internet traffic. The attacker takes control over several compromised devices such as computers and IoT devices and uses them as the source to create fake traffic. These individual devices are often referred to as bots, and the group of bots that are connected is called botnets. Due to this unexpected traffic on the network target to a specific server, the server becomes inaccessible to legitimate users for any services they rely on. The main motive of a DDoS attack is to prevent the website or web services from working correctly.

Healthcare professionals face severe difficulties as a result of this type of attack. Technically, there are two types of DDoS attacks based on the layer of the OSI (Open System Interconnection) model.

- **Application Layer Attack:** This attack targets the traffic at layer 7 of the OSI model. A simple HTTP request is easy to process on the sender side, but it places a significant computational load on the server to send the requested webpage, as the server often needs to read multiple files and run multiple queries in the database to complete the webpage. The attacker controls the botnet remotely and sends several HTTP requests to the targeted web server offering the services. These HTTP requests flood the server network and result in denial of service to legitimate users.
- **Protocol Attacks:** This attack targets the traffic at layers 3 and 4 of the OSI model. These attacks are often referred to as state-exhaustion attacks, causing a service disruption by over-consuming the server resources or network resources like firewalls and load balancers. In this layer, the network is flooded with synchronization (SYN) packets. This attack exploits the transmission control protocol (TCP) handshake, which is the mechanism to establish a connection between two devices and to exchange the packet and finally terminate the connection. Here the flooded SYN packets create several connections until the device cannot handle any more connection requests, and these connections

never close, leaving the target system inaccessible for the legitimate users.

- **DNS Amplification Attacks:** In this attack, the attacker uses the compromised botnets to send spoofed IP addresses to the DNS server. The DNS resolver tries to send the reply to the IP address, which is the IP address of the victim. So, the victim will receive several responses from the DNS servers that occupy the entire bandwidth resulting in a denial of service.

  In many cases, the DDoS attacks are targeted at medium to large-sized organizations to deny services to their customers, which in turn affects the reputation of the company, impacts the business, and lowers the reliability among the customers.

Insider Threats: It is not necessary that the attack should have originated from outside the organization, as sometimes an insider can also be the reason for the attack. In many cases, the insiders pose a threat because they have access to sensitive information of the organization, and they will be exempted from various cybersecurity defence mechanisms such as intrusion detection systems and physical firewalls. In addition to this, a malicious insider will have a stronger knowledge of the network setup and the vulnerabilities in the organization than any other outsider. Insiders typically involve current or former employees. There are various types of insider threats:

- **Malicious Insider**: A person who intentionally shares or sells legitimate credentials or steals sensitive and protected information with a motive of financial benefits.
- **Careless Insider**: An innocent person who unintentionally exposes sensitive credentials/information to outsiders.
- **A Mole**: Someone pretending to be someone else. Although this individual is technically an outsider, he or she has managed to get insider access to a secure network.

  These are the few attacks that the healthcare industry faces, but it is not an exhaustive list of attacks. In addition to the abovementioned attacks that threaten the healthcare sector, scams are another major threat to this industry. The scammers use the spoofed email to trick the employees into initiating money transfer, or stealing sensitive login credentials, or installing the malware into the network or victim's device. The attacker is almost successful every time because the healthcare industry is not completely equipped with all the security countermeasures related to threats. The second reason is that the healthcare industry allocates a very minimal budget for securing the organization's infrastructure from cyber threats. And finally, the employees and stakeholders of the healthcare sector are least educated about the safety practices to be followed to avoid most of the cyberattacks like sharing passwords, using weak passwords, accessing organization networks from untrusted networks and devices, clicking malicious links sent by any phishing or scam emails, etc.

10.6   RESEARCH TRENDS IN CYBERSECURITY FOR THE HEALTHCARE SECTOR

With lots of innovation and transformation, healthcare 4.0 has coined the word "Digital Health," where the health records of the patients are stored in the electronic form. We should accept the fact that the industry is not well equipped with data security systems that safeguard the organization from alarming cyberattacks. Protecting healthcare records is not as easy as we think. Healthcare associates have to balance the quality of patient care and meet the strict regulatory policies coined by HIPAA and other regulatory bodies [14,15].

Security Challenges in the Healthcare Sector: Understanding the real and practical challenges in the healthcare sector helps the researchers to formulate or to come up with an innovative solution.

- **Raising Ransomware Attacks**: The major challenge in the healthcare sector is the rise of ransomware attacks, and the cost of the ransom has also exponentially increased over decades. These ransomware attacks literally shut down the entire system of patient care, and lots of patients' lives are at stake.
- **AI-Based Cyberattacks**: Technological advancements are not only for the good guys. They are in the hands of a few bad guys as well. Nowadays, attackers are becoming tech-savvy in handling the technologies and initiating more sophisticated attacks. The AI and ML models help the attackers to initiate attacks that are not possible by human means. These types of attacks are often hard to detect and counterfeit unless the organization has proactive security measures implemented.
- **The Emergence of IoMT and Health Devices**: All the features of healthcare 4.0 are made possible with the usage of connected devices such as the Internet of Medical Things (IoMT) and health monitoring devices. The technological advancement is marching towards the increased usage of BYOD (Bring Your Own Device), leaving the security doors open for the attackers to gain access over the networks. Hence, these devices should be properly managed, monitored, and tracked by security professionals to identify any malicious intruders.
- **Increased Exchange of Information**: With the help of integrated systems and data modernization, patients can now play a crucial role with the use of healthcare devices, mobile applications, and web-based services. This has increased the enormous amount of data being exchanged in the network across several systems and applications. This comes with a downside that there are lots of chances of data exposure. The healthcare industry can survive only if they implement secure communication algorithms to prevent the data from getting into the wrong hands.

These are a few predominant security challenges that the healthcare industry is facing while advancing with the technology. Any quality research that leads to overcoming these challenges will be greatly welcomed to sustain and advance healthcare without compromising security.

10.7 CONCLUSION—DEFENDING HEALTHCARE SECTOR FROM CYBERATTACKS

The dependency of healthcare on technology is inevitable. Similarly, the amount of information collected, shared, and analyzed is also getting increased drastically, which automatically prioritizes the need for cybersecurity and data privacy. It's a hard time to realize that cybersecurity and privacy are not an option anymore or just for the sake of regulatory norms. The healthcare sector can defend itself from cyber-attacks by practicing regular safety measures such as

- Upgrading and replacing the legacy systems,
- Educating the health professionals regularly on cybersecurity awareness and conducting frequent training programmes,
- Increasing the budgets for adopting cybersecurity infrastructures for data protection,
- Strictly adhering to the regulatory policies imposed by the government,
- Risk analysis and assessments,
- Hiring security professionals for penetration testing and the list goes on and on.

Evolution in the healthcare industry from healthcare 1.0 to healthcare 4.0 sounds promising by integrating all the technologies. But, at the same time, it's really a tough challenge for security professionals in managing, securing, and monitoring the fleet of medical devices that are interconnected to provide quality patient care and monitoring.

REFERENCES

1. Li J, Carayon P. Health Care 4.0: A Vision for Smart and Connected Health Care. *IISE Trans Healthc Syst Eng* 2021; 11(3):171–180. https://doi.org/10.1080/24725579.2021.1884627
2. Sriram RD, Subrahmanian, E. Transforming Health Care through Digital Revolutions. *J Indian Inst Sci* 2020; 100:753–772. https://doi.org/10.1007/s41745-020-00195-0
3. Chute C, French T. Introducing Care 4.0: An Integrated Care Paradigm Built on Industry 4.0 Capabilities. *Int J Environ Res Public Health* 2019; 16(12):2247. https://doi.org/10.3390/ijerph16122247
4. Sony M, Antony J, McDermott O. The Impact of Healthcare 4.0 on the Healthcare Service Quality: A Systematic Literature Review. *Hosp Top* 2022; 21:1–17.
5. Murugadoss M, Saini S, Singh R. Influence of Big Data in the Healthcare Sector. In *2019 3rd International Conference on Electronics, Communication and Aerospace Technology (ICECA)*, 2019, pp. 1335–1341. https://doi.org/10.1109/ICECA.2019.8822146
6. https://www.confluent.io/learn/distributed-systems/
7. https://insidebigdata.com/ 2016/10/27/distributed-system-architectures-for-healthcare-and-life-sciences/
8. van Steen, M., Tanenbaum, AS. A Brief Introduction to Distributed Systems. *Computing* 2016; 98:967–1009. https://doi.org/10.1007/s00607-016-0508-7
9. https://www.splunk.com/en_us/data-insider/what-are-distributed-systems.html
10. Abouzakhar NS, Jones A, Angelopoulou O, Internet of Things Security: A Review of Risks and Threats to Healthcare Sector. In *2017 IEEE International Conference on Internet of Things (iThings) and IEEE Green Computing and Communications*

(GreenCom) and IEEE Cyber, Physical and Social Computing (CPSCom) and IEEE Smart Data (SmartData), 2017, pp. 373–378. https://doi.org/10.1109/iThings-GreenCom-CPSCom-SmartData.2017.62.

11. https://swivelsecure.com/solutions/healthcare/cybersecurity-threats-to-the-healthcare-industry/
12. https://www.hipaajournal.com/largest-healthcare-data-breaches-of-2021/
13. https://swivelsecure.com/solutions/healthcare/healthcare-is-the-biggest-target-for-cyber-attacks/
14. https://swivelsecure.com/solutions/healthcare/securing-patient-information/
15. https://www.cisecurity.org/insights/blog/cyber-attacks-in-the-healthcare-sector

11 Improving Cardiovascular Health by Deep Learning

Shiva Tushir
Panipat Institute of Engineering and Technology (PIET)

CONTENTS

11.1 INTRODUCTION

Medical technology includes various tools and techniques to empower health professionals, leading to an assessment of quality of life for the society in general. The life of any patient can be improved by early diagnosis of diseases, treatment optimization, and the selection of less invasive treatment options, along with a reduction in patient hospitalization. Before the existence of smartphones, biosensors, wearable medical devices, and medical communications systems, only classical devices like stents, implants, prosthetics etc. were considered part of healthcare technology. The medical system and medicines in the pharmaceutical sciences industries were revolutionized with the inclusion of artificial intelligence (AI) in portable medical devices of small size. Any area dealing with large amounts of data can benefit from the techniques of AI for the solution of complex problems. It is a part of computer science. The second "4P model" of medicine, including preventive, predictive, personalized, and participatory properties, has been enabled by the power of AI with healthcare technologies leading to patient independence (Zhao et al., 2020) and an electronic medical record is the best example, as the data of any patient can be filled and distributed on smartphones with its sharing between the patient and the medical practitioner. The use of biosensors for monitoring various vital functions of the human body helps in the selection of personalized medicine therapy with better patient compliance (Alam et al., 2018; Guk et al., 2019). Augmented medicine is a relatively new field in which the technology of augmented reality is used for the betterment of patients. The Food and Drug administration (FDA) has approved various algorithms in the last 10 years based on AI that can be considered for clinical practice. There are various kinds of supportive tools for augmented medicine along with AI-based technology (Kelly et al., 2019).

11.2 MACHINE LEARNING

Machine intelligence is also known as AI, as it can mimic the process of response generation in the human mind. Although the idea was proposed in 1950, even in today's scenario, it is considered a branch of computer science with a multidisciplinary approach that helps to improve the quality of human life (Brenner, 2012).

Machine learning (ML) can be defined as a subfield of AI technology and can be explained as the capability of any machine to mimic human behaviour. With the help of AI, complex tasks can be performed in a manner very similar to that of humans. ML is the most commonly used AI technique. The basic principle of ML is to discover any kind of regularity in the pattern of reported data and build a model by interpreting the concerned data. This will help the machine make predictions about the future (Ghahramani, 2015).

11.2.1 MACHINE LEARNING CLASSIFICATION

ML can be classified further into three types, as shown in Figure 11.1.

    a. **Supervised Machine Learning**: In this type, labels are set manually, helping to achieve a result by machine. This type of learning plays a crucial role in the operation of biological networks, including artificial neural networks,

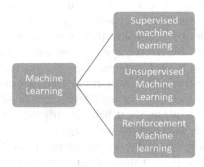

FIGURE 11.1 Classification of machine learning.

which supports its application in the medical diagnosis field with its clinical importance.

b. **Unsupervised Machine Learning**: It is different from the previous one as the label is not carried by a given dataset but the machine has to search for the label itself. It has application in various fields, like prediction of the risk of cardiovascular diseases and image analysis.

c. **Reinforcement Machine Learning**: The main goal of this type is to increase the rewards for any particular model during the process of learning. In the case of supervised and unsupervised learning, we have to propose any goal and AI is required to fulfil the same. But, the achievement of a goal is not a mandatory task in this type because its aim is not to meet the goal defined but to increase rewards. This helps in the optimization of the process of patients getting rid of mechanical ventilation in intensive care units (ICU) at hospitals.

11.3 NEXT GENERATION MACHINE LEARNING

Deep learning was proposed by Geoffrey Hinton as a subtype of ML. Learning from big data and automatic programming of algorithms can be enabled by deep learning. An artificial neural network, including artificial neurons and nodes, can be trained by this. Processing of image, audio, video, and voice-based data is significantly affected by this and can be applied in the field of medical imaging and radiography (Gulshan et al., 2016; Camacho et al., 2018).

11.4 APPLICATIONS OF ARTIFICIAL INTELLIGENCE FOR CARDIOVASCULAR HEALTH

Cardiovascular disorders are one of the most prominent causes of death throughout the globe, and AI can be used in their management. Deep learning technique can be used in the field of cardiovascular research in many ways, including personalized or precision medicine, imaging analysis, robotic tools, and accurate predictions for patients.

11.4.1 PRECISION MEDICINE

Precision medicine, or personalized medicine, is the new concept in patient-oriented therapy. Techniques of AI are used as reminders for the medication to be taken by patients, for real-time counselling of diseases to patients for their own betterment, along with warnings for the early symptoms of any disease and follow-up of patients in remote areas. AI applications are not limited to patients; it also aids clinical practitioners in the collection of patients' medical histories as well as the collection of all patients' data for compilation and interpretation. Clinicians are able to customize treatment plans for individual patients (Krittanawong et al., 2017).

11.4.2 Clinical Predictions

More accurate clinical predictions for patients can be made by the application of AI through big data. In a study conducted by magnetic resonance imaging scans and blood tests of 256 patients with heart diseases, it was found that the time period of death can be predicted for the patients with heart disease by AI technology. This technique stores a record regarding the movement of 30,000 expressions observed on the structure of the heart during each heartbeat. Combination of these data with previous medical history of patients in the last 8 years helps to predict abnormal conditions, if any, responsible for the death of patients along with prediction of the chances of survival of patients for the next year. Similarly, in another study by Motwani et al., the risk of death in the coming 5 years for patients with coronary heart disease was predicted and data were accessed from approximately 10,000 patients. Results confirmed that AI-based risk assessment is more precise than the conventional method of judgement by doctors (Motwani et al., 2017).

11.4.3 Image Analysis

With the introduction of deep learning in AI technology, there is a wide scope for the analysis of cardiovascular system–related images. It also helped a lot in the analysis of angiography and electrocardiograms (ECG). This technology enables the identification of blood plaque inside the walls of arteries that supply the heart with blood in a more precise manner than clinicians. Accurate identification at an early stage is very important because plaque build-up causes narrower arteries and slows down the flow of blood through them. In addition, this can be used for the analysis of echocardiographic images, which includes cardiac chamber size measurement and left ventricular function assessment. This technology also helps in the assessment of structural heart diseases, which is very crucial to identify as these are the defects caused by birth in any individual or are developed due to injury or infection, and helps to understand the causes of diseases and to find out the particular stage of disease (Madani et al., 2018). Deep learning in combination with AI can predict the survival rate of patients by analysis of echocardiography, e.g., intravascular ultrasound, which is a kind of medical imaging analysis. Coronary arteries are targeted more frequently for this as intravascular ultrasound is used to access the amount of blood plaque to be deposited in the coronary artery and can access both the volume of plaque as well as the degree of artery narrowing. Image diagnostics techniques can be more accurate and faster with the inclusion of deep learning and can benefit the medical field in various ways.

11.4.4 Surgical Robots

The introduction of surgical robots in the medical field helped a lot of clinicians. Surgeons can do complex procedures in a precise and flexible manner with better control than traditional surgical techniques. Robotic surgery is a less invasive technique in nature and is preferred throughout the globe. Surgical robots consist of a camera arm and a mechanical arm attached to surgical instruments. Surgeons are able to control both arms through AI-based computer technology just by sitting near the operation table. A computer screen or panel provides a high-definition, three-dimensional view of the body organ where surgery took place, and other team members can assist the surgeon during the operation. Robotic surgery is a minimally invasive procedure and successful completion of this leads to quicker recovery of patients, a smaller and less noticeable scar of surgery, less pain, and very minimal blood loss, along with fewer chances of infection after surgery (Kelleher et al., 2018). In the future, automated surgery will be helpful in the reduction of hospital stays of patients with improved patient safety. In special cases where exposure to radiation is involved, AI can perform cardiac interventional surgical operations without the assistance of surgeons. Involvement of reinforcement learning can help in many ways, especially in surgical repetition drills, and surgeries can be performed at a faster rate than human clinicians, which could be a revolutionary step in the healthcare industry.

11.4.5 HEALTH INFORMATICS

ML is very useful in the medical industry for making accurate decisions, especially collection of a large quantity of health-related data. ML-related software and algorithms have proven to be effective aids in decision-making in various aspects of healthcare. Prognosis of any disease depicts a chance or probability of the occurrence of new illness or disease based on medical observation and experience of the health practitioner, and it is very difficult for cardiovascular system–related diseases due to different kinds of risk factors like blood pressure of patient, diabetic status, cholesterol level, pulse rate, etc.

Detection of any kind of abnormality in the heart at an early stage could save life. Health informatics is the field of science or medical technology, which deals with collection, study, review, and management of health data with the help of information technology. It aims for better healthcare to the patient, and ML helps in optimal usage, storage, and retrieval of data, which lead to optimization of medical decision on the basis of predictive values in large size data with the help of various techniques of ML. For example, in case of the prediction of any illness or disorder related to cardiovascular system, various aspects are considered like pulse rate, cholesterol level, gender, smoking, etc.

Prediction of heart disease can be made possible by the help of seven types of algorithms Naive Bayes, linear model, logistic regression, decision tree, random forest, support vector machine, and hybrid random forest with a linear model (Ayon et al., 2022).

a. **Native Bayes**

According to the Native Bayes algorithm, independence should not exist between multiple traits that are comparable to one another, despite what numerous predictors have shown.

b. **Linear Model**

Linear combination of independent variables can be represented by the dependent variable with the help of the generalized linear model, which is also known as simple linear regression. Simple linear regression can be executed well whenever the distribution of dependent variable is normal. Assumption of normally distributed dependent variables may cause damage in real-world situations. In case of generalized linear model, response predictor's linear combination mean value was correlated by the use of link function.

c. **Logistic Regression**

Logistic regression is appraised as one of the ML algorithms organized in a better way and binary classification can be explained with its use. Variable number of problems can be solved with the help of logistic regression, which can give different types of solutions. It utilizes a dependent and decisive variable, which is very similar to binary variables that depict either pass or fail.

There are two types of logistic regression technique. The first is the multinomial logistic regression technique in case of existence of greater than one outcome for the variables. If multiple categories are presented in a systematic manner, it is called an Ordinal Logistic Technique.

d. **Decision Tree**

One of the supervised learning algorithms is named as the decision tree and its techniques are utilized by classification problems. Decision tree will generate continuous performance by producing the natural features of this basic concept.

e. **Random Forest**

The random forest algorithm is one of the most well-known and supervised ML algorithms. This approach may be used for both regression and classification problems, with classification jobs yielding superior results. In this random forest approach, the many decision trees are used before the outputs are generated. As a result, a group of decision trees is evaluated. The random forest approach is used to classify the data on the basis of assumption that a larger number of trees will lead to the correct choice. The categorization includes a voting method, which is used to determine the class. The mean of all outputs is taken into account in the regression approach, which is based on the choice of each tree.

f. **Support Vector Machine**

The support vector machine approach is the most often used supervised ML technique. This strategy uses a predetermined target variable that functions as a classifier and predictor. The hyperplane in feature space is used to distinguish between the classes in the classification feature. The support vector machine model is represented by the feature space, which is made up of points known as training data points. These points are organized such that they belong to different groups and are separated by a margin. This margin will have the greatest separation distance feasible. The technique of classifying the data using support vectors is very well defined and the test data points are then mapped inside the same area, and categorization is based on which side of the margin they fall.

g. **HRFLM**

This is a novel technology that stands for Hybrid Random Forest with Linear Model. HRFLM denotes a hybrid of random forest and linear forest models. A computational technique is used in HRFLM, which uses three connectivity rules of mining: apriority, predictive, and Tertius. The three mining rules may be used to find the parameters linked with the UCI Cleveland dataset based on heart disease. HRFLM's inputs are made up of 13 clinical characteristics that are processed using an ANN with backpropagation. The outcomes of traditional procedures are evaluated and compared to the ones obtained. This approach yielded high covariance vectors, and the feature dimension was reduced via vector projection.

11.5 FUTURE SCOPE

AI is the next big trend in the healthcare field. Integration of AI technology into the medical field requires a lot of professional expertise along with substantial investment. In the future, AI-based healthcare projects can be handled by big technological agencies like Google, Microsoft, Apple, etc. to enhance productivity in clinical setups. Project "Apple Heart Study" was launched recently by Stanford and Apple. Sensor technology, along with ML, is one of the best examples of AI application in healthcare. A medical device named "Apple Watch Series 4.0" was launched for the measurement of ECG, which has been approved by the USFDA (United States Food and Drug Authority) for clinical use. Patients with any heart-related illnesses are assessed for risk by life sciences committed to the study and development of life sciences using the machine learning (ML) approach. An algorithm was successfully developed for the analysis of the images of the eyes of patients and accurate analysis of health data, including age, blood pressure, and smoking habits of individual patients, and this can help to find out the risk of the occurrence of a new disorder. This algorithm was written and trained by statistical analysis of data collected from over 30,000 patients. The results were 70% accurate and very close to the result by the conventional method of risk assessment by the method of blood cholesterol measurement (Poplin et al., 2018).

11.6 CHALLENGES

A major challenge in the frequent usage of AI technology for healthcare is that a large amount of high-quality data is required and this is not an easy task. Another limitation is the inability of AI to make differential diagnoses. Healthcare is considered as one of the best choices for the application of AI, but its use is limited due to superficial understanding of the processing and working of the human brain, bad-quality data collected to be used for algorithm generation, complex process of computation and there is a need for higher quality standards of AI technology for clinical applications as compared to other fields.

11.7 CONCLUSION

Modern techniques for the prediction of any type of heart disease include methodology of ML and deep learning along with data mining. This technique can be utilized for the predictions on the basis of data from the medical industry. In the technique of AI, pattern of disease occurrence is recognized by computers, which is converted to the form of structural data for prediction. Doctors can take better decisions by automation of techniques like ML and deep learning. Automated prediction of disease helps in the creation of any single platform for retrieval of data leading to efficient patient care. The technique of deep learning lies in between ML and AI and is able to learn unsupervised forms of data. If learning algorithm is not working in an accurate manner, there is the need to feed more data for model training. As this may cause an issue of scalability, Deep learning techniques are preferred as a solution for data handling issues due to their ability to learn representation of unstructured data with multiple levels of abstraction. Hierarchical level of artificial neural networks very similar to human brain are utilized by deep learning techniques for the execution of ML process and data are processed in a non-linear manner as compared to others, which follow the linear way of processing. This technique is able to perform fast and precise analysis of data, which supports its quick adoption in the field of healthcare. It can take decisions with minimal human involvement and minimal pre-processing of data is required as compared to other techniques of ML. For e.g., normalization tasks and filtering tasks are performed by human programmers in the case of ML, but the network of deep learning techniques is able to do them by itself. Heart disease can be diagnosed effectively on the basis of knowledge from the data collected and time taken for diagnosis is also reduced by this technique and leads to a reduction of medical errors. Disease diagnosing is very important task as it is dependent on knowledge and experiences of doctor. Diagnosis can be made more accurate and efficient by training of the machine to learn algorithms in order to behave like humans (Mukherjee and Sharma, 2019). Accuracy in disease diagnosis is very important in the case of the model adopted by ML techniques and trustworthy text analytics can be represented by deep learning techniques even if the data available is biased and skewed. Various deep learning techniques are important for prediction and decision-making as some advanced methods are combined for power increment and the creation of new methods. Personalized treatment of cancer and type 2 diabetes patients are examples of its application. Majority of the population with cardiovascular disorders are unaware about their illness and living (Swathy and Saruladha, 2022). Prediction of diseases well in advance helps in the reduction of associated consequences. Medical imaging and chatbots are utilized by deep learning techniques for the identification of a specific pattern of diseases along with associated symptoms. One of the deep learning techniques named as neural network working on graph topology consists of multiple nodes and possesses a distributed information processing structure. Each node is correlated to neurons and associated weight is correlated to the edge. Various hierarchical layers are present, which help in decreasing the time required for the solution of any problem. Single output connection of individual node is branched further into various connections. One input and one output is included by the layer of Neural Network. Real-time problems over a wide range can be solved with ease by the combination of Neural Networks and Fuzzy Logic also known as Neuro-Fuzzy. Various branches of medicine like cardiology, clinical chemistry, pathology, ophthalmology, and gynaecology can benefit from Artificial Neural Networks and research is being undertaken to study their application in the diagnosis of cardiovascular diseases, as the issue of prediction is very sensitive and predictions that are not accurate may lead to false assumptions affecting patient health. One of the advantages of deep learning techniques is that the processing of images as medical images can be done with the help of Neural Networks, which can be further read and analyzed, and diseases can be predicted. Analysis of MRI Scans and X-Rays can be done with Convolution Neural Networks. This type of network is operated on large-sized images in a more effective manner and can bypass the manual diagnosis by doctors. CNN and RNN (Recurrent Neural Networks) are preferred for the Prediction Systems of cardiovascular diseases because detection of ED and ES frames using an automated image-driven method is the first criteria for prediction. This technique can detect the crucial features for the prediction networks in an automated manner and manual intervention is not required (Dezaki et al., 2018). Image feature extractions can be done by CNN and their in between temporal dependencies were understood by RNN as these are computationally efficient as compared to any other technique. This type of model is also suitable for the prediction of time series type of data, e.g., diagnostic history of patients and E-prescriptions of patients, as information is remembered throughout the network (Ambekar and Phalnikar, 2018). Effective diagnosis of cardiovascular diseases with accuracy would help in the selection of suitable therapy for patients. This technique plays a very important role by analyzing the patient based on various information.

Cardiovascular diseases under the category of non-communicable diseases are still a serious health issue that affects people all over the world, particularly in low- and middle-income nations. In the next two decades, it will remain the leading cause of death. Artificial intelligence, particularly deep learning, has shown considerable promise in the prevention and management of various types of cardiovascular disorders. As professionals have a better understanding of the condition, AI's capabilities will improve. AI cannot replace doctors, so clinicians must continue to learn in order to increase their capacity to assist patients, and they must avoid relying too much on computers and AI. Doctors remain the cornerstone at any time, and AI can assist them increase the effectiveness of their treatments.

REFERENCES

Alam MM, Malik H, Khan MI, Pardy T, Kuusik A, Le Moullec Y. A survey on the roles of communication technologies in IoT-based personalized healthcare applications. *IEEE Access*. 2018 Jul 5;6:36611–31.

Ambekar S, Phalnikar R. Disease risk prediction by using convolutional neural network. In *2018 Fourth International Conference on Computing Communication Control and Automation (ICCUBEA)* 2018 Aug 16 (pp. 1–5). IEEE.

Ayon SI, Islam MM, Hossain MR. Coronary artery heart disease prediction: a comparative study of computational intelligence techniques. *IETE Journal of Research*. 2022 Jul 4;68(4):2488–507.

Brenner S. Life's code script. *Nature*. 2012 Feb;482(7386):461.

Camacho DM, Collins KM, Powers RK, Costello JC, Collins JJ. Next-generation machine learning for biological networks. *Cell.* 2018 Jun 14;173(7):1581–92.

Dezaki FT, Liao Z, Luong C, Girgis H, Dhungel N, Abdi AH, Behnami D, Gin K, Rohling R, Abolmaesumi P, Tsang T. Cardiac phase detection in echocardiograms with densely gated recurrent neural networks and global extrema loss. *IEEE Transactions on Medical Imaging.* 2018 Dec 24;38(8):1821–32.

Ghahramani Z. Probabilistic machine learning and artificial intelligence. *Nature.* 2015 May;521(7553):452–9.

Guk K, Han G, Lim J, Jeong K, Kang T, Lim EK, Jung J. Evolution of wearable devices with real-time disease monitoring for personalized healthcare. *Nanomaterials.* 2019 Jun;9(6):813.

Gulshan V, Peng L, Coram M, Stumpe MC, Wu D, Narayanaswamy A, Venugopalan S, Widner K, Madams T, Cuadros J, Kim R. Development and validation of a deep learning algorithm for detection of diabetic retinopathy in retinal fundus photographs. *JAMA.* 2016 Dec 13;316(22):2402–10.

Kelleher C, Hakimi Z, Zur R, Siddiqui E, Maman K, Aballéa S, Nazir J, Chapple C. Efficacy and tolerability of mirabegron compared with antimuscarinic monotherapy or combination therapies for overactive bladder: a systematic review and network meta-analysis. *European Urology.* 2018 Sep 1;74(3):324–33.

Kelly CJ, Karthikesalingam A, Suleyman M, Corrado G, King D. Key challenges for delivering clinical impact with artificial intelligence. *BMC Medicine.* 2019 Dec;17(1):1–9.

Krittanawong C, Zhang H, Wang Z, Aydar M, Kitai T. Artificial intelligence in precision cardiovascular medicine. *Journal of the American College of Cardiology.* 2017 May 30;69(21):2657–64.

Madani A, Arnaout R, Mofrad M, Arnaout R. Fast and accurate view classification of echocardiograms using deep learning. *NPJ Digital Medicine.* 2018 Mar 21;1(1):1–8.

Motwani M, Dey D, Berman DS, Germano G, Achenbach S, Al-Mallah MH, Andreini D, Budoff MJ, Cademartiri F, Callister TQ, Chang HJ. Machine learning for prediction of all-cause mortality in patients with suspected coronary artery disease: a 5-year multi-centre prospective registry analysis. *European Heart Journal.* 2017 Feb 14;38(7):500–7.

Mukherjee S, Sharma A. Intelligent heart disease prediction using neural network. *International Journal of Recent Technology and Engineering.* 2019;7(5):402–5.

Poplin R, Varadarajan AV, Blumer K, Liu Y, McConnell MV, Corrado GS, Peng L, Webster DR. Prediction of cardiovascular risk factors from retinal fundus photographs via deep learning. *Nature Biomedical Engineering.* 2018 Mar;2(3):158–64.

Swathy M, Saruladha K. A comparative study of classification and prediction of Cardio-Vascular Diseases (CVD) using Machine Learning and Deep Learning techniques. *ICT Express.* 2022 Mar 1;8(1):109–16.

Zhao G, Li Y, Chen D, Xiong Y. Biomedicine big data—trends and prospect. In *China's e-Science Blue Book 2020* 2021 (pp. 15–42). Springer, Singapore. Compiled by key organizations, institutions, and government agencies of China.

Index

Printed in the United States
by Baker & Taylor Publisher Services

Printed in the United States
by Baker & Taylor Publisher Services